TABLE OF CONTENTS

442921

Branding Yourself

How to Use Social Media to Invent or Reinvent Yourself, Second Edition

ERIK DECKERS

KYLE LACY

800 East 96th Street,
Indianapolis, Indiana 46240 USA

Branding Yourself: How to Use Social Media to Invent or Reinvent Yourself, Second Edition

Copyright © 2013 by Pearson Education, Inc.

All rights reserved. No part of this book shall be reproduced, stored in a retrieval system, or transmitted by any means, electronic, mechanical, photocopying, recording, or otherwise, without written permission from the publisher. No patent liability is assumed with respect to the use of the information contained herein. Although every precaution has been taken in the preparation of this book, the publisher and author assume no responsibility for errors or omissions. Nor is any liability assumed for damages resulting from the use of the information contained herein.

ISBN-13: 978-0-7897-4972-7
ISBN-10: 0-7897-4972-6

Library of Congress Cataloging-in-Publication Data is on file.

Printed in the United States of America

First Printing: July 2012

Trademarks

All terms mentioned in this book that are known to be trademarks or service marks have been appropriately capitalized. Que Publishing cannot attest to the accuracy of this information. Use of a term in this book should not be regarded as affecting the validity of any trademark or service mark.

The double C in a circle, the words and logotype "Creative Commons" and the Creative Commons license buttons reproduced in this publication are trademarks of Creative Commons. For more information about Creative Commons, visit http://creativecommons.org/

Warning and Disclaimer

Every effort has been made to make this book as complete and as accurate as possible, but no warranty or fitness is implied. The information provided is on an "as is" basis. The authors and the publisher shall have neither liability nor responsibility to any person or entity with respect to any loss or damages arising from the information contained in this book.

Bulk Sales

Que Publishing offers excellent discounts on this book when ordered in quantity for bulk purchases or special sales. For more information, please contact

U.S. Corporate and Government Sales
1-800-382-3419
corpsales@pearsontechgroup.com

For sales outside of the U.S., please contact

International Sales
international@pearson.com

Editor-in-Chief
Greg Wiegand

Senior Acquisitions Editor
Katherine Bull

Development Editor
Romny French

Managing Editor
Kristy Hart

Project Editor
Andrew Beaster

Copy Editor
Apostrophe Editing Services

Indexer
Cheryl Lenser

Proofreader
Sarah Kearns

Technical Editor
Pierre DeBois,
Zimana, LLC

Publishing Coordinator
Cindy Teeters
Romny French

Book Designer
Anne Jones

Compositor
Nonie Ratcliff

Que Biz-Tech Editorial Board
Michael Brito
Jason Falls
Rebecca Lieb
Simon Salt
Peter Shankman

658.
827
DEC

442921

About the Authors

Erik Deckers is the co-owner and vice president of creative services of Professional Blog Service, a ghost blogging and social media agency. He has been blogging since 1997 and speaks widely on social media topics. He is also a newspaper columnist and award-winning playwright. Erik coauthored *No Bullshit Social Media: The All-Business, No-Hype Guide to Social Media Marketing* with Jason Falls.

Kyle Lacy is a principal of Marketing Research and Education for ExactTarget, a leading global provider of interactive marketing solutions. He has an in-depth understanding of the application of social and interactive media for both small and large businesses and regularly speaks on topics ranging from social media adoption to interactive marketing trends across email, mobile, and social media. Kyle has been recognized as one of Indiana's 40-under-40 by the *Indianapolis Business Journal*, Anderson University's Young Alumni of the Year, and TechPoint's Young Professional of the Year. Learn more about Kyle at KyleLacy.com.

Deckers and Lacy coauthored the first edition of *Branding Yourself.*

Dedication

Erik
To Toni, Madison, Emmalie, and Benjamin.

Kyle
To my family and wife, Rachel.

Acknowledgments

We often say that social media is a community, and this book is no different. We couldn't have done it without some very special people.

The words "thank you" don't do justice to our appreciation for your help. First, thank you to Katherine Bull, our acquisitions editor at Pearson, for taking a chance on us *a second time.* Thanks also to Brandon Prebynski, Leslie O'Neill, Karen Gill, and Jovana Shirley for the first edition of this book. And thanks to Pierre DeBois of Zimana, LLC, Andrew Beaster, San Dee Phillips, and Romny French for their outstanding work on making the second edition even better.

We also want to thank the people in our lives and our community who helped us gain the knowledge, experience, and insights to produce this book. We appreciate everything you have ever done for us. So thank you, in no particular order, Paul Lorinczi, Brandon Coon, the wonderful people that make up ExactTarget, Lorraine Ball, Hazel Walker, Douglas Karr, Jason Falls, Tony Scelzo, Noah Coffey,

Shawn Plew, the whole Lacy clan of Dan, Rainy, Kayla, Zach and Kelly, Lindsay Manfredi, Jay Baer, Sarah Robbins, Mike Seidle, and Scott Wise.

Erik would also like to thank Kyle for asking him to help with his first writing project, which led to this one, and hopefully will lead to many more.

Erik would like to give a special thanks to his wife Toni and his three children, Maddie, Emma, and Ben, for giving him the support and love to write this book. Hopefully those 2:00 a.m. bedtimes will pay off. Kyle would like to especially thank his wife Rachel for being okay with the late nights and working weekends.

We Want to Hear from You!

As the reader of this book, you are our most important critic and commentator. We value your opinion and want to know what we're doing right, what we could do better, what areas you'd like to see us publish in, and any other words of wisdom you're willing to pass our way.

We welcome your comments. You can email or write to let us know what you did or didn't like about this book—as well as what we can do to make our books better.

Please note that we cannot help you with technical problems related to the topic of this book.

When you write, please be sure to include this book's title and author as well as your name and email address. We will carefully review your comments and share them with the author and editors who worked on the book.

Email: feedback@quepublishing.com

Mail: Que Publishing ATTN: Reader Feedback
         800 East 96th Street
         Indianapolis, IN 46240 USA

Reader Services

Visit our website and register this book at quepublishing.com/register for convenient access to any updates, downloads, or errata that might be available for this book.

Why Do I Care About Self-Promotion?

Welcome to the Party

A story.

When Erik Deckers moved to Indianapolis in 2006, he knew one person. When an expected job didn't quite work out, he searched for another, relying on job boards. He finally found a job at the Indiana State Department of Health.

Erik worked there for nearly 16 months and got to know a number of people in the agency and a few people in other agencies. Rarely, however, did he ever have the opportunity to work with people on the outside. Consorting with the private sector was almost frowned upon, and attending business-related events during work hours was not allowed. Needless to say, Erik's professional circle was limited to his co-workers and a few journalists around the state.

When Erik left for a private sector job in 2007, selling direct mail services (interestingly, he got this job through the one guy he knew when he moved to Indianapolis), he realized the people he knew in his old job weren't going to help him in his new efforts, at least not right away.

So, rather than spending every day on the phone, Erik started attending Rainmakers meetings (a local networking organization), a business book club, and the Chambers of Commerce in Indianapolis and Fishers, a suburb to the northeast. He attended at least two and sometimes three events a week, at 7:30 in the morning or 5:00 in the afternoon. The idea was that by meeting other people in the business world, he could learn about new opportunities, meet possible new clients, and find new partners who can act as evangelists, a sort of "freelance salesperson" to their clients.

At the same time, he attended a half-day seminar on social media and blogging put on by a local Internet marketing company. Erik had been blogging infrequently up until that point, but he began to take it seriously. He studied blogging by reading other blogs and books about blogging and trying some of the new ideas and techniques he was learning.

As part of his networking, Erik would have coffee or lunch with people he met. He tried to learn as much about them as he could and asked if they could refer him to anyone else who would be interested in learning about his services. Many times, they asked about blogging and social media, and he would tell them as much as he could. He spent a lot of time online, blogging, promoting his blog, and communicating on Facebook, LinkedIn, and Smaller Indiana, a niche social network.

Those connections have led to many opportunities—sales, speaking opportunities, blogging opportunities, a job, and even this book—that never would have happened if Erik had limited his job search to just the job *boards—and especially if he hadn't drunk enough coffee to float a battleship.*

When Kyle and Erik were discussing how to write this book, Kyle said, "We need to write it for you, the you from 2007. We need to tell that guy how to brand himself and promote himself online."

What Is Self-Promotion?

Self-promotion is just what it sounds like: promoting yourself, your events, your accomplishments, your victories, and even your defeats, problems, and lessons you have learned. You do it so you can increase your visibility to and awareness by others, increase traffic to your website, increase sales, and get more speaking opportunities, exhibitions, and gigs—more of whatever it is you're looking for.

You promote yourself so you can get even more opportunities, which you can then tell people about.

Self-promotion is also called *branding yourself*, because that's actually what it has become. (That, and it's what we wanted to call the book.) We prefer to think of it as personal branding because you need to think of yourself as a brand, just like Coca-Cola, McDonald's, Google, or Facebook.

Why Is Self-Promotion Important?

You can't count on people calling you out of the blue to hire you, buy your service, or book you for an event if they don't know about you. The only way to get people to know who you are and what you do is to tell them. And you want to tell as many people as you can who are actually interested.

Self-promotion can help you make those important connections that will further your career and improve your professional standing. It can be as simple as introducing yourself to the organizer of a conference and telling her you are interested in speaking at her next conference, or it can be as involved as writing a book or two and then spending a day emailing every conference organizer you can to get as many speaking deals as you can.

`@kyleplacy:` Is that a shot at me?

`@edeckers:` No, not at all, Mr. I-Don't-Have-Time-for-Lunch-Today.

What Self-Promotion Is Not

Self-promotion is not bragging or boasting. It's not being something bigger than you are. It's just letting people know who you are and what you do.

It's perfectly acceptable to promote yourself without looking like an arrogant jerk. People are going to be out promoting themselves and their personal endeavors and small businesses. If you're not, you're missing good opportunities, and others are going to beat you in the competition. They're going to sell their art, get their speaking gigs, get more web traffic, or whatever they're competing with you for.

What Can Self-Promotion Do for You and Your Career?

Without question, self-promotion can make you successful. And if you're already successful, it can make your personal brand huge. You don't get to be a success without knowing a lot of people and having a lot of people know you. If you want to be stuck in a little, gray cubicle for your entire career, never rising above lower middle management, keep your head down and don't attract attention. Actually, put this book down. Stop reading! But if you want to make a name for yourself, establish a good reputation, finally get that corner office, or even own your own successful business, you need to promote yourself.

To do that, you need to be passionate about two things: the work you do and yourself. If you're not passionate about what you do, find the thing you're passionate about. If you're not passionate about yourself, seek professional help. The person you should love the most, admire the most, and treasure the most is you. And when you have that confidence in yourself, others see it, too. When you share that confidence with other people, they feel confident about you as well.

So don't sit in your cubicle any longer. Figure out what you want to do, make it happen, and then start telling people about it. Let them know that you are good at what you do. Let them come to you for answers and information.

Personal Branding

If you ask 100 people what personal branding is, you'll get 100 different answers. But the answer we're going with is that it is an emotional response to the image or name of a particular company, product, or person.

Think of some corporate brands you have positive or negative feelings toward: McDonald's, Starbucks, Coca-Cola, Wal-Mart, Indianapolis Colts, Chicago Cubs, BP. These brands are popular because they have created a lot of positive feelings in their fans, even if they also engender negative feelings in their detractors.

Similarly, people have emotional responses when they see you or meet you for the first time. These responses can be feelings of joy, pleasure, love, dread, fear, or anger. When they hear your name again, they will either have new experiences and emotions, or they will relive the old ones. The kinds of emotional responses they have depend on you.

 Note

A brand is an emotional response to the image or name of a particular company, product, or person.

What Is Personal Branding?

Branding yourself means that you create the right kind of emotional response you want people to have when they hear your name, see you online, or meet you in real life.

The "right" kind doesn't mean being someone you're not. It's your personality, your voice, your interests, your habits—everything about you that you want people to know. This means that the information you show to other people, the things you say, and the photos you post should all fit within that theme of your personal brand.

If you're a stand-up comic, your brand is "funny." You want people to see that you actually are funny, which means posting some of your jokes and posting links to videos of your routine and even to your blog.

If you're a freelance graphic designer, your brand is "creative." You want people to know you have creative skills, so you'll show people samples of your work through an online portfolio, possibly a blog.

If you're a cost reduction analyst, your brand is "saving companies' money." You can demonstrate your knowledge by answering questions on LinkedIn, writing useful articles on your blog, and giving talks to Chambers of Commerce.

Go Brand Yourself

Ask yourself: What do I want to be known for? What qualities do I want people to associate with me? What is the first thing I want to have pop in their heads when they hear my name?

Next, create a list of those qualities. Write down everything you can think of in five minutes, even if you think you're repeating yourself. Don't edit yourself, and don't leave anything off. This is not a time to be humble or to think, "No one will think of me that way." Come up with every adjective and noun you can think of, no matter how far out or weird it may seem. It may just spur another idea that actually does fit.

Let's say your list looks like this:

Creative	Funny	Interested in people
Musical	Well-read	Detail-oriented
Networker	Outgoing	Singer
Knowledgeable	Songwriter	Teacher
Intelligent	Dedicated	Organized

From here, you need to start grouping things that are similar. In one group, we have musical, songwriter, singer, and creative. In another, we have knowledgeable, intelligent, well-read, and teacher. In a third, we have networker, outgoing, and interested in people.

You can call these groups anything you want, but let's stick with Musical, Knowledgeable, and Networker. These groups are the start of branding yourself. They're the areas you should concentrate on being known for—the areas that can define what people know you for. They may know you for more—being a good cook, a budding actor, someone who's fun to hang out with at parties—but those are reserved more for your personal friends, not something you want to focus on, at least not at the moment. These latter attributes can be an additional side to your brand once in a while, but they shouldn't be the main focus of your personal brand.

How to Build Your Brand

The remaining 14 chapters of this book focus on how to build your brand. You're going to learn what you need to do to promote your personal brand with each of the social media tools and real-world events discussed, whether it's writing a blog post, posting messages on Twitter, or giving a speech.

Before you start, however, you need to understand the foundation of personal branding.

PERSONAL BRANDING CASE STUDY
SHAMA KABANI

Shama is one of the premier thought-leaders in the world of social media marketing. She has practically built an empire using the tools we talk about in this book. We wanted to sit down with Shama and get a better idea of what she used and how she has accomplished so much at a young age. Find out more about Shama and her company at ZenOfSocialMedia.com.

How did you decide to go out on your own? When did you find your entrepreneurial calling?

Shama: I was in graduate school doing my thesis on Twitter. This was when Twitter had 2,000 users, not 500 million like it does today. Upon graduation, I felt strongly that social media would have a huge impact on businesses. The corporate world didn't seem to share my view. So, I started my own company. Now, almost three years have gone by. We have a team of 25 and serve as a full-service web marketing company for clients around the world.

How did social media play a role in your personal brand? What tool did you start using first?

Shama: I started using social media first as an academic observer. I wanted to see how this online "jungle" functioned. As I learned more, I started building my own brand. We are at a unique point in history [in which people] with something of value to share can create a brand for themselves. I started with a WordPress blog. I blogged about social media, business, and shared my own lessons. I later started video blogging. Facebook and Twitter were great tools in allowing me to share my content and meet new people. And these tools remain in my arsenal today.

What social media tool has been the most successful to help you build your brand and your company?

Shama: Facebook has been an excellent tool for branding. With 900 million users, it makes sense to use Facebook to the fullest. By simply sharing good content, we've been able to really drive the brand.

If you had one piece of advice for someone building their personal brand, what would it be?

Shama: Consistency and patience are key. A personal brand isn't created overnight. It is an amalgamation of posts, updates, and pictures. At the end of the day, it is about capturing attention by providing value to the greater audience. If you can do that, you have a brand.

The Five Universal Objectives of Personal Branding

Whoever you are, whatever techniques you use, whomever you want to reach, there are five basic ideas, five *universal* objectives, that are the same for everyone who wants to grow their personal brand.

Discover Your Passion. (Passion Is Fundamental to Achieving Your Goals.)

What do you love to do? What gets you out of bed in the morning, fires your imagination, and revs you up? What do you think about when you're daydreaming and spend all your free time doing or pursuing?

Some people are passionate about their work. They love what they do, and that's where they focus their time and energy. These people—usually entrepreneurs—have found a particular niche that makes them happy, and they want to find a way to make money from it. They wake up early, stay up late, and spend every waking minute thinking about, talking about, or actually doing their work.

In his book, *Crush It!*, Gary Vaynerchuk talks about how he spends hours and hours leaving comments on other people's blogs talking about wine. It's not because he likes leaving comments or because he wants to boost his web traffic. It's because he loves wine. He loves selling it, talking about it, and writing about it. His love of wine has turned him into a celebrity and helped him sell plenty of wine for his family's liquor store.

Others are passionate about their hobbies. Whether it's painting, playing in a band, fixing up classic cars, analyzing baseball statistics, or collecting vinyl records, some people love their hobbies and pursue them with an obsessive fervor. They view their day job as a means to an end to fulfilling their passion.

And still others haven't found their passion. Or they have no passion at all. They go to work, they come home, they eat dinner, they watch TV, they go to bed. And then they do it all again the next day. The idea of enjoying life has been drummed out of them.

These people are dead inside, whether they know it or not. The only thing that gets them out of bed in the morning is the alarm clock and the fear that they'll lose their jobs if they don't. They eat for fuel, not pleasure. They have friends out of habit, not because they love being around people. They watch TV not because there's anything good on, but because they're afraid of what they'll learn if they're left alone for too long with their own thoughts: There is nothing in their lives that is truly exciting or enjoyable.

You need to have at least one passion in your life. It can be something you are known for, something you build your personal brand on. Or it can even be something you never tell anyone about, preferring to do in private. But the great thing about sharing your passion is that you can get to know people who share your interest and create some beneficial relationships.

All this is our way of saying you need to find your passion if you want to achieve your goals. More important, your goals need to tie into your passion because that's how you will achieve them.

If you want to be fulfilled and enjoy what you do, make sure your goals are achievable *through* your passions. For example, if your long-term goal is to own a million dollar home and drive an expensive car, you probably won't get there providing knitting lessons to at-risk teenagers.

We won't tell you to change your passions because that's not something you should give up. If you love giving knitting lessons to at-risk teenagers, by all means pursue it. Just understand that there's not much money to be made giving knitting lessons, so getting an expensive car this way is probably not feasible. But if that's what you love to do, rethink your goals.

If your passion is to create a new social networking tool, and you devote every waking hour to programming and promoting it, there is a good chance you can achieve your goal of the big house and expensive car.

It's a matter of making sure your passions and your goals are in alignment and that you can achieve the one through the other.

We hope you have already found your passion because this book is based on your actually being passionate about at least two things: 1) yourself and 2) something else.

Be Bold. (It's Okay to Talk About Yourself.)

Despite what your parents and teachers told you, you *can* tell people about your accomplishments. Actually, we want you to do that.

We understand that it's hard to do. We've been taught that talking about ourselves is bragging. We're supposed to be humble and quiet about our accomplishments and let our actions speak louder than words.

Think about the past several times you saw somebody boasting about his success, his money, his love life (at networking events, parties, night clubs, and high school reunions). We can imagine some of the words you used in reference to that person, none of which were flattering, and none of which our editors will let us publish here.

In the movies—*Mallrats, Karate Kid, Gladiator, The Princess Bride*—the braggart always gets his comeuppance at the end, receiving some cosmic justice. "See?" we tell ourselves. "This will happen if *I* brag about what I do."

The problem is that we associate self-promotion with bragging. We believe telling others about our accomplishments is the moral equivalent of bragging about how much money we make. We associate letting people know we published an article or are giving a talk as the equivalent of showing up at our high school reunion in a $70,000 Italian red sports car.

Nothing could be further from the truth.

We've found self-promotion seems to be especially hard for people from the Midwest, where we live. We're your typical Midwesterners, only we got over it. We realized we had to be bold without being arrogant. We knew if we wanted to make a name for ourselves, and earn reputations to attract bigger clients and bigger opportunities, we had to overcome this Midwest shyness and be willing to talk about ourselves. A lot.

Self-promotion is just letting people know what's going on in your lives, keeping people apprised of your special events, occasions, and accomplishments.

Table 1.1 shows a few key differences between bragging and self-promotion:

Table 1.1   The Difference Between Self-Promotion and Bragging

Self-Promotion	Bragging
A Twitter message that says, "I just published my book."	A vanity license plate that says, "Gr8 Writer."
Announcing the birth of your child.	Announcing the birth of your eight children at a national press conference.
Telling your friends you're engaged.	Telling people how much he spent on the ring.
Telling your colleagues about your promotion.	Demanding undying fealty from your underlings.

The biggest difference between self-promotion and bragging is the motivation behind why you're telling people. If it's something you're proud of, something you're excited to tell people about because you "just gotta tell someone," that's okay. That's self-promotion. If it's something you want people to do, see, visit, or even buy, that's self-promotion.

If you announce something so other people will be envious, jealous, or just think you're cool, that's bragging, and people won't like you.

Creating your online personal brand means showing your personality. What makes you unique and interesting? Why should we want to spend time with you? Why should we care what you have to say? If you're a fun person, show it. If you're interested in a lot of different things, share them. If you like to create new relationships, seek out other interesting people.

The important thing is to realize that a) people are interested in what you have to say and b) it's perfectly all right to say it.

Tell Your Story. (Your Story Is What Makes You Special.)

This is the tricky part. We just told you it's okay to talk about yourself, but now you have to do it without talking about yourself.

@kyleplacy: Huh?
@edeckers: Be patient.

Effective personal branding isn't about talking about yourself all the time. As much as we'd all like to think that our friends and family are eagerly waiting by their computers hoping to hear some news, any news, about what we're doing, they're not. Actually, they're hoping you're sitting by your computer, waiting for news about them.

Believe it or not, the best way to build your personal brand is to talk more about other people, events, and ideas than you talk about yourself. That's because if you talk about other people and promote their victories and their ideas, you become an influencer. You are seen as someone who is not only helpful, but is also a valuable resource. That helps your brand more than if you just talk about yourself over and over. Then, you're just seen as boring.

But there are other ways you can tell your own story, without saying a word. You don't tell people what you believe; you show it by living it.

The next chance you get, watch people. Study what they wear, what they eat, what they drive. Play a little Sherlock Holmes to see if you can make any deductions by what you observe. You can get a clue to their personalities by noticing simple things like clothing and cars.

That woman over there wearing the New York Knicks T-shirt is probably a basketball fan. The skinny guy wearing the running shoes is a runner. The guy wearing a Green Lantern T-shirt likes comic books. And the woman who drove by in the Toyota Prius with the "Love Your Mother (Earth)" bumper sticker wants to help the environment.

We've learned a small part of their personal stories, but they didn't say a word. These symbols we wear and brands we support tell a story for us. They let other people know, "This is something I believe in, and I want you to know about it."

It's the same for telling your own story. Rather than wearing a sign that says, "I love comic books" or sending daily emails to your friends about your obsession with comics, you could write a blog about the comics industry and your favorite titles and characters, or you could publish your own web comic. You could produce a weekly podcast about comic publishing news, cover the news from local and national comic conventions, and even interview other comic artists and publishers. By blogging or podcasting about your favorite topic, you tell the world your story—"I love comic books"—without actually saying it over and over or being a pest about it.

Besides, the sign starts to chafe after a while.

Create Relationships. (Relationships Lead to Opportunities.)

The thing that we have marveled about social networking and real-world networking is that you never know what kind of opportunities are going to come your way as a result of using it. Without sounding too mystical or cosmic, you must leave yourself open to the opportunities that may arise because of your efforts.

Erik jokes that this is "faith-based networking": You will meet the right person at the right time for the right opportunity. As long as you continue to put yourself in the situations where those possibilities can arise, sooner or later, they will eventually come.

The creation of this book is a prime example of the right people meeting in the right place at the right time. We both belong to a social network called Smaller Indiana (www.SmallerIndiana.com; see Figure 1.1), having joined within the first couple weeks of its creation. We met at the first event that the founder, Pat Coyle, organized on Martin Luther King Day 2008.

During our initial meeting, which was already filled with friendly teasing and Kyle accusing Erik of carrying a "man bag" (something Erik flatly denies even now)—

```
@edeckers:  It was a leather messenger bag, I swear!
@kyleplacy: Okay, whatever.
```

we arranged to get coffee together the next week. In the following months, we continued to bump into each other, get coffee, get lunch, attend the same networking meetings, collaborate on projects, and refer speaking and work gigs to each other. Eighteen months later, Kyle asked Erik to help with another book he was working on, and that led to this one. But it all started with being at the same place at the same time in January 2008.

Figure 1.1 *The front page from SmallerIndiana.com*

Whether you're online or out in the real world, treat every person you meet as a possible future resource. You never know if the person you meet at the Chamber of Commerce meeting will become your next employer. The person you have coffee with one day (or even the one who serves your coffee) could become your business partner. And the person who connects with you on Twitter could end up hiring you to speak at an event two months later.

You need to treat each of these new relationships with care. Nurture them, help them grow, and tell people your story.

"But how will we have time to grow those relationships?" people usually ask. "We have work to do."

That's the beauty of social media. It lets you stay in touch with people in between the times you meet face to face. It lets you share your story without doing a big information dump in the first 30 minutes of a one-hour appointment. It lets you find out about a lot of other people all at once, without buying lunch every day. It lets you learn about the details of your lives so that when you do get together, you get to spend more time talking about deeper issues and bigger ideas. And *that* is where those opportunities are going to come from.

Take Action. (Even a Small Step Is a Step Forward.)

There's an old saying that if you hit a rock with a hammer 1,000 times, it wasn't the 1,000th blow that broke the rock; it was the 999 that came before it.

All the plans in the world don't amount to much if you don't actually put them into action. If you want to be someone notable or be considered an authority in your field, you have to start somewhere.

Although you're not going to become famous with a single blog post or a single YouTube video, you can't start without your first one. It's a matter of writing post after post, creating video after video. It's publishing those 999 posts or videos that makes the 1,000th so effective.

Ask people who found some success in what they do. All of them will tell you that they worked hard—harder than anyone else. They got up earlier, stayed up later, and worked longer in between.

Earlier, we mentioned "faith-based networking" and the idea that you will meet the right person with the right opportunity at the right moment. Whether that meeting was divinely inspired, you also met the right person because you've been to hundreds of meetings talking to thousands of people and communicating the same thing: the kind of opportunities you're looking for.

Just like the rock that took 1,000 blows to break it, you had to meet 999 people before you finally met that one person who changed your life.

We wish we could tell you the secret phrase or handshake that would let you meet that 1,000th person in the first 24 hours of your new personal branding adventure. Unfortunately, we can't. There isn't one. But if you follow even half the steps outlined in this book, you'll eventually get there, and you'll have fun doing it.

Who Needs Self-Promotion?

Everyone needs self-promotion and personal branding. It's how you're going to grow your business, advance your career, and expand your personal network. There are few people who don't need self-promotion of some kind. (Actually, all we could come up with were spies and hermits.) Even if you work for a large government agency in some half-forgotten division, sequestered away in the basement, working on some underfunded project (*especially* if this is the case; see Chapter 15, "Personal Branding: Using What You've Learned to Land Your Dream Job"), you need to brand yourself.

Self-promotion is for everyone, not just business people trying to get a job or earn a promotion. Even those outside the corporate world can benefit from promoting themselves.

- **Book authors**—Although your publisher—your kind-hearted, giving, generous-to-a-fault publisher

```
@edeckers:   Forget it; they said we already blew the
             promotions budget on the launch party.
@kyleplacy:  Seriously? I knew we shouldn't have served the
             lobster.
```

will be doing everything it can to promote your book, it's also up to the authors to make sure they're promoting their book, with websites, blogs, Twitter and Facebook accounts, YouTube videos, and several other social media tools and real-world networking opportunities.

- **Musicians**—Musicians are at a personal branding advantage because they're already promoting themselves as a brand. Think of your favorite band and everything you like about them: their music, T-shirts, interviews, website, fan pages, and anything else you can find. All these things go toward maintaining their public image and persona. As a musician, you'll want to explore every free social media tool where your fans are gathered. It could be Facebook and MySpace, posting videos of your last show, or even a social network devoted strictly to bands in your city or state.

- **Public speakers**—All public speakers, except for the big-name celebrities who belong to speakers bureaus, must promote themselves to conference organizers, meeting organizers, trade associations, and anyone else who hires speakers. You need to provide evidence of your speaking abilities, but thanks to social media, gone are the days of sending out video tapes or DVDs of your talks. Instead, you can refer people to your website where they can watch videos of your talks, download your *one sheet* (a single sheet about your qualifications as a speaker), and even read some of the articles that you discuss in your talks.

- **Entrepreneurs**—This will end up being one of the best marketing campaigns you could run. By equating you with your company, you both become a synonymous brand. When people hear your name, they think of your company, and vice versa. By offering yourself as an expert in your field on a blog and Twitter, people will come to see you as a resource, and someone they need to hire for a project or even a long-term contract.

- **Salespeople**—We're seeing a major change in the way sales are done around the world. A lot of sales coaches and experts are telling salespeople to put down the phone and quit making cold calls. They're inefficient, ineffective, and just plain boring (cold calling, not the coaches). Nowadays, salespeople are building relationships rather than databases, providing information and knowledge, and networking with as many people as they can. We understand that many salespeople still have to slog out their time on the phones, but by keeping track of your sales funnel (see Chapter 11, "Measuring Success: You Like Me, You Really Like Me!") and finding where your best customers are coming from, you may learn that networking and branding yourself are much more effective than cold calling some name from a list.

- **Job seekers**—These are people who need personal branding the most. Every element of a job search is focused on what people think of when they hear your name. You email a PDF or word processing document with your skills and experience on it. You have three or more conversations with several people about how your skills and experience can help their company. And nowadays, you're searched online by people who make a hiring decision based on what they find. By carefully planning and creating your personal brand and then living up to it, you can greatly improve your chances to find a new job, compared to those people who still think FaceSpace is just for teenagers and perverts.

Meet Our Heroes

We talk to a lot of people about social media, especially in the small business world. And we have met people who are or were in the same boat as Erik, trying to redefine, or even define, themselves—to launch a new phase of their career, to make a name for themselves, or even just to reach people they have never had to reach before. These are four fictional people we created to help illustrate the different lessons in each chapter. You can see how each of them can apply what we discuss in their own lives.

- **Allen (influencer)** was an account manager for a marketing and advertising agency for 14 years but was laid off six months ago after his agency lost its biggest client. He has many contacts in the agency world and is a member of a professional marketing association. He is an influencer because he may switch jobs, but he stays within the same industry. Influencers are usually hired because of their network and industry knowledge. A lot of salespeople tend to be influencers, hopping from company to company, but staying within their industry and not actually moving up the career ladder.
- **Beth (climber)** is a marketing manager for a large insurance company. She has been with this company for 10 years, but this is her second insurance company. She has moved up the ranks in this company, as well as with her last employer. Beth is a climber because she changes jobs to climb her career ladder, but she will stay within the same industry and even the same company to do it. Her ultimate goal is to become the chief marketing officer of an insurance company, preferably this one.

- **Carla (neophyte)** is a former pharmaceutical sales rep who was laid off after eight years with her company. She is interested in working for a nonprofit, either as a program director or a fund-raising specialist. Carla is a neophyte because she is not only changing jobs, but changing industries. This means she is starting over in terms of knowledge, influence, contacts, and even possibly her skill set. A new college graduate would also be a neophyte.

- **Darrin (free agent)** is an IT professional who leaves his job every two or three years in pursuit of more money. He is a free agent because he'll stay at roughly the same level of job, regardless of where he goes, but he can make more money because there are bigger companies requiring his expertise. Darrin is not considered an influencer because he jumps industries every time he jumps companies, which means it's harder for him to make a name for himself in that field.

2

How Do You Fit
in the Mix?

Can you remember at least one piece of information from
Erik's story from Chapter 1, "Welcome to the Party"? This
is what Chris Brogan, one of the top branding and social
media experts on the Internet (www.chrisbrogan.com),
calls the storyteller's promise. The storyteller's promise is
an agreement that the reader and storyteller/author make
at the onset of a story.

What does a storyteller's promise state? According to
Brogan, it says, "I'm here as a consumer of your content (or your personal brand). You will give me what
I've come to see/read/experience. You won't try to trick
me, unless that's part of what I've signed up to see."[1] In
this case, Erik's storyteller's promise is that he will tell
you how to build your network through social networking, not about the time he took his dog for a walk and
shenanigans ensued. Erik is going to give you what you
expected to see when you bought this book and read the

---

1. www.chrisbrogan.com/presentation-and-storytellers-promises/

first chapter. You believe we are not trying to trick you by filling the pages with dog stories and shenanigans.

It would be safe to say that you remembered at least one portion of Erik's story about networking and personal branding; that is the storyteller's promise. When developing your personal brand, you are entering into an agreement with the individual experiencing your brand. You are creating a storyteller's promise.

When we tell a story, people listen. It's extremely important that your story is not terrible. You don't want to tell a story that people will frown upon or never remember. Stories are what drive memories. They are intricate to the development of a person, and they're extremely important in the world of personal branding.

It's safe to say that there is a story in all of us. It's also safe to say that stories are what make each of us different. For example, Erik may have had an encounter with a wild animal at a local restaurant. The wild animal (let's say it was a bear) stole all his food and proceeded to drink all his water.

This is a story, albeit untrue, but it's still a story. The story is unique to Erik, and Kyle could never claim to have experienced the wild animal at the same restaurant, under the same circumstances.

@kyleplacy: I did have a talking bear in a green tie
            steal my picnic basket one time, though.

@edeckers: I think you're thinking of a Yogi Bear
            cartoon.

The stories that surround us all are the first ingredient in building a strong personal identity that enhances our overall brand. We'll discuss how our four heroes from Chapter 1 can use storytelling to enhance their personal brand. In fact, you'll meet them in every chapter of this book.

This chapter can help you define and build your personal story. You do not need to write a book, maybe a few pages. This chapter is not meant to be a guide on how to write a research paper but a guide to help you discover your personal brand story.

How do you start? Where do you begin this journey to further refine your personal brand story to help you fit in the mix? How do you define your identity? Read on.

The Basics of Building Your Personal Brand Story

The important part to build a personal brand is telling your story. That's a phrase you'll hear a lot from personal branding and social media speakers: "telling your story." (That's because it sounds so much more interesting and cool than "narrating your personal history" or "relating your background.")

Telling your story is what makes you unique and helps you succeed in your marketplace and your career. Your life story, your professional story, or whatever story is most relevant to establishing your personal brand can help you stand out from those people who never figure this out.

Writing Your Personal Brand Autobiography

All autobiographies start with (are) a story. Norman Rockwell has a story, and Bill Clinton has a story. They both have written their autobiographies, and the books/ stories have helped guide their personal brand in the public's eyes.

Have you tried to write your own autobiography? You don't need to write a book—just a simple bio. You might not even have enough content to write a book, but how about a paragraph?

Your personal brand biography is important because it is your overall personal sales pitch. There are three different types of personal branding biographies: shortest, shorter, and short. You have a 1-sentence pitch, a 100-word pitch, and a 250-word biography. These are important because they help you prioritize and figure out what is most important about *you*. What skills are your best? What's your passion? What are you best at in your career? What makes you *you*? The personal brand biography is also used in your elevator pitch, which is discussed later in this chapter. Let's look into how you can write your personal brand biography.

Prioritizing When Writing Your Personal Brand Story

The hardest part about writing a personal brand is that you are talking about yourself. It may be easy to talk about yourself, but when you are writing down your accomplishments, it can be more difficult. Don't fret. Most people don't know where to start, either from being modest (don't be; you can't afford to be modest or downplay your accomplishments) or lack of direction. (Write for the audience you want to reach.)

We'll give you some examples to work from. You don't have to do this alone, and certainly not from scratch. Let's look at Kyle's bio and try to break down what is best and worst of the personal brand biography.

@edeckers: Wait, why are we doing your bio?

@kyleplacy: Because we opened the whole damn book with yours!

@edeckers: Oh yeah.

> *Author of two acclaimed books,* Twitter Marketing For Dummies *and* Branding Yourself, *Kyle Lacy is a Principal of Marketing Research and Education for ExactTarget, a leading global provider in interactive marketing solutions.*
>
> *He has an in-depth understanding of the application of social and interactive media for both small and large businesses and regularly speaks on topics ranging from social media adoption to interactive marketing trends across email, mobile, and social media. Kyle has been recognized as one of Indiana's 40-under-40 by the Indianapolis Business Journal, Anderson University's Young Alumni of the Year, and TechPoint's Young Professional of the Year.*

Let's break this down. The bio starts by announcing that Kyle has written two books and spends his time working in marketing research and education at ExactTarget. This automatically tells you exactly what Kyle does on a daily basis. And it talks specifically to the people he wants to reach: people who work in interactive marketing, CMOs, or people who need to do social media for enterprise systems.

After this, Kyle's bio establishes him as an author and speaker in the field. This tells you exactly why he is an expert in the field. He wrote two books and regularly speaks because he's an expert.

The rest of the bio mentions different accolades and his speaking topics. It covers everything he thinks a potential customer or event organizer would need to know to take the next step in the relationship.

That next step is crucial. It could be something small like deciding to follow Kyle on Twitter or connect with him on LinkedIn or hiring him to give a talk. A good bio should answer any question someone else may have, even if that answer is "no."

Writing Your Personal Brand Biography

We talked about the three different lengths of biographies earlier, and this is your chance to do it. Each biography you write, whether short, shorter, or shortest, has its place. You may be at a networking event and have only 5 seconds to give your pitch. Every type of personal brand biography has its place in the world of building your personal brand.

We're a little tired of elevator pitches, even though they're all the rage with all the networking groups we attend and all the sales coaches we talk to. Elevator pitches are 30-second speeches you're supposed to give to explain who you are or what product you sell.

The problem is they're about 25 seconds too long. If it takes you 30 seconds to explain yourself to someone, you're probably not going to notice his or her eyes glazing over after the first 15 seconds.

If you are introduced to someone, you should be able to say what it is you do or what you're looking for in a single sentence. If you have time, you can give a longer pitch. And if the person is either unable to escape, or actually interested, you can hit him with an even longer pitch.

Practice the short, shorter, shortest model with your pitch. Let's say you're a former newspaper reporter who is looking to break into the PR field. Here's how your bio would look:

- **Shortest**—I'm a former newspaper reporter trying to get into public relations.

- **Shorter**—I'm a former newspaper reporter trying to work as a public relations professional. I worked for the *Pawtucket Times* as a news reporter for four years, as a sports reporter for another three, and then covered the business beat for six. I've been spending a lot of time volunteering as the PR director for our local Oyster Shuckers Rehab Center and I wrote a book about Thomas Gardiner Corcoran, one of President Franklin Roosevelt's advisors.

- **Short**—I'm a former newspaper reporter trying to get into public relations. I worked for the *Pawtucket Times* as a news reporter for four years, as a sports reporter for another three, and then covered the business beat for six. I also served as president of the Rhode Island Journalists Association and spoke at our annual conference about the growth of small-town media. In addition, I'm a part-time professional historian, and I wrote a book about Thomas Gardiner Corcoran, one of President Franklin Roosevelt's advisors and part of his brain trust. Because it was a self-published book, I had to do all my own PR work. I scheduled a series of radio and TV interviews, and the book reached Amazon.com's Top 1,000 for 16 weeks in a row, bumping some Twitter marketing book out of the ranking. Finally, I've been serving as the volunteer PR director for our local Oyster Shuckers Rehab Center, garnering us about $100,000 in earned media.

The following examples should give you a good idea of what we're talking about. And you'll notice that the longer ones might seem a little more suited for a written bio, rather than a verbal introduction. When you write your bio, you don't need to recite it word for word. Just make sure you hit the high points.

So what should you do and what should you say during your introduction? Here are a few points you need to remember:

- **Introduce your professional self**—What would you say to a stranger who asked who you were? Kyle would say, "I'm an interactive marketing strategist." This helps in the development of your one-sentence biography.

- **What do you do?**—Of course, you have to tell people what you do, or they will have no idea how to use you in their current state or setting. People need to know what you do before you discuss all your accomplishments to further solidify your importance as a personal brand: "I am an interactive marketer and thought leader who specializes in communication through social, mobile, and email." We now have our one-sentence elevator pitch (more about that in Chapter 9, "How to Network: Hello, My Name Is…").

- **What have you accomplished?**—What is the most important thing you have accomplished? For Kyle, it is writing a book and being listed as one of the top business professionals under 40 years old in Indianapolis. Don't list all your accomplishments, no matter how cool they all are. Just pick your top three, and let them tell the story of your brand.

- **Write in third person, talk in first**—Your bio is used by other people. Your bio is for other people to tell your story. Be sure you write it in third person and make it sound like someone else is describing you. Just, please, don't do this when you're actually speaking to someone. It sounds pretentious.

- **Ask a friend for advice**—Don't believe that you have written a perfect biography. Kyle and Erik have each asked other people about their opinions of their personal brand biography. Have someone else read it. Ask them to tell you what's missing and what should be taken out. Having another set of eyes to help with the process is going to be the difference between a good and a great bio.

- **Don't forget it**—You cannot ignore your biography any more than you can use the same résumé that you left college with. You're constantly changing and growing, and so is your story. Every project you work on and every client you come in contact with will change your story. You'll have changes in experience, skills, and opinions on your industry. Your top three accomplishments will change as you add new successes. And your career path will change. Your bio needs to change and update as well, both in the written and verbal form.

You need to use specific language and ideas when you're discussing your bio. Please, oh please, don't buy into that "use memorable, creative terms" or "use an opening statement that will make people ask questions" advice that some networking consultants give.

Many times they'll tell you to use an elevator pitch like "We can help your company stand out from the competition." The problem is, everyone helps you stand out from the competition. It could be a marketing or advertising agency. It could be someone who sells custom logo apparel. It could be the company that does full-color car wraps. It could be the guy who dances outside your store waving a giant sign telling people that you'll buy their gold.

The problem is, all these people will help a company stand out from the competition, so offering something that vague and generic as an elevator pitch will not encourage people to ask questions; it will make them ignore you in favor of someone who's more interesting, or at least more specific.

How Do Our Heroes Use the Personal Brand Biography?

You need to apply some of the principles of telling your story to our heroes from Chapter 1. They're all transitioning from their current role to a new one and must state their desires and past in their personal bio. If you ran into them at a networking event, what would be their one-sentence pitch? Would you remember it?

- **Allen (influencer)** was an account manager for a marketing and advertising agency for 14 years but was laid off after his agency lost its biggest client. The layoff wasn't his fault, but he was a casualty of the loss.
  What should his one-sentence biography say?

  *I'm a creative professional in high-level marketing and advertising, and I
  have worked for one of the top agencies in the country.*

  What is positive about this? It says Allen is creative and professional,
  has an established marketing and advertising career, and worked for
  a top agency. A person would come away with the idea that Allen is
  good at what he does.

  What's missing? You could argue that Allen could have included
  something about the kind of job he's looking for, but that could come
  in a follow-up sentence like, *"And I'm looking for a job in a marketing
  agency as an account executive."*

- **Beth (climber)** is a marketing manager for a large insurance company.
  She has been with them for 10 years, but this is her second insurance
  company. Remember, Beth wants to move up the ranks within the
  company and eventually become CMO. What would be a good one-
  sentence biography for Beth?

  *I am a marketing manager for Inverness Insurance and have been
  ranked as one of the top marketing professionals in my industry for the
  past three years by* Insurance Marketing *magazine.*

  What's important about mentioning that she is one of the top marketing managers in her firm? Is it true? We assume she is for one reason:
  She verified her experience by putting in the recognition from a media
  source.

  If you worked outside the insurance industry, you would have no idea
  whether Beth was lying, but you would automatically trust the media
  placement. This doesn't mean you should make up traditional media
  names to verify your existence. A liar is a liar, plain and simple. Don't
  lie on your one-sentence personal brand biography—or ever.

  What is the difference between Beth's written and a spoken one-
  sentence biography? For one thing, we hope Beth wouldn't drop the
  whole "ranked as one of the top marketing professionals" phrase in the
  middle of a conversation. That sounds a little arrogant. However, it's
  perfectly acceptable to say this in written form.

- **Carla (neophyte)** is a former pharmaceutical sales rep who was laid off
  after eight years with her company. She is interested in working for a
  nonprofit, either as a program director or a fund-raising specialist.

We're actually torn here, because Carla almost needs two different bios:

I'm a sales and marketing professional who specializes in the development of relationships between customers and the organization.

and

I'm a former pharmaceutical salesperson trying to make the leap to the nonprofit world.

Remember, Carla is not searching for a job as a pharmaceutical rep. She wants to work as a program director or fund-raising specialist for a nonprofit. So the second bio is more of a conversational introduction—something she would use when meeting someone in person. The first one is better suited to the written form, especially on a résumé or on LinkedIn (see Chapter 4, "LinkedIn: Networking on Steroids").

By creating the first bio to highlight that she is a marketing professional specializing in the development of relationships between customers and organizations, Carla is not discounting her last job, but she's not overtly saying she was in pharmaceutical sales. She's pointing out the similarities between what she used to do and what she wants to do now. The more important part of this one-sentence biography is that she is a relationship builder. People want relationship builders.

What's missing? The second bio doesn't say as much about what Carla wants to do. We can easily add *"as a fundraiser or program director,"* and that will fix it. But this is generally short enough to capture someone's interest.

- **Darrin (free agent)** is an IT professional who leaves his job every two or three years in pursuit of more money. He is a free agent because he'll stay at roughly the same level of job but he can make more money if he decides to pursue bigger companies on his own.

Darrin is going to be writing his one-sentence biography with as much validation as possible to win him the largest projects. Darrin needs to talk extensively about his accomplishments while touching lightly on his profession of information technology.

I'm an IT professional who has worked for six of the top corporations in the city.

Darrin's biography is less about his profession as it is about his professional accomplishments. It is also key to use the word *trust* when you are trying to sell yourself as a professional. When people trust your opinion, you are bordering on the ability to become a thought leader to the person who is reading (or hearing) your one-sentence biography.

What's missing? Darrin needs to be prepared to talk about what he's looking for and what kind of IT work he has done. Darrin also needs a verbal bio, and "I'm in IT" is not going to cut it. That's fine when he's meeting his wife's friends at a party who will end up asking for help with their email, but it doesn't tell a potential employer a single thing. Something like, "*I'm a network security specialist*" is more appropriate to tell someone who's in his same field.

Telling Your Complete Brand Story

Your personal brand sentence and biography will give you your start in formulating your personal brand story. This is the author's agreement with the reader, where you give the reader what he was expecting. You have to flesh out the story, but in other locations. All your content—your photos, blog posts, and status updates—should center on telling your story.

The following points are more than just a checklist. Your content should fall within one of these groups—these "buckets"—as you live out your personal brand. By relating the right content in the right chapters, you'll tell your story to your readers. And as you put more and more content into each chapter, even the latecomers will follow your story. The following points are a guideline to help you form your personal brand biography. If you hate writing, use the following points to help guide you in telling your personal brand story:

- **The beginning**—This is where you take the time to define yourself. Where did you come from? How did you get here? Where are you going? Write out the answers to each of these questions concisely in a couple of sentences. This is just the definition of who you are and want to be as a brand. People want to know your story. All you have to do is write it. You should end up with two sentences for each question.

- **How do I help?**—What situation did you help solve? This could be a situation that you helped solve at the office or any problem you solve on a daily basis. It is up to you as the writer to define the problem. Basically, people want to read a story with a problem that needs to be solved. Novelists, playwrights, and screenwriters are taught to write about conflict, about problems to be solved. Solve the problem by the end of your biography, and you have a real story.

- **Your emotional context**—Engage with people on an emotional level. Tell stories that tap into a person's emotions, rather than relying on statistics and facts. This will help people connect with you. For instance, what significant event took place to make you choose the career path you now have? Use this to let people see you as unique and real. It's not about how 20% of all people do the thing that results in the other thing; it's about how your high school English teacher said you had real skill as a writer, and you should think about pursuing it.

- **Keep with consistency**—Build your story by being consistent in the types of stories you tell and the theme around them. All good stories have a rising theme or a story arc. Define your niche (your theme), and build around it. Don't jump all over the place in what you do or talk about; if you are living and writing about your dream of running your first marathon, don't switch gears by writing about your dream of becoming a travel writer. When you're consistent, your story will stick, and your message will reach your intended audience.

- **Leave no room for questions**—Don't make people read between the lines. When creating your story, be completely clear. Leave no room for questions or blanks. You, as your brand, must be completely defined along with your audience and your expertise.

- **Remember you**—Don't get too caught up in the words and forget to care about why you're doing this to begin with. When building your story, remember those moments in your life that shaped the brand you've become. Tell people those moments and get them fired up about your brand. It'll motivate you and make others understand why you're so great.

- **Keep the steam going by firing up others**—You've gotten people interested...or at least gotten their attention. Don't lose steam. Build your story by building up others. The same people who are fired up about you should be the ones you brag about. Shout out to them on Twitter, engage them in conversations, and boast about their accomplishments louder than they do. You want your audience to be loyal, so be good to them first.

- **Connect on their level**—Make your story relatable. Remember, you're not writing science fiction. You're dealing with real life and real situations. Put yourself in others' shoes, and cater to your market. You defined who your audience is and know what it is they need and want. Give it to them.

- **Keep them interested**—At this point, people know who you are, what you're about, and what you do. Now is the time to make sure they know you're good at it. Share your success stories to reinforce your abilities, and continually invest time in finding new stories. You're only as good as others say you are. Invest in them so that in turn they invest in you. Build your story around an audience that needs you.

- **Edit your work**—Where are you confused? Where are you confusing to others? You can define and redefine your brand if it makes sense. Look back through your story to proofread and fix any nuances you may have forgotten.

After you finish writing a couple of sentences for each point, you will have a basic understanding of what you want to accomplish and how you are defined as a person. You will end up with a short bio to help describe, define, and relate to individuals in the professional world.

The Law of Anecdotal Value

Peter Sagal, the host of "Wait, Wait, Don't Tell Me," a comedy quiz show on public radio, once said that he was told by a professor to "Choose the experiences in life that offer the most anecdotal value—that is, look for the opportunities that have the most likelihood of producing a cool story." He said he has tried to live by this directive, which he calls the Law of Anecdotal Value.

This is an important piece of advice, and one we thought worth offering here, because it encourages us to actually do stuff that's interesting and worth repeating to others.

Remember, the whole basis for your personal brand is to build an interesting personal story—to actually do things that you enjoy telling other people about. It means getting out of the office and doing things. It means going out for drinks, coffee, or dinner once in a while, instead of going home. It means going to conferences and spending time meeting new people. And best of all, it means not watching television night after night.

We have yet to hear an interesting story that starts with, "One night, while I was watching TV...."

We want to encourage you to do the things that add value to your own life. Throughout the rest of this book, we're going to tell you to share interesting things that are of value to the people in your network. But we don't want you to spend all your time amassing other people's interesting information. We want you to be a source of interesting information and stories yourself.

Living an anecdotal life—a "story-worthy" life—usually means having passion about some things you enjoy doing, or want to achieve, and then working and thinking about how to get it done. We talk about passion in Chapter 1, but it's worth mentioning again: You will not be following the Law of Anecdotal Value if you just sit around and watch TV night after night, or sit in your cubicle day after day without dreaming of, and working toward, your next big thing.

There are plenty of people who live lives without passion and without doing any-thing. They don't have anything to inspire them, and they don't try anything new. There are people who eat the same food, go to the same restaurants, drive the same route to the same job they've had for 20 years because it's easier to do that than to work a little harder to accomplish something a little better.

These people don't want More. They are happy with Good Enough. Good Enough is easy because it doesn't require any work. But the problem with Good Enough is that it sucks the life and motivation right out of you. Once you have achieved it, there's never a reason to reach for More.

If you want to follow the Law of Anecdotal Value, it means you won't accept the status quo and do only what you need to do to earn the next paycheck. It means you'll actually do something that takes some time and effort. This book is filled with case studies and testimonials from people who have worked to do more in life, and as a result, have dozens of stories to tell. We've chosen a few of our favor-ite social media professionals and asked them to share one of their stories with us.

Surround Yourself with People Who Have Passion

If you want to lead that story-worthy life and have stories and interesting things to share, surround yourself with people who have a passion for something in their life. It doesn't have to be the same passion as yours. You want to surround yourself with people who love what they do as much as you love what you do, if not more.

Whether it's someone who loves their work or loves their hobby, find a way to spend time with that person—they'll sweep you up in their energy, and you'll add their fuel to your own fire. Their energy will be contagious—as yours will be to them—and you can feed off each other's ideas and passion.

As you spend more time with these people, and learn from them, you'll learn new stories to tell, discover new ways to tell them, and best of all, you'll create your own stories. Now you have to share them with other people to get them to stick.

Sharing Memories and Stories

There are a lot of different tools and technologies that you can use to tell your story. We actually cover them in Chapters 3 ("Blogging: Telling Your Story") and 7 ("Say Cheese: Sharing Photos and Videos"). But here, we want to tell you why it's important.

Think about your family's best stories. What are the stories that get told and retold during family gatherings—those stories that are passed down from generation to generation, father to son, mother to daughter. These are the stories that family legend are made of.

There is no reason you can't have stories like that, or that they need to stay only with you. One of the cool things social media has let us do is to share those stories with each other.

Both of us have heard stories from friends and industry colleagues like Dan Schawbel and Jason Falls that we repeat to our own audiences. These stories have become memorable—and occasionally legendary—in their retelling because they are interesting things that actually happened to these people.

But here's the important thing: You have to tell these stories. You have to be willing to share those stories with people—whether it's writing it up as a blog post, posting it on Facebook, or letting your videos and pictures tell the story for you and putting them online for others to see and share.

If you're not comfortable sharing certain parts of your life, don't share them. No one said you had to tell everything you were doing, show photos of every aspect of your life, or reveal every personal detail you'd rather keep private.

"There are just some things I don't want people to know about," we often hear from social media resisters.

That's fine; don't share those things. If you don't want people to know where you live, don't put your house on Foursquare. If you don't want people to know you're on vacation, don't post photos to Facebook while you're out.

Choose the parts of your life you want to share with people, and make it available for people to read, watch, and enjoy. Share the parts of your life that you feel comfortable sharing, and keep the rest of the stuff private. Rather than relying on the ever-changing, always-complex Facebook privacy settings to keep your stuff hidden, just don't put it up.

Just remember that to build relationships with people and get them to know and like you, you need to reveal some parts of yourself to make yourself seem more human. That's where sharing your memories and stories, through blogging, status updates, tweets, photos, and videos, are all going to help you with this.

Do's and Don'ts of Telling Your Story

There are certain rules that everyone should follow when embarking on their personal brand journey. Read, reread, and read again the points made in this section of the chapter. They will help guide you through the situations you will face while building your personal brand.

1. Don't Post Pictures That Would Shock Your Mother

Every social networking site lets you post pictures. Whether you're on Facebook, Twitter, or LinkedIn, you can post pictures of yourself to help tell your story. Don't be stupid when it comes to your picture posting and professional storytelling. It's safe to say that an employer doesn't want to see you doing a keg stand or flashing a concert goer. Post pictures that relate and strengthen your professional story, and completely avoid pictures that you would be ashamed to show your mom. The general rule of thumb is to imagine your mom, your boss, and your biggest client are in a car together, driving by your billboard with your photo on it. If you would be embarrassed for them to see it, don't post it.

2. Don't View Your Personal Brand Story as a Sales Pitch

There are plenty of people who dislike getting sales calls during dinner—or ever. The same is true with your personal brand. Don't create your story as a sales pitch. Make it a story. If you treat your personal brand as a conversation rather than a sales pitch, your readers will trust you.

3. Don't Post Something You Will Regret Later

Imagine a situation in which an employee posts something extremely negative about a client, a business partner, or even a whole city she's visiting, and it's viewed and picked up by hundreds of people on the Internet.

We know a few people who have posted a nasty or negative comment, said at a time when they frankly should not have been posting anything, and when they had been trying to cultivate an image of being a respected professional.

The people used Twitter or Facebook to share their comments and meant them as a joke. They then realized the error of their ways and deleted the offending posts. However, it was too late because several people had copied the posts, taken screen shots, or even retweeted them and shared them with hundreds of other people, which became thousands of people.

Would you fire the person? More than likely. Would you do business with them? Doubt it. Would you ever hire them? Absolutely not.

The old World War II phrase "Loose lips sink ships" is appropriate here. Everything on the Internet is saved, whether it's on Google's cached pages or Archive.org (a site that takes a picture of Internet pages as they're created. Erik has found stuff he posted back in 1996 in Archive.org). Remember that everything is being read, and everyone is listening to what is being posted. Be careful what you post.

4. Don't Ask for Things First. Ask for Things Second

Your role in building your personal brand is twofold. To help other people, and then to help yourself. When we help others, we all succeed, not the other way around. When Erik offers to help Kyle with a project, Kyle is more likely to help Erik when he needs it. If Erik asks for help first, Kyle may be busy at the time and can't help out. Later, if Kyle needs help, Erik will remember that, and he'll be "busy" as well.

@kyleplacy: Is that why you couldn't help me set up that blog site last week? You're so selfish.

@edeckers: How hard is it to help people move? I spent 12 hours loading and unloading that damn truck.

@kyleplacy: I was at my sister's wedding!

The important lesson is to give before you ask. By doing so, you'll build up good-will, and people will be more willing to help you. (We'll talk more about this idea in Chapter 9.) When you ask for things all the time, you will fast become the boy who cried wolf instead of the boy who everyone loves.

5. Don't Get Distracted

It's easy to get distracted when you work on personal branding. There is so much to do, so much to say, and so much to accomplish that it can be hard sometimes to focus on a specific task. It's so easy to get distracted by all these things you "ought" to be doing and tools you "ought" to try. But being active does not mean being effective.

@edeckers: Squirrel!

@kyleplacy: RT @edeckers: Squirrel!

Remember that focus is key when it comes to telling your story. If you lose focus and slip, brush yourself off, drop the thing that distracted you, and refocus your efforts. By refocusing your efforts, you can assume responsibility to meeting your goal.

6. Don't Underestimate the Power of Your Network

Your current network should mean everything to you. These are people who know about opportunities, deals, and projects that you may never hear about otherwise. They are the people who will connect you with individuals who could change your career, your company, and your life. Rather than trying to figure things out on your own, ask your network for help. If you want to be connected, you have to let your network do its thing. However, remember to not badger your network into helping you all the time. The boy who cried wolf screwed up the first three times. Ask for help when it is needed.

7. Do Invest in Yourself

Invest in yourself by always staying informed about what's going on in your industry. Read industry blogs, read blogs from allied industries, attend seminars, read books, and listen to audiobooks and podcasts.

You want to be ahead of the game and ahead of content compared to your peers. Read and talk to people to improve your knowledge. Investing in yourself is one of the more important aspects of your personal brand.

8. Do Invest in Other People

When you invest in other people, they invest in you. This could be as simple as forwarding an email or sending a Twitter message for someone in your network. When you give, you will receive. When you help other people grow and find new opportunities, they'll return the favor. If you ignore them, they'll ignore you when you need their help.

9. Do Be Visible and Active

It's just as important to stay visible in the world of storytelling and social media as it is to invest in yourself. In fact, staying visible and involved is a form of self-investment. By being visible, you share information about yourself on a daily basis and staying in front of the influencers, clients, and network connections that matter. By being visible, you maintain awareness of your personal brand.

10. Do Take Some Time for Yourself

Read this last one carefully: You will most certainly be overwhelmed with the amount of information you receive, content being processed, content being shared, and stories being developed. You need to take some time for yourself. This means turning off everything you're doing and doing something with family or friends. If you don't take some time for yourself, you'll get caught in the never-ending process of personal branding and be completely void of personality after a couple of years of grinding yourself into the dust.

Your Network Is Your Castle—Build It

3

Blogging:
Telling Your Story

Blogging is an easy way to publish your thoughts, ideas, and insights, and it can be done without Hypertext Markup Language (HTML) coding. A blog—short for web log—is an online diary that you're willing to let others read and comment on.

Anyone with a computer and an Internet connection can start a blog: You sign up for a free blogging platform and start writing blog posts. When you are comfortable with navigating around your blog, you can add a template to make it look the way you want, buy a domain name to make the name easier to remember, and start promoting it to your friends and families on your different social networks.

Blogging should be at the center of your social media campaign. Everything we talk about in this book hinges on blogging. You need to have a blog as a part of your online identity, because it will serve as the anchor for all your efforts.

Your blog is the collection of all your knowledge, the hub of your personal branding wheel, the virtual spot where you plant your personal branding seed and say, "This is where I will grow." You need a single destination to refer people to, so it should be a blog. Your blog is the place where you show your knowledge and share your accomplishments.

If you're an artist, you can upload photos of your work to your blog. If you're a consultant, you can write your thoughts about your industry. If you're looking for a job, you can write about industry issues to demonstrate that you understand what your potential employer is dealing with. And if you're a nonprofit, what better way to keep donors up to date with what's going on without sending out 2,000 newsletters every month?

Now, it's not impossible to have a personal branding campaign that doesn't have a blog, but it's difficult. You need a place to refer people and a way to showcase your thoughts, ideas, and work.

We have heard arguments from some people that "large corporations don't use blogs, so why should I?" Although this might be true, you are not a large multimillion dollar corporation. You are launching a personal brand, and we recommend that you use your blog as your hub. (That, and there are already a lot of corporations that use blogs, so there!)

Remember, two of the personal branding universal objectives (see Chapter 1, "Welcome to the Party") are to tell your story and to be bold. You need to tell people about yourself, and a blog is going to be the easiest, best way to do it. You can keep a record of what you've done, where you've done it, and what you were thinking when you did *it. It's a journal of your professional accomplishments to show your value to an employer, to a client, or to your industry in general.*

What Is Blogging?

To start blogging, you need to register on a blogging platform, like Blogspot or WordPress. Today's blogging platforms make it easy for anyone, even non-programmers, to share photographs and videos online, and to post articles for the world to read.

Before we had these different blogging platforms, any web updates had to be done via HTML coding. If you wanted to post a new article, you had to place your new article above the old one, format it via HTML, and upload it via File Transfer Protocol (FTP). If you were really good, you could add a new prewritten article in about 15–20 minutes. Now, it's just a matter of entering text in a window that looks like an email window, formatting it, and clicking the Publish button. Take a look at Figures 3.1, 3.2, and 3.3 for examples of what an email window, a Blogger window, and a WordPress window look like.

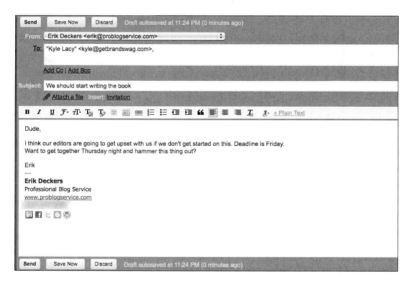

Figure 3.1   *A Gmail window.*

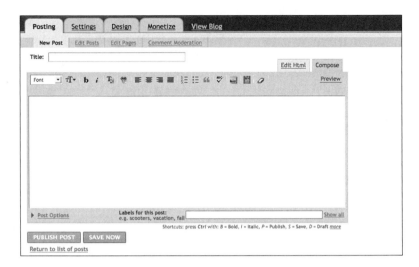

Figure 3.2 *A Blogger.com window. Because Google owns Blogger and Gmail, these two look similar.*

Figure 3.3 *A WordPress window. Whether you use WordPress.com or WordPress.org, the window looks like this.*

Most blogging platforms are just as easy to use as Gmail or other email programs. Your subject line is your headline, and you type the content in the body. You format the text with the formatting buttons, which look an awful lot like the formatting buttons you will find at the top of any word processor. In an email, you click Send, and your recipient receives your email in seconds. In blogging, you click Publish, and your blog post is published in seconds.

Note

At our last count, there were more than 40 different third-party and self-hosted blogging platforms out there. Rather than review all 40, we're going to stick with the most popular ones in the United States: Blogger, WordPress, and Tumblr. We'll mention others at times, but when we discuss blogging, we're primarily thinking of these three, but especially WordPress because it's what we use for our clients.

A Clarification of Terms

There is a difference between a blog and a post. People use the terms interchangeably, but there are actually two strict definitions. A *blog* is the collection of blog posts. It is *not* a single article or post. An *article* or *post* is a single entry in a blog, similar to an entry in a diary.

- Wrong: "I wrote a new blog today."
- Right: "I wrote a new post today."
- Also right: "I blogged today."

The first one means you created an entirely new blog. The second one means you just published a new article on your existing blog. The third one sounds like you picked up a virus somewhere, but it's still okay to say.

Why Should You Blog?

There are as many reasons to blog as there are blogs. People have their own reasons to start one, but they can usually be boiled down to a few major categories. See if one of these categories fits why you want to start a blog.

- **You want to establish your expertise**—You could start a blog to help your chances in a job search, to launch a public speaking career, or to show all those jerks from high school that your knowledge of mollusk mating habits was not esoteric and useless. This is also a good way to improve your own knowledge in your field. You need to keep up with what's going on to tell your readers about it. So, if nothing else, blogging forces you to stay current in your industry.

  Although the rest of these are important reasons to blog, this is a book about building your personal brand for career success. So most of this chapter will assume this is why you're writing your blog. However, keep in mind that blogging for these other reasons is just as important in branding yourself.

- **You want to market or sell something**—One reason businesses have a blog is to make money. Another is to engage with their customers. They use their blogs to engage directly with their customers and to help them make buying decisions about their products or services. You may not sell anything on your blog, but you can sell things because of it. You can showcase your products and drive people to your website and shopping cart, which can increase sales. Many businesses are embracing blogging as a new marketing tool, which is why we know it isn't going away any time soon. When the business world picks something up, it'll be around forever. Many businesses still use fax machines, if that tells you anything....

- **You have something to say**—Whether it's personal observations about life, political beliefs, or knowledge you want to impart, you want a place to publish your thoughts. Even if you write your blog for just three people, it's important that you have a platform to stand on. Blogging lets you do that. We know bloggers who started out writing for only a few friends and now measure their readers by the thousands each month.

  It is worth noting that sharing personal beliefs on a blog for professional branding can backfire. Potential employers may read your blog, and getting too personal or too controversial can keep you from getting the job.

- **You want to share your passion**—Many blogs are about a passion or hobby someone has. Photographers, collectors, and writers have all showcased their talents or acquisitions through blogging. Whether it's the photographer who uploads her best wedding photos or the antique tractor collector who's showing off his latest steering wheel, bloggers have shared their passions with other people like them.

- **You want to be a part of a community**—The great thing about sharing your passion is that people who share that passion will soon find you. If you write about marble collecting, other marble collectors will find you on the search engines and any networks where marble collectors hang out. You can share information via your blogs, talk about upcoming events, and eventually meet face to face at the Marble Collecting Convention. (Yes, there actually is one.)

- **You want to make money**—You can make money from blogging, but it can be difficult. There are three basic ways: ad sales, freelance blogging, or affiliate blogging. Our good friend, Doug Karr (MarketingTechBlog.com), is one of the most widely read bloggers in Indiana, and his blog is one of Ad Age's Top 150 blogs (#119 as of this writing). But he makes just a small amount of money from ad sales each year.

Freelance blogging, or **ghost blogging**, is where you write blog posts for other companies, and they pay you for it. Erik's company is a ghost blogging company.

Affiliate blogging is basically where you sell things for other companies through your own website or blog. For example, you set up a system where you are an affiliate for Amazon.com. You create a page that has a link to this book in Amazon's system. If a visitor to your page buys our book, you make a small commission. There are people, like Heather Sokol, who have built small businesses that do nothing but affiliate sales (see Figure 3.4). They create several blogs, write posts about different products for them, and then promote them via search engines and social media so people will buy their affiliate products or services.

Figure 3.4   *Heather Sokol runs Inexpensively.com as part of her affiliate blogging network. This is one possible way to make money from blogging.*

Choose Your Blogging Platforms

Several free blogging platforms are out there. A Mashable.com article from 2007 listed 40 different free sites (http://mashable.com/2007/08/06/free-blog-hosts/), and we even thought of a couple they missed. We're only going to discuss a few in this book—Blogspot, WordPress, Tumblr, Posterous, TypePad—the ones we work with the most frequently. Check out the Mashable article if you want to find any others.

All the platforms we discuss in this chapter, except for one (TypePad), are completely free to use. Some of them have additional upgrades you can purchase, but they are optional, and you can run your blog without ever buying them.

If you're not technically savvy, or don't know anyone who is, we recommend that you start your new blog on Blogspot, WordPress.com, Posterous, or Tumblr. You can set one up in less than 30 minutes, and the hardest part of the entire experience will be choosing which template you want to use (graphic design elements, such as background, colors, and photos). But after you're up and running, it's a breeze to add new content.

Blogspot.com/Blogger.com

Blogspot was called Blogger before Google purchased it in 2003. Now, typing in either URL will get you to the same place. It's one of the most widely used blog platforms around the world, it's easy to use, and it integrates seamlessly into other Google properties like Picasa (photo sharing), FeedBurner (RSS creator), and Google Analytics (web analytics software).

Basically, if you sign up for a free Google account of any sort, whether it's Gmail, Picasa, Google Analytics, Google Docs, or even iGoogle, you have a Blogspot account.

Blogspot is also a hosted blog site, which means your blog lives on Google's servers. You don't have to mess with server storage or updating and maintaining software, and it doesn't cost anything.

Although many advanced bloggers look down their e-noses at Blogspot, it's the most widely used of all the blogging platforms because it's easy. However, its ease of use also means it's limited in what it can do. It doesn't have the add-ons and plug-ins that WordPress does, although it does now allow users to create several pages.

 Note

> Let's define a few terms:
>
> *Add-ons* and *plug-ins* are things you can add on or plug in to a blog to increase its functionality. *Pages* are extra pages you can add to a blog, which are accessible from the front page. This lets it work more like a website than a traditional blog. This is a fairly new development in the blogging world but is not available on every platform.

The URL for your blog will look like http://bobscrumrunner.blogspot.com (or whatever name you choose; this is a fake one), but Blogspot has a feature that lets you "cloak" your blog behind your purchased domain. (See the later section "Purchasing and Hosting a Domain Name" for more information.) The upside of cloaking is that your domain, BobScrumrunner.com, is always visible.

The downside is that there are no specific URLs, like http://bobscrumrunner.blogspot.com/2009/12/18/my-trip-to-the-twine-museum. html. The original domain is the only one to show up in the address bar. This means you can't copy the longer URL that sends someone to a specific post.

Erik runs his personal blog, ErikDeckers.com, on Blogspot.

WordPress.com and WordPress.org

While Blogspot is quite easy, WordPress is more advanced because it's a powerful and sophisticated platform. WordPress is *open source* software, which means there is a community of users and developers working to improve it and add new features. You can actually choose from two versions of WordPress, depending on how much effort you want to put into it:

- **WordPress.com** is a hosted blog site, like Blogspot. You don't worry about server space, paying for usage, or maintaining a server. WordPress.com is a little more basic than WordPress.org, which means it's suitable for the beginning blogger who is happy with using templates and having limited functionality. WordPress.org is a better fit for more technically inclined bloggers who want to learn new software.

  A WordPress.com URL looks like this: http://bobscrumrunner.wordpress.com, but WordPress.com will also, for a fee, let you choose your domain name (but won't cloak the longer URLs, which is good; see the previous Blogspot section for more information), buy extra storage, post videos with a WordPress player, and eliminate ads. But other than those options, it's free. (If you have a WordPress.com blog already, go to the dashboard and click the Upgrades button for pricing.)

- **WordPress.org,** on the other hand, is software that you download and install onto your server—it's *self-hosted.* This takes some technical know-how. If you're technically savvy, have the patience and willingness to learn, or can bribe a geeky friend with a nice lunch, you can tackle WordPress.org. If you plan to become a blogger of some note, or plan to have a lot of features, you need a self-hosted WordPress blog. You don't have to start here, but you'll want to get here sooner rather than later.

WordPress.com and WordPress.org both let you create pages. Rather than writing code to create different pages, you can create a new page for any topic or subject, like speaking videos, photos of your art, or any products you sell. Creating a new page is as easy as creating a new blog post. Just click a button, and you're ready to start.

Note

Posts are regular blog posts listed in reverse chronological order on the home or blog page. Pages are static and not listed by date. An About page is a good example of a static page.

A WordPress.org post will have its own URL—http://www.bobscrumrunner.com/blog/2010/04/12/I-met-Elvis-at-conference—and the long URLs won't be cloaked. This is crucial to help your blog posts be more easily found on search engines.

The great thing about WordPress.org is that it's fully customizable and has literally thousands of plug-ins and add-ons for your blog. With these plug-ins, you can do all this and more:

- Block spam comments.
- Ask readers to take a survey.
- Optimize your blog to be better found on search engines.
- Integrate your Picasa or Flickr account.
- Create an ecommerce site.
- Create your own URL shortened based on your domain name.
- Show visitor locations and stats.
- Post your workout results.
- Post the Turkish lira exchange rates in your sidebar.

Basically, we could write an entire book with nothing but WordPress plug-ins, and it would be out of date the second we sent it to the publisher. That's because new plug-ins are constantly developed and released, and old ones are dropped by their developers all the time.

Both of us use WordPress.org for client blogs. We also have our work blogs on WordPress.org. Kyle's is at KyleLacy.com; Erik's is at ProBlogService.com.

Other Blogging Platforms

At least 40 other blogging platforms are available. All of them are free, although some of them offer premium upgrades as WordPress.com does. Our two favorites out of the 40 are Posterous and TypePad.

Posterous

Posterous is fairly new to the blogging scene, arriving in May 2009. That's pretty late to the party, considering Blogger.com started nearly 10 years earlier. However, Posterous is cool for a number of reasons:

- Posts are made by emailing text and photos to the site; they automatically populate to your blog, which creates your individual posts. You just write the text or snap a photo on your smartphone and email it, and Posterous does the rest. This makes it ideal for people who need to do blog posts quickly, such as crisis communications professionals or frequent travelers. (Yes, the other blog platforms let you do this, too, but this is Posterous's *raison d'être*—reason for being.)

- Your posts are distributed automatically to other social media tools. (You need plug-ins or third-party apps (applications) to do that with the other platforms.) So if you email a video to your Posterous feed, that video is then forwarded to your YouTube account. Upload a few photos, and they'll be added to your Flickr or Picasa account. And if you write a full-blown post, you can even forward that content—including photos and videos—to a Blogger, WordPress, or even Tumblr blog.

- Posterous has its own URL shortening service, post.ly.

- Posterous lets you point your domain name to your Posterous account. So, you can point www.BobScrumrunner.com to your Posterous account, and it'll host it for you.

- You can follow several Posterous blogs and have the new posts emailed to you in a daily digest. This is a great way to keep up on all your Posterous blogs at once.

Erik has been testing Posterous as a possible platform for crisis communications professionals and mobile bloggers. He often takes photos at conferences with his mobile phone and uploads them to Posterous, which is how many crisis communicators and first responders would use it. (But at real crises, not at conferences. At least not the ones he attends.)

 Note

As we were writing this second edition, Posterous was purchased by Twitter. Many people are speculating that this will mean the end of Posterous completely. If you're thinking about using Posterous, keep an eye on the tech news or on Posterous' own blog, for the updates to its continued existence. Or just use Tumblr or another "short form" blogging service.

Former Apple evangelist Guy Kawasaki, technology reporter Leo LaPorte, blogger iJustine, and the TED Fellows (fellowship holders and members of TED.com, a nonprofit that brings together people from Technology, Entertainment, and Design) all use Posterous.

Tumblr

Tumblr (no "e") works just like Posterous: You can post text, photos, and videos just by emailing them to your *tumblelog* (a Tumblr blog). Unlike the other platforms, however, users can "follow" each other and see their posts aggregated on their own dashboard. Basically, if Kyle follows Erik's blog, both blogs appear on Kyle's dashboard. If he follows a third blog, his dashboard includes that one as well, but Erik's does not. You just need to click the Follow button in the upper-right corner (see Figure 3.5) to follow someone's tumblelog.

Figure 3.5 *A Tumblr blog. Note the Follow button at the top right of the window. That's how you follow a Tumblr blog.*

Tumblr has been embraced by younger users as an acceptable substitute for WordPress—it's great for anyone who wants to have a blog presence but doesn't want to mess around with a self-hosted WordPress site. Plus, Tumblr has some themes that lend it more readily to the micro-blogging service that Twitter was originally supposed to be. (Twitter was originally designed to be a place where you could write short posts about what you think; it has turned into an ongoing communication tool, like a public Instant Messaging service.)

Tumblr lends itself to the rapid response, on-the-go blogging that a lot of mobile phone users want without all the hassle of messing around with something bigger and more complicated like a WordPress blog. If you snap a photo on your mobile phone, or have a random thought, or even write a short article (100–200 words), it's great for Tumblr. They even have a dedicated iPhone app, and you can email any text, audio, video, and photos from any mobile phone (just like Posterous).

Another reason Tumblr has been embraced by a lot of younger users and social media thinkers is that it's a community. Like we mentioned, it's easy to follow each other's tumblelog (just like Twitter), which lets you connect with other users, building your own community of favorite Tumblrs. And as you follow other Tumblrs, you will see their own blogs in your feed. However, there's no way to divide Tumblr feeds into separate groups like Twitter (see Chapter 5, "Twitter: Sharing in the Conversation"), so if you follow a lot of people, you'll be overwhelmed by the resulting feed.

You can also integrate your Tumblr blog into your Google Analytics, auto-promote new posts on Twitter and Facebook, and fully optimize it for search engines.

On the downside, Tumblr is not a great fit for long-form writing, and it doesn't have any plug-ins. It's intended to be a simple micro-blogging service, rather than a full-blown blog or extensive communication tool.

Tumblr has the same potential for crisis communications professionals and mobile bloggers that Posterous does, but Posterous has some additional social media functions.

If you want something for short, pithy comments, and lots of photos and videos, Tumblr is a great tool for the beginning blogger. But if you want to write longer blog posts, it can't handle the posts as easily. And if you decide to export your tumblelog to another blogging platform, such as WordPress, it can be rather convoluted.

Gary Vaynerchuk (creator of WineLibrary.tv and author of *Crush It*, one of our favorite social media books), Lenny Kravitz, Katy Perry, and Justine Bateman are famous Tumblr users.

TypePad

Our friend, Rodger Johnson of GetSocialPR.com, *loves* TypePad because that was the first blogging platform he used. We've tried to talk him into WordPress or Blogger (we even bribed him with a damn dollar!), but he won't budge. So we decided to include it in here so he won't feel left out.

TypePad takes the best of Blogspot, WordPress, and Posterous, rolls it into one package, and then charges $8.95 (or more) a month for it. There's also a *TypePad for Journalists* program, which offers a free blog package for professional journalists. (You have to prove you're one.)

Rodger is so insistent on TypePad that we figured there had to be something to it. TypePad does the same things that all the other blogging sites do—they all do, really—but TypePad has garnered a reputation for providing world-class support, stability, ease of use, and protection from spam. That can be important if you need stability and reliability because your job depends on it.

Über-marketer Seth Godin (author of *Tribes* and *Linchpin*), Dave Barry, Zachary Quinto (*Heroes* and *Star Trek*), as well as several corporations (Coca-Cola, Rubbermaid, GE, Patagonia, and the *Los Angeles Times*) use TypePad.

Which Platform Should You Choose?

So which platform is best? We're going to give you one of those maddening answers that people give when they don't want to make a choice.

It depends.

It depends on what your level of commitment will be, what your level of technological expertise is, and how much time and money you want to spend on your blog. Table 3.1 shows a few questions to ask yourself before you choose your blogging platform.

Table 3.1   Choosing Your Blogging Platform

Issue	Platform
Money is a concern. You want free.	Blogger, WordPress.com*
You want stability and ease of use.	Blogger, TypePad, WordPress.com
You need convenience and speed.	Posterous, Tumblr
You want to customize.	WordPress.org
You want to use your blog as an ecommerce site.	WordPress.org
You need multiple pages, like a website.	Blogger, WordPress

WordPress.org is free as well, but it's your server hosting that actually costs money.

Setting Up a Blog

Setting up a blog can be quite easy. Blogging companies want to get as many people to sign up as they can, so they make it as easy as possible to use. Basically, if you have ever set up another social network profile, even Gmail, Twitter, or Facebook, you can set up a blog. Like we said earlier, the hardest part of the process is choosing a template to use.

Just go to one of the blog platforms we listed, or any of the others we didn't, and follow the step-by-step instructions. It is that easy. No programming, no coding, no dealing with technical issues (unless you choose WordPress.org). Just fill in the blanks, and you're done. But we can give you a few hints to make your blog more successful.

- **Choose an easy-to-say URL**—When you tell people where your blog is, you want something that you can actually pronounce without difficulty. No special characters, weird spellings, or special abbreviations. When Erik set up his Blogspot account, he made the mistake of getting a URL with a dash: http://laughing-stalk.blogspot.com. After a few years, he got so tired of telling people "laughing dash stalk dot blogspot dot com" that he had to purchase his name as his domain name—ErikDeckers.com—and forward it to the website. Of course, now he has to make sure people spell his first name correctly, but it's a lot easier than explaining that stupid dash.

- **Choose a professional-looking template**—If you keep the default template that comes with your new blog, you'll be branded as an amateur or a poseur until you change it. Pick something you like but is easy to modify and customize. Depending on which template you choose, this can actually be one of the hardest parts about blogging. It's hard not because you need any technological wizardry to make it happen, but because there are so many templates to choose from. There are dozens, hundreds, or even thousands of choices, depending on which platform you pick. (WordPress.org has the most.) Find one you like, and stick with it. If you're going for a serious, professional image, and are using WordPress.org, be willing to spend a little money on a theme. They're professional looking, well-designed, and optimized for search engines and well worth the cost.

- **Don't moderate your comments**—Blogging is a two-way conversation. You write a post, your readers write a comment, and you comment back. If you shut off comments, you limit this conversation with your readers. On the other hand, it's okay to require people to create an account or give you their name and email address before leaving a comment. Although this won't completely eliminate spam, it helps you reduce it greatly.

 Tip

WordPress.com and WordPress.org actually come installed with an anti-spam plug-in called Akismet. Follow the directions on your blog dashboard for installation. Even if you have a WordPress.org blog, you need a WordPress.com account to activate Akismet.

- **Set up an RSS feed**—Regardless of which blog platform you choose, we recommend FeedBurner.com as a way to measure your RSS feed. (RSS stands for Really Simple Syndication, and it's the way you get your new blog posts to your readers, who can see them on an RSS reader, like My Yahoo! or Google Reader.) Most blog platforms already offer a way to syndicate your blog content, but we like FeedBurner because it also tells you how many people subscribe to your blog.

Purchasing and Hosting a Domain Name

Your domain name is crucial when you set up your blog. This is the first thing search engines key in on when they index a website or blog. If your domain explains what it is you do, who you are, what you sell, and so on, you get a lot more *search engine juice*. (That's one of those technical terms we use to sound cool.)

You don't need to purchase a domain name when setting up your blog. But you may find that as you get further into blogging and become more proficient, you want to have a special domain name. You can purchase this before or after you set up your blog.

For example, if you sell abstract French art, you should get the domain name AbstractFrenchArt.com. That will tell the different search engines what your site is all about, and they'll know how to index the site. They'll know what keywords and hyperlinks to look for, and they'll make sure the "best" hyperlinks to and from your site are about abstract French art.

 Note

Generally, it's a good idea to purchase your name as a domain name. That makes it easier for people to remember, helps you when you try to showcase your professional self to hiring managers, and even helps you be found more easily on search engines.

We strongly recommend that you use a domain registrar like GoDaddy (GoDaddy.com), Network Solutions (NetSol.com), or other independent registrars, as opposed to purchasing a domain through a blog hosting provider. You could run into a couple of dangers with the latter:

- They charge more than your typical registrar for a domain. (You can get them for $9.95 or less from GoDaddy.)
- They may try to keep your domain if you ever try to switch to a different provider.

If you work with a reputable domain registrar, you can avoid those problems.

Getting Inspired

First, if you've never considered yourself a writer, now is the time to start thinking of yourself as one. You're writing blog posts; therefore, you're a writer. And writers have processes. They have procedures. They have their favorite places to think, their favorite ways to find ideas, and their favorite ways to get inspired.

Pay attention to where you get your ideas, and start writing them down. Maybe you like to come up with ideas sitting in a coffee shop with a Moleskine notebook in front of you; so get a latte and buy yourself a notebook. Maybe your ideas come in the middle of the night; keep an index card and pen on your nightstand, and write down ideas when you wake up. (Do *not* try to remember them the next morning. That just doesn't work.) Maybe you get inspired in the shower, so get a low-flow shower head and take longer showers. Or maybe a meeting with a colleague triggers an idea, so send yourself an email, or write in your notebook, as soon as the meeting wraps up.

Whether it's music, exercising, or meditation, you need to find the things that inspire you to write, and then you need to start doing them. Combine those with your preferred sources for material, and you can start creating more blog posts than you'll know what do with.

What Should You Write About?

Uh, so now what?

You've got your blog set up. You followed most of the advice we've laid out so far, and you're ready to start writing. Maybe you even wrote the obligatory "This is my first blog post" post. (Go back and delete that.)

Hopefully you've figured out what to write about before you set up your blog. If you didn't, and you've waited this long to figure it out, we'd like to commend you on following our advice so closely.

We'd also like to ask you to buy five more copies of this book.

Figuring out what to write about can be what makes or breaks your blog. Although your subject matter is up to you, we can tell you that having a focused, specific topic is going to make your life much easier than if you have a broad, general topic. That seems rather counterintuitive, but it's true. You will have much more to write about if you narrow your focus to something small than if you write about something huge.

Say you want to blog about marketing. What's there to write about? Well, for starters, there's advertising, direct mail, marketing campaigns, marketing strategy, billboards, and Internet marketing. Most general bloggers we know can generate 10–20 posts about "marketing," and then they're tapped out. The topics are too broad to cover without either going overboard and writing 50,000 word textbooks or getting stuck after writing their "this is my first marketing blog post" entry.

But if you make your blog about marketing strategy, you're getting somewhere. Your blog can be about creating strategies, critiquing other strategies, and even doing case studies about a company's strategy. Drill down a little more. How about "social media marketing strategy for nonprofits?" Even better. Now you can focus strictly on that one small niche and how nonprofits can improve their marketing efforts and raise more money.

By focusing on this single niche, you are more likely to catch the attention of non-profits who want to improve their fund-raising and marketing. And—get this—they will want to hire the person who told them how to do it: you.

That's right. You've been giving a certain nonprofit all this free advice, and it figures there must be a whooooole lot more rattling around in your head. That's why it'll pay you a lot of money to show what that "more" is and to help it get better at what it does.

 Tip

Check out the book *Free: The Future of a Radical Price* by Chris Anderson for an explanation of why giving stuff away for free will end up making you more money than if you charged for that same information in the first place. Believe it or not, if you blog about social media marketing strategy long enough, you'll be asked to give talks at nonprofit conferences, get hired to consult to nonprofits for $100 per hour, and be asked to write a book, where you package your blog posts and your conference talks into easy-to-carry book form and sell it for $19.95...uhh, we've said too much.

Greg Fox writes the Donor Power Blog (DonorPowerBlog.com; see Figure 3.6), where he tells nonprofits how to raise money from donors by "(sharing) power with them, not treating them like passive ATMs." He does this by writing about 11 different topics, including branding, demographics, donor psychology, and the recession. He doesn't write about how to run a nonprofit, how to coordinate volunteers, or how to organize special events. He writes about getting donors to, what else, donate money.

Figure 3.6   *Greg Fox writes the Donor Power Blog to boost his personal brand in the nonprofit arena.*

Greg works for a company that specializes in donor acquisition, donor loyalty, and donor management for nonprofits. So by showing his own expertise in this area, he also establishes his employer's expertise, which makes his employer an attractive solution to nonprofits who want to improve donations.

By focusing on his niche, Greg can delve really, *really* deeply into the topics that matter to his niche: nonprofits that need help raising money from private donors.

Use these examples in Table 3.2, comparing a general topic versus a narrow topic versus a tightly focused niche to help you figure out how to find your own niche.

Table 3.2   General to Narrow to Niche—Finding Your Specialty

General	Narrow	Niche
Cooking	Italian cooking	Gluten-free Italian cooking
History	American history	Civil War history
Business	Sales	Selling to large corporations
Marketing	Internet marketing	Email marketing
Finance	Personal finance	Personal finance for Gen Y
Writing	Journalism	Running a weekly newspaper

If you're not sure how to focus your niche, ask your Twitter network (see Chapter 5) what areas they think you should focus on. This is especially helpful if you're following a lot of people in your chosen industry.

Finding Subject Matter

One of the best places to find subject matter and writing topics for your blog is other blogs. This is especially true as you try to establish your place in your field. You want to be noticed by other bloggers (so they'll write about you and introduce you to their audiences), and the best way to do this is to write about them.

If you want to establish yourself as an expert in your field, writing about the latest developments in your chosen niche is the best way to show that you're keeping up with the advancements in thinking and technology. You can become a resource to your readers and network by being the first one to tell them about all the great stuff you've been reading. Not only should you forward those articles to your network via Twitter, but you should write about them on your blog. This lets you add your own thoughts to their ideas and helps you set yourself apart from the Me Too crowd of people who are only repeating what they've heard.

Here are some other places to find blogging ideas:

- Newspapers
- Trade journals
- Questions from customers
- Comments on previous posts
- Something you heard on the radio or saw on TV

How to Write a Blog Post

When you find your niche, figuring out your subject matter is very easy. But your blog is more than just a regular opinion column. You can use different formats that can actually drive your topics and determine what you write about:

- **Personal versus professional topics**—Many bloggers who try to create a professional image worry about whether to write personal posts. They don't want to put too much information about themselves in public or confuse their personal life with their professional life. We don't think that's an issue. Social media has blurred the line between our personal and professional lives anyway, so there's nothing wrong with letting some of your "public personal" life bleed over into your professional life.

As dreadful as some people may think personal blogging is, it's going to make you more accessible and, well, personal. People will get to know you, and feel a closer connection to you, by reading what you think about personal topics like your favorite TV show or your adventures in finding a babysitter to watch the kids on a Friday night. Although this may not seem as important—because it frankly doesn't do squat for your credibility and expertise—it lets people get to know you. When they get to know you, they'll trust you. And when they trust you, they'll want to be a part of what you're doing.

Remember, as part of our personal branding objectives (see Chapter 1), we're creating relationships. To create relationships, we need to be personable. Personableness and personality build trust, which leads to the opportunities we're trying to create.

- **List posts**—This is a big favorite with blog readers, and it seems to generate more traffic for bloggers than any other type of post. "Five Secrets to Successful Blog Writing" always gets more attention than "How to be a Successful Blog Writer" or even "Secrets of Successful Blog Writing." People are attracted to these because they're finite, they hold the promise of being short, and they're an easy read.

  List posts let you to spend a little time on several topics and explore a few different ideas at once. Later, if you're ever stuck for a topic, you can come back to your list post, pick one of the items, and expand on it.

- **Authority posts**—These are similar to how-to posts because they establish your authority on a particular topic. These are your "messages from on high." In an authority post, you can pontificate, philosophize, and predict. Talk about industry trends. Predict what issues your industry will face in the coming year. Review new books or technology, and give an opinion about whether you think they're great or suck.

- **How-to posts**—These are more specific and factual than authority posts; they're for teaching processes, while authority posts are about expounding on viewpoints. Check out the message boards for questions in your field or industry. Answer customer emails, especially ones you have to answer over and over. (In the future, just send customers a link to that post.) Write out step-by-step instructions whenever you can, and include diagrams or photos, if possible.

- **News article and blog responses**—Find a post by someone in your field that you can respond to. State whether and why you agree or disagree (be polite), and present your own thoughts. Don't just say, "Here are Greg Fox's five reasons why nonprofits should send donation letters on Monday" and then repeat Greg's five reasons. List a couple of them, but then add a couple of your own. Now you've contributed to Greg's conversation, and maybe given him something to think about. You've also added to the body of knowledge about nonprofits and sending donation letters.

As an added benefit, if you link back to Greg's post, he will see the link, which can increase the chances of Greg linking back to you and participating in your conversation as well. Plus, any mentions Greg makes of your blog will introduce you to his readers.

- **Product reviews**—Review new products, services, restaurants, companies, software, tools, whatever you happen to be involved in. Because you're the expert, you're going to teach people about what's out there. Introduce people to the new offerings in your industry, and give an unbiased opinion about them. If you blog about open-wheel racing (that is, Indy Car and Formula 1 racing), write about new websites that have formed to help fans keep up with live races or points standings. If you're in home maintenance, talk about the new tools available from Stanley or Porter-Cable.

Writing for Readers Versus Writing for Search Engines

Some of the notable social media and blogging professionals believe that quantity of posts is more important when it comes to blog writing. Others believe that quality of writing is more important.

Generally, people who try to write a lot of posts are concerned with winning search engine rankings—how high they appear on Google, Yahoo!, or Bing results pages—because higher rankings mean more visitors. People who try to write better posts are more concerned with winning additional readers.

They concern themselves more with keywords, backlinks, and making sure their sites are fully optimized, using every search engine optimization (SEO) trick they can think of or learn about. If they think it can give them the tiniest boost in their SEO rankings, they're willing to try it.

Don't get us wrong. There are certain SEO rules you'll want to follow—we discuss them later in this chapter—but beyond that, you don't want to sweat all the different SEO details unless you're going to become an affiliate blogger.

It's About the Quality of the Writing

You can tweak your blog's SEO to win search all day long, but if people don't like what you have to say, or you say it poorly, they're not going to stick around, let alone come back on a regular basis. Just because they showed up once doesn't guarantee they'll show up again. That's where quality writing comes in.

It *is* true that it takes search to bring a person to your blog, where you can hook them with good writing. But there are so many additional ways to bring them around: Twitter, Facebook, speaking opportunities, networking, business cards, and so on. Bringing them in via search is great, and some of our search engine optimization colleagues point out that search is still the most popular source of website traffic for most people.

Bottom line: This is a fine line to walk. We don't think you should ignore SEO and focus only on being a good writer because search engine traffic is going to be a big part of your audience. But at the same time, we don't think you should ignore writing well for the sake of tricking search engines into ranking you higher.

It's possible to do quality writing *and* SEO at the same time, and you need to strike that balance. If you had to lean to one side or the other, err on the side of quality writing, but without forsaking SEO completely. They're two different horns on the same bull. Ignore one, and you'll get gored.

Google Expects You to Write Good Stuff

In early 2011, Google updated its search engine algorithms with a new version they called Panda, and with it, they started paying closer attention to the quality of a site. They wanted to make sure that people were writing good copy and designing good-looking sites.

But do they measure that? Google is not paying attention to how good looking your sites are, or grading your text to see if it's well-written and grammatically correct. (Although we keep hoping for that day.)

Instead, Google measures the users' data to see if a site is well done. Basically, they look at things like time on site, bounce rate, and even click-through rates.

- If people spend only a few seconds on a site, Google assumes they didn't like what they saw or read, so they assume it's poorly designed or written, and lowers the page's placement for those keywords. They do this by counting when people click a link to visit a site and then hit the Back button to return to the results. They also look at the Google Analytics if it's present on that particular blog or website.

- If people bounce on a site (visit one page and then leave again; visiting a *second* page means they did not bounce), Google assumes the site wasn't easy to navigate or wasn't good enough. Again, they measure whether a user hits the Back button, or by looking at Google Analytics, to determine bounce.

- If people don't click a site when it's near the top of the search engine rankings, the Google bots assume the description wasn't even interesting enough to get people to visit the site. (It's like having a store that wasn't even interesting enough for people to walk into.) Because Google can measure whether people click a result, they can also tell when people don't click a result.

So, if you want your site to do well on Google, make sure you write great content. Make sure it's good looking and easy to navigate. Include photos, videos, and other content to get people to stay on the site for a while. Include Previous Post/Next Post links to get people to navigate around, as well as Related Posts links that lead to similar posts on your site. (There are WordPress plug-ins to help you do this; there aren't for most of the other blog tools we discussed previously.) In short, be a good blogger, and you'll be doing good SEO. You don't even have to be awesome at it. Since most people do not do a great job of blogging, you can do a passable job and surpass most bloggers out there.

How Often Should You Post?

One of the questions we're asked the most often is how often to blog. Once a week is the bare minimum for a personal blog, and business blogs should post two or three times a week, but once a day is even better. (One post per weekday is fine, and skip the weekends.) Anything less, and you look like you can't commit to a simple blogging schedule, you don't have good follow-through, or you've just abandoned the blog completely. And because you're trying to create a positive personal brand, this is something you want to watch out for carefully.

But don't limit yourself to the bare minimum. You need valuable content, and you need to post with some frequency. Posting once a day is possible, but it's hard work. The tendency is to write as quickly as you can, and the quality of your writing drops off. However, the more you post, the more search engines will find you (and love you).

Regular posting makes it easier to be found in the search engines for your particular search terms because search engines want fresh, new content on a regular basis. The more you post, the more they visit your blog. The more they visit your blog, the higher your possible ranking.

More important, you need to post *consistently*. If you post once a week, publish on the same day. If you post daily, post it at the same time. That way your readers will know when and how to find you, and your readership will build more quickly and reliably than if you were to post every 7–15 days, without rhyme or reason, or on any regular schedule.

How Long Should Your Posts Be?

A lot of new bloggers worry about the length of their posts, fretting about writing 750 word manifestos on a daily basis. Actually, a decent blog post should be in the 350–450 word range.

"350 words?!" new bloggers exclaim. "I can knock that out in a quick email."

When you consider that the average newspaper column runs about 550 words, and the average blog post runs anywhere from 150–450 words, you can see why blogging is becoming so popular: It's because your average blog reader is like your average newspaper reader. They have the reading level and attention span of a 6th grader.

Now, this isn't true of everyone, and we're not suggesting you dumb anything down. We're also *not* suggesting that people are dumb. (Not all of them anyway.) Rather, people have grown to expect most text to be written at this reading level.

Think of it this way: When you're jogging or riding your bike, you can probably run or ride one or two miles per hour faster than your usual pace, but you don't because it doesn't feel comfortable. You want to stick with a rate that feels good, so you can keep doing it.

Our brains work the same way. Yes, we can read at a higher level. We all learned to read, and most of us graduated from high school. But that doesn't mean we want to read at a high school reading level all the time. Thanks to years of journalists and marketers writing at the sixth grade level, we have an expectation of it. The reading is easier and requires less mental bandwidth; we're more likely to stick with something at our accustomed reading level.

If you want to make your posts readable, write them like a newspaper article. Not only are they at a sixth grade reading level, they're written for someone who gets impatient and abandons an article halfway through it.

Newspapers are also readable because of the tone and voice the writers use. That's why many newspaper columnists have regular readers—because of their writing style. Adopt your own style, but make sure you're friendly, conversational, and factual. Your style can be anything from your frequent choice of certain words, the length of your sentences, and complexity of your words. It can be the tone you take when discussing certain issues, or even ending every question with "huh," because your "?" key is broken. Find a style that suits you, stick with it, and hone it until it's something you and your readers enjoy.

Newspapers figured out a long time ago that people abandon articles around the halfway point, so they started putting the most important information first, second most important information next, and so on. Most newspaper articles get boring about halfway through because they're giving nothing but background information, so you can skip that part. Likewise, when you're blogging, just stop writing when you get to the less important information and you'll be around 350–450 words.

Now, there's no magic number of what a blog post "should" be. We just recommend 350–450 words because that's all people will typically read, especially if they're reading your blog on a mobile phone.

But My Posts Are Too Long

This is another frequent problem we see: What do I do if my blog posts are too long? In some cases, bloggers want to cram as much information into a single post as possible, as if they're trying to make up for lost time.

Don't worry about lost time. You'll have plenty of opportunity to get your information out to people. Besides, you want to stay under that 450-word mark if you can help it. But if you want to write longer posts, go ahead. Like we said, there's no hard and fast rule about how long a post should be. You just need to make sure your writing style and your subject matter are compelling enough to keep people engaged to the end.

If your posts are too long, the problem may not be too many words; it may be too many ideas in one post.

In our blogging talks, we recommend that people follow the mantra: *one idea, one post, one day*. Talk about one idea, not two or three, put it in one post, and do it once per day. If you try to double up on any of those areas, you're going to have problems keeping readers around because your posts will become cumbersome and complex.

As you're writing, see if there is a natural "crease" in your writing. Is there a place where it would be easy to break the post into two places? Maybe you're talking about the importance of getting durable, hard-wearing luggage for business travel, and you start talking about choosing the right kind of luggage for different styles of travel.

If you look closely, you could probably split the post into two different ones: one for durable luggage and one for suitable luggage for different types of travel. There's no need to combine the two, so just split them into two separate posts, which takes care of two days of writing.

SEO Through Blogging

Search engine optimization (SEO) is the art of making your blog appear at the top of the search engine rankings. By focusing on one or two keywords and optimizing your blog and posts for them, you can improve your chances for appearing at the top of Google, Yahoo!, and Bing.

We may have come down a little hard against SEO earlier, but we still think it's important. You don't want to ignore SEO completely, but at the same time, you don't want to focus so much on SEO that your writing sucks.

Rather than ignoring SEO for the sake of focusing on high-quality writing, you need to focus on both. Otherwise, the search engines will have no idea what your site is about. Using SEO will tell them everything they need to know about your site and its content.

- **Keywords**—Everything is based on keywords, or the words or phrases that each post is about. That's the thing the search engine zeros in on. Choose your keywords carefully, but don't go for the big, generic keywords, like "history" or "marketing." You'll never win that search. Instead, go for long-tail keywords, like *19th century Midwest agricultural history* or *email marketing best practices.*

 Note

The term *long-tail* is from Chris Anderson's book, *The Long Tail* (LongTail. com). It's the 20% in the 80/20 rule. Or as Anderson says, the 2% in the 98/2 rule. Think of it as a special sales niche: 98% of people want to buy a big generic product, and every store is fighting to be #1 in that market. But by appealing to the 2% who don't want the generic product, you can expend less energy and comfortably sell to that 2%. So, this means that if you can win enough long-tail searches, you'll do as well or better than the one person who tries to win a single search for the 98%.

- **Headlines**—This is the first place to put your keyword. If you're writing about direct mail response rates, your headline should be something like "5 Tips for Improving Direct Mail Response Rates." (Notice we used the 5 tips list post idea.) This tells the search engine what you're writing about and tells the spider what it should be looking for when it crawls your site.
- **Anchor text**—Search engines also pay attention to whether you put your keywords in your hyperlinks. If you're writing about direct mail response rates, you need to create a hyperlink with those words—direct mail response rates—that also leads to a site about the same thing. Never link to phrases like, "Click here for more information." Unless you're blogging about the word "here," avoid using it as your hyperlink. The one exception is if you're using it like this: "You can find out

more about direct mail response rates *here*. And *here, here*, and also *here*." The alternative is to try to use the keywords in a link at every possible opportunity. But when you do that, it looks more like you're trying to spam the search engines if you try to work keywords into every link. If they think you're spamming them, they'll drop you from their index.

- **Body copy**—The actual text of the blog post needs your keywords. If you're writing for SEO, you want to shoot for about a 1–2% keyword density. That is, out of every 100 words, you should use your keyword one or two times. One percent is okay, but don't try to go too much higher than 2% because it can make your writing sound stilted, like you crowbarred in your keywords. So, a 300-word post should have no more than six occurrences of your keyword.

- **Backlinks**—This one is important for SEO. The more links that point *back* to your blog, the more important Google thinks your site is. So you want to build up your backlinks by leaving comments on other people's blogs, using your blog URL in your email and forum footers, and, of course, writing quality content that gets other people to write about you. The best way to do this is to write about other people. If you do this often enough, they'll return the favor.

In his book *Crush It*, Gary Vaynerchuk says other people's blogs are the best place to spend most of your time. Visit other blogs in your field, or who have written a single post about your niche, and leave intelligent comments on the different blogs several times a day, every day. He used to spend many hours a day doing this. Although you may not have the hours that Gary devoted to his site, you should consider following the same strategy, even if you spend only 15 minutes a day doing it. Even if you only left 3 comments a day, at the end of 7 weeks, you will have left 100 comments with 100 backlinks.

By leaving all these comments, you've essentially introduced yourself to 100 new people. That's 100 new readers, 100 new fans, 100 people who will talk about you to their friends and followers, which in turn leads to even more readers and fans.

Backlinks in blog comments do not carry much impact on your total SEO. Where the real backlink power comes from is when other people write about you or link to you on their blog. It also introduces you to new potential readers and social media connections, thus expanding your network.

How Does This Apply to Our Four Heroes?

We've been saying blogging is important, that it's for anyone who wants to build their personal brand. So let's see how our four heroes would use blogging to find a job or further their career.

- **Allen (influencer)** spent 14 years as an account manager in a marketing agency, so he has a lot of expertise in account management, marketing campaigns, and ad creation. He's also looking for a job. Blogging is going to be a great benefit to him, for two important reasons: 1) Hiring managers use search engines to research candidates. Allen wants to make sure that hiring managers find him, instead of finding absolutely nothing. 2) Allen wants to show that he knows a lot about account management and agency life. He can use his social networks to drive people back to his blog, which means fellow marketing agency professionals can see the quality of Allen's work and thoughts, and may refer him to an opening in their agency. If he wants to, he would write about things agency professionals can use.

- **Beth (climber)** wants to be the chief marketing officer in the insurance industry, possibly at her current company, but not necessarily so. Insurance marketing is a specialized niche, which makes it ideal for blogging. Beth can write all kinds of posts about marketing campaigns, lessons learned, new marketing technology, or anything else that can help her reach out to other insurance marketing professionals.

- **Carla (neophyte)** has left a career in pharmaceutical sales and wants to become a program director or development director at a nonprofit. Although the for-profit and nonprofit world are quite different, some of the ideas are the same, like getting people to give you money in exchange for something. Carla can use her blog to explore the connections between sales and fundraising, which will be of interest to other fundraising professionals. And because there are so many openings already in fundraising, Carla can use this blog as an introduction to potential bosses, as well as use it as a selling point when she's asked an interview question like, "So how do you think you can use selling techniques to help you with fundraising?"

- **Darrin (free agent)** is an IT professional who spends his days troubleshooting computers, and he moves from employer to employer every two or three years. He's almost a commodity in the IT field, so he needs to distinguish himself from every other IT professional. A blog is the best way to do it. Darrin can write about things like balancing the need for network security and the growing use of social media in the corporate setting, or providing basic computer security information written for non-IT personnel who don't have an IT background. By adopting a style that's friendly and easy to follow, Darrin can become the computer troubleshooting expert, which makes him more attractive to larger corporations with IT professionals who do nothing but fix computers.

Do's and Don'ts of Blogging

We asked our Twitter friends to give us some do's and don'ts about blogging for newbies. (See, this is the kind of thing you get if you follow us on Twitter: We ask you to help write our book, and you might be put in it!)

And our friends came through for us. They gave us a lot of great advice, which we include here.

What's not so surprising is that we got more do's than we did don'ts. More people have good advice of things to do rather than things to avoid. Either that, or we just know some really optimistic people.

Do's

- Write from the heart. —@dave_kellogg
- Write about something you have passion for! —@mandyboyle
- Blog on a regular basis—at least once or twice a week if not more when you first start your blog. —@dave_kellogg
- Blog often. Don't worry about perfection. Just get your words out there! —@robbyslaughter
- Invite guest bloggers and submit guest blogs to others.
- Always check a twitter handle or blog URL before mentioning, might not be the right business or person. (Learned myself the hard way.) —@kellyjknutson
- Maintain a consistent posting schedule. Readers and search engines both love fresh, interesting content. —@mandyboyle
- Read a variety of others' blogs to see how tones, styles, and content types can vary. —@aims999
- Blogging is about community. Don't expect people to read your blog if you aren't reading and commenting on theirs. —@JustHeather
- Top 10 Lists are your friend, everybody loves a list. —@BannedLibrary
- Re-read each post before you click Publish. It will save you some embarrassment. —@4ndyman

- @4ndyman I try to sit on a new piece for 24 hours then re-read, but I still post mistakes. —@randyclarktko (said in response to @4ndyman. Conversation abounds!)
- Unless you are a copy editor, use and trust one. —@randyclarktko
- Start slow and build up. Once a week, then twice a week, etc. Don't burn yourself out trying to go every day out of the gate. —@DanOnBranding
- Use alt text with images. Most people forget to. It can boost SEO and help when browsers don't display images. —@mandyboyle

 Tip

Alt text, or *alternative text*, was originally created so people who used screen-reading software (software that lets people who are blind use a computer) could tell what was in a photograph. If you post a photo of your daughter riding her bicycle, you would write an alt tag that says "My daughter riding her bicycle." That way, the screen reader users would know what this photo is about.

However, search engines also use alt text, so you can give yourself an SEO boost by including alt text inside your photo descriptions. However, don't go nuts and try to cram keywords and search terms into each photo.

Putting "Kyle Lacy talks about social media, social networks, social marketing, blogging, Twitter, and Facebook marketing at his KyleLacy.com blog" into every alt text of each photo may trigger alarms on the search engine, and you'll be penalized for keyword stuffing. At the very least, your blind readers will hate you.

Don'ts

- Don't assume people are as smart as you are. Spell terms and ideas out once in awhile. —@sunnysocial
- Don't think of topics all by yourself. Find help from Google Reader, StumbleUpon, guest posts to share the load + inspire. —@DanOnBranding
- Don't leave spam or half-hearted comments.
- Don't make your blog one big commercial.
- Don't neglect grammar and spelling. —@dave_kellogg

Tip

One problem that Microsoft Word users have is that copying a post from Word and then pasting it into a blog window adds a lot of extra HTML characters that are viewable when published. One way to eliminate this is to copy the Word version, open Notepad (the free word processor on Windows), paste the text into Notepad, and then copy it again. This strips out all the extra HTML, and you can then paste it into the blog window.

Our favorite tip came from our friend and fellow blogger, Meghan, who summarized this entire chapter in one tweet.

- Do be social. Do ask questions. Do have a sense of humor. Don't be boring. Don't blog at people. Do blog to engage. —@meghanbarich

A Final Note on the "Rules" of Blogging

When we were first writing this book, Erik had a meeting with Jason Falls, a noted social media consultant and writer (and Erik's eventual co-author on *No Bullshit Social Media*), on a day he was writing this chapter. Erik asked Jason, "What's a do or don't for blogging newbies." Jason is a seasoned blogging expert, so we'll just let him speak for himself:

> *Take all of the "rules" with a grain of salt. I've seen not only with my own blog, but with some of the most notable blogs in the world, that sometimes the rules don't apply. Until recently, I've never tried to win search terms, so there's never been a concentrated effort to optimize my blog at all. I win a lot of important search terms, but I've never focused on that. I focus on providing great content and let everything else take care of itself.*

In other words, Jason says, you can ignore everything we've said in this chapter. As long as you're writing with passion and providing well-written content, people will come to you.

4

LinkedIn: Networking on Steroids

Imagine this.

You walk into a networking event and you are pleasantly surprised to see your closest business contact and friend standing at the front of the room talking to one of your clients. You are also surprised to see the majority of the people being close connections of yours.

At first, you think this is a surprise party and you are about to look for your mother, but then you notice another group farther away from all your friends (who are now smiling at you). You recognize some of the faces but can't place their names. Looking more, you become aware of multiple groups spread wide throughout the building who you've never seen before.

Suddenly your friend walks up to you and asks if you would like to meet the second group of people. Absolutely. After all, you're there to network.

You follow your friend and are introduced to each person in the second group. As you meet people in that group, it grows larger, and more people enter the room. One by one, you're introduced to every one of them, and your network just keeps growing.

Finally, money starts falling from the ceiling and you smile because, hey, free money.

No, this isn't some creepy dream. (Although the money thing would be pretty cool.) It sounds funny but this is how LinkedIn works to build your personal brand.

LinkedIn is networking on steroids. It's an adrenaline junky, passion-infused, connection-building, and market-leading networking site for the professional person. Erik calls it "Facebook for Grown-Ups," and Kyle calls it the "White Collar Connection Point."

It's like playing Six Degrees of Kevin Bacon, but without the bacon.

@edeckers: Mmmm, bacon...
@kyleplacy: Not that kind of bacon.

LinkedIn gives you the opportunity to connect with people who can push your personal brand to new heights. It's a social networking site much like Facebook but with 700 million fewer people and higher incomes. LinkedIn boasts a membership size of approximately 161 million users[1] with an average income of $109,000.[2] Talk about a professional networking site.

What makes this site valuable? LinkedIn is exactly what it sounds like: A networking site that helps you "link" to other professionals or connections and build a web of

---

1. http://press.linkedin.com/node/1191
2. http://socialmediastatistics.wikidot.com/linkedin

ultimate personal branding domination. LinkedIn gives you the opportunity to connect with people who can connect you with other people who can connect you with other people, and so on. And those can be your connection to a former co-worker leading to him/her connecting you to a potential employer.

To start in the world of LinkedIn, you need to understand the basics of building a profile and your personal brand.

The Basics of LinkedIn

Your LinkedIn profile is the window into your professional soul. You can technically view the profile as your online résumé, but it is so much more than that. Résumés can be extremely boring, but a LinkedIn profile is enhanced because of the networking ability.

Your LinkedIn profile is a way to promote the professional side of your personal brand. It's the link to your best skill sets, the recommendations of your peers, your professional personality, and your knowledge. It's the one place on the web where you can demonstrate every aspect of what makes you valuable to an employer or a client. We have talked extensively about how your personal brand builds trust and tells a credible story. Your LinkedIn profile is another aspect of that story.

One of the more powerful aspects of LinkedIn is that you can indicate how closely connected you are to the individuals listed in your database. LinkedIn groups them by three different degrees. Here is the basic breakdown.

What's in a LinkedIn Profile?

The first step to establishing your presence on LinkedIn is creating a profile. After you create a profile, you can start adding connections to people you know who are also on LinkedIn.

The Employment Section

The profile usually focuses on employment and education history (see Figure 4.1), not a list of your hobbies or your favorite movie. We're going to leave that to Facebook. Remember, this is about your professional brand.

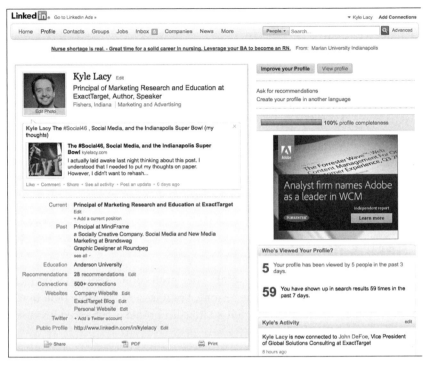

Figure 4.1   *This is an example of a completed LinkedIn profile with all the information associated with your personal brand.*

To fill out your profile page, begin by filling in information for your current and former jobs. Some of the entries will include job title, employer, industry, dates, and a short description of what you accomplished at the job. You should plan to set aside 30 to 60 minutes to fill out your LinkedIn profile. Remember, it is an easy form to fill out, but the profile needs to be completed fully to support your personal brand.

LinkedIn also looks up your employer to see if they are in the LinkedIn database. It can then help you find people who used to work at the same company and are still currently employed with the company. So, if you worked for a large corporation, LinkedIn finds other people who also worked at that corporation and allows you to connect. This feature comes in handy later when you try to grow your network. You can also add the school you attended to obtain a list of alumni currently using LinkedIn for networking purposes.

After you have filled out your professional information, be sure to upload a professional picture, and then fill out your educational experience.

Your Photo/Avatar

Let's first talk about your photo (also called an avatar) because we know you cringe at the thought of posting a picture to your profile. We have (and will) talk extensively about avatars throughout the book because they are extremely important to your personal brand and brand consistency. It's vitally important that you use the same picture on every social network site on the Internet. If you meet someone on the street, you are going to want them to remember it. What's the point of not having a picture on a professional networking site? It's like going to a networking event with a mask on.

You can decide to take a professional head shot or hire a photographer to take the head shot for you. We recommend the latter. We are assuming that you understand the concept of professional. A professional photo does not involve a swimsuit or a keg stand.

The Education Section

After you figure out your picture situation, you are asked to fill in your education experience. You list the different schools and learning institutions you attended after high school, including their name, degree earned, years attended, awards won, and any other awesome accolades you want to add. Remember, the more information you list, the better. You never know when you share something in common with a potential employer.

 Note

LinkedIn uses all this employment and education history later to help you search former and current colleagues and classmates.

The employment and education information make up the basics of your LinkedIn professional profile, but you also have the chance to fill out a short summary to help people understand exactly what you do and why you do it.

The Summary

Think of this as a networking pitch. (We'll talk more about your networking pitch in Chapter 12, "How to Network: Hello, My Name Is... .") Your summary is what makes you unique and gives someone a reason to connect with you. It's basically a short description of your professional experience and skills. Remember your personal brand story discussed and built in Chapter 2, "How Do You Fit in the Mix?" This is a great place to use it. This is the traditional "career objective" you would put on a résumé, but you get to add a little more and make it more thorough than you have room for on a paper résumé.

LinkedIn uses keywords to help track and categorize profiles for use in searching. An employer may be using LinkedIn to search for job prospects, or a fellow net-worker may be searching you! Be sure you use the keywords you want to be known for or searched for by hiring managers. Don't overload the Career Summary by using the keywords over and over, but be sure you use the words that describe your position, your field, and any useful skills.

An effective LinkedIn summary draws on the short bio you already wrote and adds keywords that illustrate who you are, like this one: *Creative and hardworking young professional focused on corporate public relations. Led two 80+ student organiza-tions while also studying as a full-time student. Worked two separate internships with a PR firm in Washington, DC. Strong written and oral communication skills with a passion for public speaking.*

What makes this an effective summary? It describes what makes the individual special and unique, who she is, and what she likes to do. She used the keywords public relations, PR, communication skills, and public speaking.

If you're following along with us, write your LinkedIn summary before moving to the next section. A good tool to use is the personal brand story you wrote in Chapter 2. Refer to your points of storytelling to help write your LinkedIn sum-mary. This can also be used across many different platforms like Facebook!

Your Websites

There's also a section to list any websites you're associated with: both personal and professional, your blog, your RSS feed, and your creative portfolio (see Figure 4.2). There's also a place for you to list interests, affiliated groups, and honors. This lets people find out more about you beyond your LinkedIn profile.

 Tip

When you list your websites and blogs, you can select My Website, My Company, My Blog, My RSS Feed, My Portfolio, and Other. If you select one of the first five options, they show up as that name (My Company, My Blog, and so on) on your profile. But if you select Other, you can spell out what that other site is. Type in the name of your blog, your website, what-ever. Then, when people see your profile, they see the name of your com-pany, the name of your blog, and so on. That link is more informative than the other five options offered.

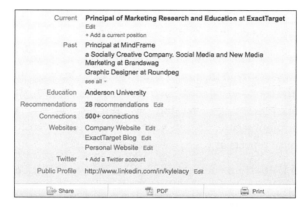

Figure 4.2 *This is an example of what is seen when a person searches for your profile. You want them to connect with you outside of LinkedIn using your website or a blog.*

 Tip

Don't link to your Facebook profile in your Website section. You want to create a boundary between your personal and professional life. Although truly industrious hiring managers may search for you on Facebook, there's no reason you need to make it easier for them. (At the same time, make sure you aren't posting anything on Facebook that could harm your professional reputation.)

After you fill out your profile, check whether it is 100% complete. LinkedIn shows you a status bar for completion on the right side of your profile. It isn't a hard thing to do to hit 100%. Just follow the LinkedIn suggestions under your status, and you will hit 100% before you know it. If only life were this easy!

If you hit 100%, you're doing great. However, if you haven't hit it yet, it's extremely important to figure out what needs to be done to reach that mark. A complete profile shows that you mean business and helps with the search functionality of the site. It shows potential connections that you're using LinkedIn properly, and it isn't just some half-finished, rarely visited network to you.

Cool LinkedIn Features Worth Examining

LinkedIn is a powerful tool. It's more than just a résumé or network-building tool. It isn't just a set-it-and-forget-it social network. You actually need to *use* LinkedIn if you want to benefit from it. Just like every other social network, you get out of it what you put into it. So, you need to use the full range of LinkedIn's features to get the most out and to make the best of your connections.

LinkedIn offers some cool features to help you build your personal brand. It is widely known (especially in the health and financial industries) that corporations limit or block the use of social media access, except for LinkedIn. Because LinkedIn is a closed system—meaning it's hard to gain information if you are not a member of the site—it is more secure. The site's extra features let you customize your profile to showcase all aspects of your professional life.

- **Personal URL**—LinkedIn lets you personalize your URL. So rather than having a long URL filled with all kinds of letters and numbers, you can have one that has your name in it, like www.linkedin.com/in/ WinstonChurchill (assuming your name really is Winston Churchill).

 Note

URL means uniform resource locator. It's just another name for the web address. You can just call it URL without ever knowing what it means. And it's pronounced "You Are Ell," not "Earl."

- **Events**—The Events tab can help you promote your events, find other cool events to attend, and give you the opportunity to see what other people are attending, whether it's a community event, a professional after-hours meetup, or even a conference or trade show. It also offers an event search and recommends events based on your profile information. You can also find out more information about attendees and updates surrounding the event.

- **Connect with Other Social Profiles**—We have talked repeatedly about the importance of linking your other social profiles to create one continuous story. LinkedIn lets you build your social business profile. After you make your connections on LinkedIn, the rest of your networks are only one click away from connecting with you on multiple platforms, like your blog or Twitter.

  Remember, it is important not to link to your Facebook profile. Personal information and pictures do not need to be shared with a perspective employer until after the initial meeting. You do not need the employer to make an assumption on your ability to deliver.

- **Applications**—LinkedIn offers a range of applications that help you make the most of your profile. SlideShare allows you share the presentations you loaded on SlideShare.net; Portfolio Display posts your portfolio entries on your profile; WordPress pulls the feed from your

WordPress blog; and tweets pulls in your Twitter feed to share with your network. (This is why it's important to be at least semi-professional on Twitter, too.) There are more applications than we listed here, so look for the ones that will be useful to you.

- **Groups and Subgroups**—Join groups (they work like discussion forums) to build deeper relationships and gain new connections. You can find groups for your community, your industry, or even your job function. You can find the best discussions and most influential contacts within your groups. They are great resources for announcements, upcoming events, discussions, and valuable information. Only join groups and subgroups because you have a genuine interest in what the group is about.

Creating Contacts on LinkedIn

Of course, a networking tool is not much good without a network. And although you can search and scour for people on LinkedIn, there's an easier way to do it.

We all have personal contacts who can build our LinkedIn network, so it's time to build that database and connect with other members. There are a couple of ways you can build your contact list, and it starts with your work database, past and present colleagues, and classmates. You also have the opportunity to search by name, company, school, and city. Finally, LinkedIn has advanced search functionality.

By searching for possible connections, you have the opportunity to view their profile and research other connections. After you search and find individuals, you can ask them to join your network by inviting them to connect with you. After you create the connection, you have the ability to search their profile and connect with people that you may not necessarily know but would be valuable for your network. Just ask your newly minted connection for an introduction.

 Tip

Please, please, *PLEASE* rewrite the introduction message—I'd like to add you to my professional network on LinkedIn—before you connect with someone. At the very least, it tells the other person how you know them, especially if they don't recognize your name off the bat. At best, it shows that you actually want to connect with that person, and aren't just too lazy to make an effort to tap out a few sentences of introduction. We know people who delete connection requests if the requester couldn't be bothered to rewrite that introduction message.

Using Your Email Database

Out of all the tools you have at your disposal, your email database is the most important. It's your initial contact list. Your email database is filled with people you have already been communicating with on a regular basis. They are the people who already know who you are and why you would want to connect with them.

The easiest way to start is to either download your email database from your email client (like Outlook, Thunderbird, or Apple Mail) or use your Gmail, Yahoo!, or AOL email account. LinkedIn offers to do this automatically, or you can click to the Connections tab to upload your email database automatically to the LinkedIn network. LinkedIn can automatically search your uploaded database and find every connection that has a LinkedIn account. The only thing you have to do is look, click, and connect. It is that easy to build your initial network.

 Tip

We recommend that you get a Gmail account and synchronize it with your work email. You never know when you're not going to have ready access to your work email address. Then make sure you keep it up to date and clean. It's useful to make this your primary email address, as opposed to an email address from your cable company, phone company, or work. If you move jobs, your email address becomes obsolete to all your contacts. Finally, every social network we have seen lets you add contacts through your Gmail account.

 Tip

Check out the LinkedIn Outlook toolbar if you're a frequent Outlook user. This is one of the easiest ways to connect your email address book to LinkedIn.

Just type in your email username and password, and LinkedIn automatically pulls all your contacts and shows each contact who has already joined the site (see Figure 4.3). This allows you to connect with your initial contact base—friends, colleagues, co-workers, vendors, and so on. The same process happens when we upload our email database, which we discussed earlier in this section. When you connect to an individual on LinkedIn, you have the opportunity to connect with their contacts! People you may not know but could be valuable to your network. Remember, these people become your best marketers. They're the people who spread your message (and personal brand) faster than anyone else in the world. However, you have a chance to confirm any connections before they're automatically made. That allows you to avoid connecting with someone you'd rather keep at arm's length.

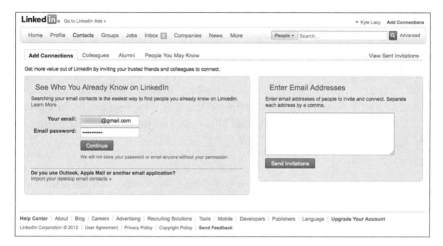

Figure 4.3 *By allowing LinkedIn to connect with your email address book, you can build your network with personal connections.*

Other Ways to Connect: Colleagues and Classmates

After you fill in all your education and work history, LinkedIn can find other people who shared these experiences with you. Whether it's the woman who worked in the cube next to you, the guy who sat behind you in your Psych 100 class, or even someone who you never met but was attending the same class, LinkedIn gives you the tools to easily connect with all of them. In the Find Contacts Wizard, you can pick and choose who you would like to connect with. When you upload the address book or database to LinkedIn, you have the ability to check or uncheck the names of people to whom you would like to connect. You can choose to bulk connect with every person in your database (automatically) or pick and choose.

You are also asked to invite nonmembers to the site by email, although we don't recommend it. The only time you should invite nonmembers to the site is when you are sure they will appreciate the invite. If they're the type of person who might freak out that you "sent another email," it's probably best to keep from sending that or any other message.

You're making some great progress. You've created a profile and connected with your database. The next step is expanding your network to grow into something that can help you and your overall personal brand. You have the ability to ask your LinkedIn network for introductions to people you do not already know. Remember the second- and third-degree system from the party at the beginning of the chapter? Let's get this party started.

Building Off Your Second- and Third-Degree Network

Building your network on LinkedIn does not stop at your first-degree connections. The power of LinkedIn is in your ability to connect with people outside of your first degree of influence (your personal connections). It defeats the purpose if you attended a networking event and chatted with people you already knew. By connecting with people you already know (the first step) you can build a platform to be introduced to their connections. This is where the second- and third-degree connections come into play on LinkedIn. First, let's define what second and third degree represent:

- **Second-Degree Contact**—This is the more important connection. Being connected to a person by a second degree means there is only one person in between you and the other individual. LinkedIn allows for contacts to connect with each other by a second degree. The only thing you need is an introduction to that second-degree contact.

- **Third-Degree Contact**—A third-degree contact is a harder shell to crack because you are not directly connected to the individual through one other contact. Being connected by a third degree means you have a contact connected to another individual that is connected to your third degree. We know, the crazy web we weave!

The second-degree contacts on LinkedIn are the more important connections to you in this web of networking. LinkedIn gives you badges (or symbols) next to an individual's name to show you the level the person is when connected with you. If you look at Figure 4.4, you can see a second-degree symbol by Abby Bergman's name on Kyle's LinkedIn profile. Jonathan could be a valuable connection based on who he is connected with. If you want to become a connection to Jonathan, you can use your initial network to ask for an introduction. Refer to Figure 4.4 to find the line that states Get Introduced on the right side of the profile. By clicking this button, LinkedIn brings up the connections Jonathan and you have in common. You can then ask for an introduction from an individual who you trust to facilitate the connection.

By gaining an introduction to second-degree contacts on LinkedIn, you can build your network past the initial contact list to individuals who could be extremely valuable to your overall brand. You can build an army of people who are and will become powerful evangelists for your personal brand. In Chapter 2, you discovered your personal brand story. You now have the opportunity to support that personal brand and take contacts and transform them to connections!

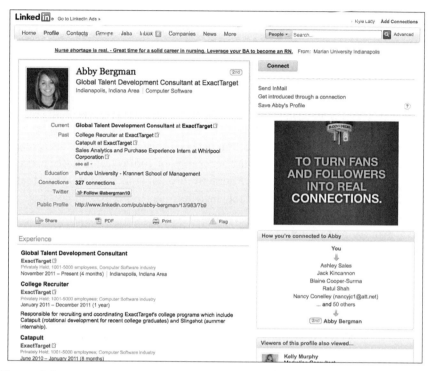

Figure 4.4   *You can connect with second-degree contacts on LinkedIn by being introduced through a first-degree connection.*

Transforming Your Contacts into Connections

So, why should you turn your contacts into connections? What does that even mean? What is the difference between a contact and a connection? And can we squeeze one more question into this paragraph? They are the same type of people, but you need to discover that a contact may be less important than an actual connection. This section is about building relationships and strong context with your LinkedIn network.

- **Contact**—A contact is an individual that you have been in "contact" with at least once and is familiar with your occupation and name. This person may appreciate the initial connection on LinkedIn but would hesitate to share her entire client list (on LinkedIn) with you. Remember, the entire point of LinkedIn is to build your network to get introductions to individuals who are second and third degrees from you. To do that, you need to get your contacts to become a...

- **Connection**—A connection is a cheerleader. Not the pom-pom kind but the rabid fan kind. A connection is someone who will share your message whenever asked and will connect you with the necessary people to make your goals and personal brand idea a reality. We want to try to turn every contact into a connection. It may not happen, but that doesn't mean you shouldn't try.

So, clearly, the important dilemma is how to turn contacts into connections.

1. Build the Trust Factor

LinkedIn was built to create connection between trusted contacts. This is huge! How do you start to build more trust between your connections? Offer them information they think is valuable. Share content through your status updates that helps your contacts on a daily basis, and they will become connections. (This is why you should try to connect with people who will actually benefit from your content, rather than trying to connect with anyone and everyone. This isn't Facebook, and it isn't a contest. Connect with people you trust and who you want to trust you.)

2. Recommend Your Friends

Recommendations make the entire experience of LinkedIn a referral reality. You must give to receive. Give out those recommendations, and you will receive them in return. By recommending the people you have worked with, your connection will grow deeper, and that contact will become a connection. People put greater stock into the LinkedIn recommendations because they know (to an extent) they are sincere. It beats putting them up on your website, which isn't always perceived as trustworthy.

3. Get Involved in Your Contact's Groups

Get involved with groups that share your common interests. This introduces you to more possible contacts, and you can identify your relationship with this individual as part of a shared group. The more groups you become involved in, the more opportunity there is for you to make contacts. (But don't just join to join; be selective about the groups you join.) Supporting a contact's group builds the deeper connection points that need to happen to strengthen your relationship with them.

4. The Power of Staying in Touch

LinkedIn offers the opportunity to connect with people who may not use sites like Twitter and Facebook. Remember, LinkedIn is made up of professionals who (usually) use it to connect only with other professionals in their industry. LinkedIn is great for staying in touch. It's updated by users, which makes it a reliable current database.

The Importance of Recommendations

Out of all the applications that LinkedIn offers, recommendations are important to your profile. Recommendations give you additional credibility with people. The best way to dominate in the personal branding world is to get qualified and stellar recommendations.

If you've had a good business relationship with another LinkedIn member, ask that person for a recommendation. Don't ask just to ask or to rack up a bunch of recommendations. This isn't a contest. You want people who know you and can honestly write a good one. Then return the favor; writing recommendations also helps complete your LinkedIn profile.

You need to give and receive the appropriate recommendations that can help further your personal brand. Do you want to be known as a great speaker? Ask people who have seen you speak to write that kind of recommendation. See Figure 4.5 for examples of recommendations. Do you want to be known as a strategist? Ask clients who have been successful because of the strategy you implemented. And remember, you must give before you receive. Give recommendations to the people who have helped you over the years, and they more than likely will return the favor.

So what makes a good recommendation? Remember our friends from Chapter 1, "Welcome to the Party"? Our four heroes are devoted LinkedIn users, and they each have gathered recommendations that are useful for their personal branding objectives.

- **Allen (influencer)** is looking for a new job after working at the same ad agency for 14 years. Allen should ask his supervisor, a co-worker, and a client he worked with for recommendations. Here is an example of a recommendation for Allen from one of his clients:

  "Allen has been nothing short of extraordinary at managing our projects with our company. They were continually delivered on time, on target, and on budget, with every detail covered. Thanks, Allen, for being such an asset to our company!"

  Notice that the recommendation feeds into Allen's strengths as an account manager and strengthens his commitment to managing customer accounts the right and successful way.

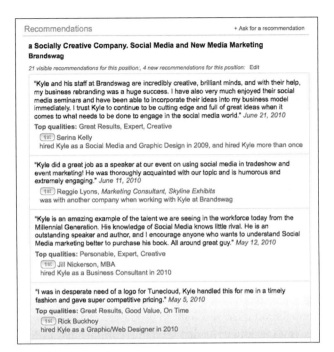

Figure 4.5   *This is an example of how your recommendations will display on your profile. Build your recommendations to create an increasingly powerful personal brand.*

- **Beth (climber)** wants to move up the ranks within her company to become CMO. How should Beth use recommendations? She needs recommendations from her superiors and co-workers to show upper management that she is fulfilling her company goals. Recommendations can help her get past the manager who may not share positive information with the higher-ups of a company. Here is an example of a positive recommendation for Beth:

  "Beth has been extremely effective at building marketing platforms that help our team at Company X. She is a go-getter and has consecutively hit her goals and expectations of my team."

  Beth has a recommendation that feeds into her ability to hit her goals, which is extremely important when climbing the ranks of any company. Remember to include information that can help in your internal promotion meetings. Also, do not hesitate to ask for recommendations from individuals of different departments within the same company. They could end up being extremely powerful for your personal brand development.

- **Carla (neophyte)** is a former pharmaceutical sales rep who left after eight years with her company. She is interested in working for a non-profit, either as a program director or a fund-raising specialist.

  Carla has an interesting problem because her previous job was as a pharmaceutical sales rep, which has nothing to do with being a program director. There are two things Carla could do. She could ask her sales manager at the pharmaceutical company to give a recommendation based on her ability to create relationships with doctors and other medical professionals, which could help her get a position as a fund-raising specialist. Or she could have him talk about her ability to manage several different clients and projects, which could speak to a program director position. Here is a good example of the former:

  > *"Carla was extremely effective in creating strategic relationships with doctors at private practices and helped in securing those relationships over an extended period of time. The relationships she handled have amounted to an increase in sales at our company!"*

- **Darrin (free agent)** is an IT professional who leaves his job every two or three years in pursuit of more money. He is a free agent because he'll stay at roughly the same level of job, regardless of where he goes, but he can make more money because there are bigger companies requiring his expertise.

  Darrin should follow the same path as Allen when it comes to asking for recommendations. He should ask a client or co-worker to give a positive recommendation to reinforce his ability to deliver for high-level clients. It is important that he gets recommendations from bigger companies because they are his target market; smaller companies will probably not help him in his personal branding endeavors. Here is a good example:

  > *"Darrin is a skilled IT professional who provided me with quality service when I knew very little about the field or my software. He was patient and knowledgeable and communicated well in explaining to me what his plans were in designing my software and internal communication solution. He listened well and provided choices for me based on the type of systems I was going for at the time."*

  You need to understand the advantages that good recommendations give to a LinkedIn profile. Remember to get recommendations from people who are going to influence your personal brand.

You may feel overwhelmed because there are so many useful tools to use for LinkedIn and personal branding. But if you want to choose one of the top features to further your personal brand, it's Recommendations. You are giving people the opportunity to tell their story of interacting with you as an individual and how you helped them. Now that's powerful!

Ten Do's and Don'ts of LinkedIn

Don't you love the do's and don'ts section of books? We do.

@kyleplacy: This is the only part of the book I'm actually going to read.

@edeckers: But isn't this your chapter to write?

@kyleplacy: Yeah, so?

There are plenty of rules to apply when building your personal brand with LinkedIn. These are the top 10 rules we share with our audiences. They are ones you should take extremely seriously if you want your personal branding campaign to be a success.

1. Do Upload a Professional Picture

This should be self-explanatory, but it is surprising how many starfish, cars, sunflowers, people standing on the beach at sunset, and dogs we witness on LinkedIn profiles. Honestly, who puts a picture of their dog on a professional networking platform?

@edeckers: Ooh, I hate the "standing on the beach" photos. Not only are they too small, they're backlit, and I can't see who they are.

@kyleplacy: What about the photo of people standing in the mountains?

@edeckers: Those too. They try to show the entire mountainscape, but the person is the size of a gnat in the photo.

It's bad enough when people do it on Facebook and Twitter, but this is a professional network.

The point of LinkedIn is to further your networking ability online as well as offline. You want people to recognize you when you walk into a networking event. And when you have a picture of your dog, that never happens. Upload a professional picture to all platforms you are building your personal brand on, whether that is Twitter, Facebook, LinkedIn, or your blog. We know you'll want to be fun and creative on those other sites, but don't do it if you're trying to create a professional image.

2. Do Connect to Your Real Friends and Contacts

Just like we tell children not to talk to strangers, the same applies to your LinkedIn profile. It's crazy to see how many people connect with strangers all over the world because they want to "build up" their network on LinkedIn. Connecting to hundreds of strangers will NOT help your network in LinkedIn. They do not care about you! They will not help build your personal brand. Why would you build a network of people you don't know and will never have a chance of knowing? Remember, you want to build a network of connections (deep relationships), not contacts (someone whose email you just happened to get). Remember, the value of LinkedIn comes in the quality of relationships you have, not the quantity. Although there are LIONs (LinkedIn Online Networkers—people who race to add as many people as they can on their profile) who abound on LinkedIn, they're not actually adding value to their network. They just have a lot of people they're connected to.

Think of it this way: If you ever have to ask someone for an introduction to someone else, it's rather a big letdown to get a message back that says, "Oh, I don't actually know them; they're just in my huge network." People like this do not provide real value, so don't become one of them.

3. Do Keep Your Profile Current

Let's use an example for this. Erik is hanging out with Kyle, and there is a funky smell coming from somewhere. Kyle asks Erik where that smell is coming from, and Erik nonchalantly says he hasn't changed clothes in three days. Does that change the way Kyle is interacting with Erik? Of course!

```
@edeckers:    Gee, I'm so glad I could help you out with this
              example!
@kyleplacy:   See what happens when you leave me alone with the
              manuscript?
```

Just like Erik neglected his appearance, the same concept applies to your LinkedIn profile. If you neglect your profile, people will tend to forget and avoid you. Neglecting your profile doesn't help you in the least, and at worst, it shows you're lazy.

4. Do Delete People Who Spam You

In life and in LinkedIn, there are bad apples. There are times when contacts or connections abuse the system and spam your Inbox with some new multilevel marketing scheme or a new product or service they're selling. It's polite to ask them to stop and rethink their strategy. They could be new to this, and maybe they made a mistake. But if they continue to abuse your connection, delete them. They're wasting your valuable time by making you wade through their mess. Get rid of them.

5. Do Spend Some Time on Your Summary

Do you ever read an email, newspaper, or blog post when the headline is terrible? Of course not. Your summary has the same effect on your LinkedIn profile. Be extremely concise and specific when writing your summary. Get people excited about reading your profile and connecting with you. Express your personal brand. Express what you are passionate about. It may even be helpful to have a co-worker or close connection review your summary.

6. Don't Use LinkedIn Like Facebook and Twitter

There is a time and place for professional and personal content when building your personal brand. We have discussed the importance of having places for both. LinkedIn is a professional network, and although it is important to share some personal content, don't use LinkedIn as a personal network. That's what Facebook is for.

7. Don't Sync LinkedIn with Twitter

Similarly, don't automatically blend LinkedIn with Twitter. LinkedIn gives you the applications and tools that allow you to connect your account with Twitter, which means whenever you post a message to Twitter, it automatically posts to your status update in LinkedIn.

Don't do this. Ever. If you're using Twitter correctly, you're communicating with connections, asking and answering questions, giving shout-outs to people across the country, and even making plans for lunch. People on LinkedIn don't want their feeds disrupted by all your tweets.

Remember, too, that not everyone uses Twitter, so your colleagues on LinkedIn may not know how to read some of the special characters and abbreviations on Twitter. (You will, after you read Chapter 5, "Twitter: Sharing in the Conversation.") So your tweets (Twitter messages) will be confusing. The same is true of Facebook: Don't tie your Twitter feed into your Facebook account.

8. Don't Decline Invitations. Archive Them

When a stranger asks you for a connection on LinkedIn, archive the invitation instead of deleting it. There could be a time when you meet this person, and you can refer to the previous invitation to connect with her. When a connection is archived, it's easier to keep track of it.

9. Don't Ask Everyone for Recommendations

There's no hard and fast rule about the number of recommendations you should have. There's no minimum, and some people think there's no maximum. Just remember that not every recommendation is important.

You do need to have at least two recommendations to reach 100% completion of your profile, but they need to be valuable recommendations. Here are a couple tips to follow:

- **Make sure you know the person**—This seems obvious, but unfortunately it is not. Basically, if you don't know the person who's asking you for a recommendation, send her a nice note that says, "I don't know you!" You don't need to give a recommendation to someone you don't know; similarly, you don't need to accept one either.

- **Ask your best clients**—Happy clients are the best referral and recommendation source for you. Make a list of 10 people to ask for a recommendation. You don't need 20 or 30 because 10 people talking about you is more than enough to strengthen your LinkedIn profile and build your personal brand.

10. Don't Forget to Use Spelling and Grammar Check

Do you use spelling and grammar check on your résumé? The same idea applies to your LinkedIn profile. Remember, your profile is technically a résumé, and we've all been taught that our résumés have to be laser perfect. Spell check everything! If you lose a job or a position because you misspelled a word, you have to buy five more copies of this book.

@kyleplacy: Ooh, and attend one of our seminars!

@edeckers: Yeah, at full price!

5

Twitter: Sharing in the Conversation

Imagine a social networking site where millions of people connect on a daily basis. You are throwing yourself into a networking event with millions of people chatting in succinct 3–5 second conversations. In 140 characters or less, they update the world on everything from the vital to the mundane, from the inspirational to the just plain silly, from the passions that drive them to what their pet ate for breakfast (which can be extremely entertaining and valuable).

We're either talking about a weird Alfred Hitchcock meets Adam Sandler movie, or Twitter. We know it sounds odd (Twitter and Alfred). We know the site is a little weird and hard to understand. We know you have no idea where to begin. It's also safe to assume that you've probably disregarded it as another site where people share things you don't need or want to know. However, the site is extremely valuable to your personal brand. That's part of the reason why you bought the book, right?

The truth of the matter is Twitter is revolutionizing the way people communicate on a daily basis, and this revolution is spreading through the ranks of blue collar and white collar professionals and over every inch of the globe.

Twitter is a platform that enables the instantaneous sharing of your blog or website's content, which means you have the opportunity to publish your opinions and ideas to a potential readership of millions, and you can do all this between sips from your latte, beer, or apple juice (for you young at heart).

Remember, it's the content that makes the personal brand, and Twitter is the perfect site for sharing those ideas and passions that make you a unique individual. The quickest, easiest way to share information and content—and thus, create your brand—is Twitter.

The question you need to answer is this one: Does the social networking site really matter to you? Isn't Twitter just another Tweeter or tweeker tool for young people? Can Twitter actually have an impact on the world of personal branding in 140 characters or less? (Hint: We wrote a whole chapter on it, so you can guess what that answer will be.)

Why Should You Use Twitter?

Do you care about 500 million people paying attention and understanding your message? Okay, maybe not 500 million, but you can get hundreds and maybe even thousands of people interested.

Let's talk about why you should use this amazing conversation tool to further your personal brand and build your already thriving network.

Twitter has been growing exponentially since its creation four years ago and now boasts upward of 500 million[1] users around the world.

Let's think about this for one second (maybe even a couple seconds): 500 million is a big number. It's bigger than the entire United States. It's more than 7% of the world's population. It's a *big box* of a million little things. It's a massive database of people to whom you can directly market your personal services or brand. Ridiculous amounts of content are shared on Twitter (upward of 200 million tweets per day[2]), and the important part of all this content is that it is dynamic. What does *dynamic content* mean? Let's talk about the amount of content shared.

According to the official Twitter blog (http://blog.twitter.com), there are 200 million tweets sent on a daily basis, or 2,340 tweets per second! Imagine the little pieces of rice yelling 2,340 times every second because you are dumping them in a vat of boiling water. (But we digress... .)

Admittedly, a few of these messages or tweets are a complete waste of time to some people, but there are others who would appreciate the references to pet food and sandwiches. For example, an individual who works for a pet food supplier would *love* to know what her customers use on a regular basis. There is so much content shared on Twitter that 100% of your tweets will be relevant to someone, just not everyone. The important tweets are changing the way we communicate to the masses and changing the way people perceive your personal brand.

Sure, this is content in 140 characters or less, but the sheer volume alone is enough to make Twitter an extremely valuable tool for building a personal brand.

What Can Twitter Do for You?

There are many reasons to start using Twitter to share your content. It's worth repeating: Twitter is one of the premiere platforms to build your personal brand for many reasons, which we discuss throughout this chapter. Remember, we discussed the objectives and goals of building a personal brand in Chapter 1, "Welcome to the Party," and Chapter 2, "How Do You Fit in the Mix?." Most important, Twitter has a lot to offer you in regards to meeting your personal branding objectives and goals.

- **You can establish your expertise**—We talked about blogging and establishing your expertise in Chapter 3, "Blogging: Telling Your Story." Blogging enables you share your story with a range of

---

1. http://www.tgdaily.com/software-brief/52284-twitter-on-pace-to-reach200-million-users-by-2011

2. http://blog.twitter.com/2011/06/200-million-tweets-per-day.html

individuals. To further your story, you need the ability to share that story, and Twitter is the perfect place to do so. Remember your fellow 500 million twitterers? You have the opportunity to share your story with hundreds of people (sometimes, whether they want to hear it).

- **You can market or sell your personal brand**—Twitter gives you the opportunity to share your expertise with millions of people across the world. And the beautiful thing about this tool is that it is a "newer" phenomenon than Facebook or MySpace. Social networking sites are still growing exponentially, but Twitter is a newer system. Even after six years, the opportunity to grow your personal brand is exponential.

- **You can have direct communication with potential clients and employers**—At the core of this social networking site, Twitter is a communication medium. People use Twitter to communicate with different types of users all over the globe. This is not only a medium to simply share content, but to discuss it as well.

- **You have access to many types of research**—You can use Twitter to research blog content or to find marketplace trends. What are your peers writing about? What are they reading? What's trending across the country or around the world? Check it out, and create your own responses. As we wrote this chapter, the National Basketball Association (NBA) had just finished labor negotiations with their players. Anyone who wanted to take advantage of it was writing about things such as "Five Things the Start of the NBA Season Means to _____" and finding readers.

  You also have the ability to research what other experts say about your product, service, or marketplace. The best part about all this is that Twitter is free. When content is shared so rapidly, it is easy to gauge trends and reap a ton of content from the site.

- **You can also track your competitors**—You'll be amazed at how much content your competitors share on Twitter. Because Twitter is fairly new to the general public, it's extremely easy to gain valuable content from your competitors, including things like, "Had a great meeting with @ABC_Widgets about possible marketing plan!" Use Twitter to make decisions on how to market yourself to the client just by watching what your competitors are sharing.

- **You can find people who share your passions**—There are plenty of different types of personal passions shared daily on Twitter. Millions of tweets are created every second of every day, and yours are in there, too. Just do a search for whatever inspires you, and start connecting with the people talking about it.

You want to connect with passionate people because they share content. It helps when you find individuals who are passionate about the same things. Both Kyle and Erik share a passion for the city of Indianapolis, and they connect with people on a daily basis who live in the city. Erik connects with other food lovers in the city to find new restaurants to attend and promote. Kyle finds new music venues by following local musicians. Our passion for our city helps us grow our personal brands because of the direct contact we have with other individuals.

You can increase traffic to your website and blog. Twitter is a content distribution and communication medium. If you send your blog posts to Twitter, you can get a hefty return in terms of clicks. People love to click different posts to read varying types of content through Twitter.

How Do You Use Twitter?

Are we past the point to prove that Twitter is a viable platform? If you've reached this point, hopefully you're ready to join the twitterati, the millions of people who use Twitter on a daily basis to build their brand. Building your personal brand with Twitter starts with your profile.

Creating a Twitter Profile

The first step in the world of Twitter is to cross the threshold and create your own profile. Your Twitter profile is your home base on Twitter much like your website is your home base for your business. It's where you connect with people and start following others to build your personal network. You can customize your settings and background and send or receive direct messages.

When you create your Twitter name, you need to make sure it is easy to remember and has something to do with your name. If your name is Adam Decker and your Twitter handle is @394ldkf, you're not going to amount to much in the world of Twitter. 394ldkf just doesn't roll off the tongue that easily.

A good example of a name is your full name in real life (@AdamDecker). If your name is actually taken, try different variations. Kyle decided to use @kyleplacy because @kylelacy was already taken by another Twitter user. He thought it was a great idea until he started receiving notes and letters to Kyle Placy.

```
@kyleplacy:  Not funny anymore, people. I've heard them all!
@edeckers:   How about Ky Leplacy?
@kyleplacy:  Shut up.
@edeckers:   Or Kyl Eplacy?
@kyleplacy:  Or Ed Eckers?
@edeckers:   Truce.
```

After you come up with your Twitter name, upload a nice photo. As a friendly tip, be sure to upload a nice photo of yourself, not your dog or a Mercedes. (We all know it's not your car anyway, so quit trying to fool people.) Besides, you need to remember that people want to get to know *you*, not your dog. Your picture should reflect that idea.

 Tip

Make sure the photo (or avatar) is a close-up of your face, and only of you, not you and your friends, or you standing on the beach or a mountain with the sun backlighting you. How do we even know that's you? Pick a photo of your face that allows people to pick you out of a crowd if they've never met you before.

Finally, fill out your profile information, including your bio. Be sure to fill it with relevant information. Your profile is there to give people the opportunity to learn what you're about and who you are. Also, add your blog URL or your website address to the profile. Remember to give people the opportunity to connect with you as many times as possible.

Getting Followers

The next fork in the road is getting actual followers to your Twitter account. Your goal may not be to have hundreds of thousands of followers, but you do need to gain a few worthy friends. If you're on Twitter and don't have friends, people assume you're a weirdo, and they don't want to associate with weirdos. (Or it could be that you're just not using Twitter, in which case we won't associate with you then either.) Friends (or followers) on Twitter give you the opportunity to share your message with other people. Followers share your content, and we love sharing content! It furthers the brand!

You can add people as followers to your account in a few ways.

First, introduce yourself by "following" people. Keep your tweets (posts) open to the public so that anyone can read them. It is likely that when you follow people, they will reciprocate and follow you back. That doesn't necessarily mean you should follow everyone. You can search for people based on keywords. Go to http://search.twitter.com, and search for keywords surrounding your industry or even your passions. Follow those people, and see if they'll follow you back.

Note

Following is Twitter jargon for "connecting with." Although it sounds rather stalkerish—"Hey, I'm following you. Are you following me?"—you'll get used to the parlance after a short while. Although it's not all puppy dogs and rainbows of Facebook—"Will you be my friend? She's my friend!"—it's not as creepy as it sounds.

Next, import your email contacts. When you start your account, Twitter asks if you want to import your contacts from email providers like Gmail, AOL, and Yahoo!. Enter your email information and watch what happens: Twitter pulls all your email contacts and cross-references them with the Twitter database. It tells you who out of your email database uses the Twitter service. Click one button, and Twitter follows everyone from your email database. And remember that if you follow all these contacts, there is the potential that they will follow you back. You will get a better response rate from people following you from your email database because they already know your name (or at least they should). This is a great way to build up your Twitter database with people you already know.

Sending Out Tweets

Let's get to tweeting! This is where the true fun begins in the world of Twitter. *Tweets, tweeting,* and *being tweeted* are less about that little yellow bird from Bugs Bunny cartoons and more about sending messages to other Twitter users.

Tweets are the brief messages you post to your profile and send out to your followers. They are the lifeblood of the Twitter universe. The 140-character post (the max amount of content per message) is the engagement tool that prompts the conversation from other users. You can essentially say whatever you want, link to whatever you want, and show pictures and videos of whatever you want. But keep in mind, as you build your personal brand, that everything you do is a reflection of you.

Remember to start conversations. You can direct tweets at other users by asking questions, sharing news, or whatever. By starting conversations, you build relationships with other Twitter users. The point of using Twitter and social networking is to build your brand, and the only way to accomplish this is to share content. Figure 5.1 is an example of a tweet.

Figure 5.1   *This is a tweet sent out by Kyle to @BrennerMichael congratulating him on the amazing content he has been sharing.*

This tweet was sent out from Kyle's account (@kyleplacy). He was replying directly to @BrennerMichael after Michael had shared a blog post with valuable marketing information. When Kyle sent the tweet, all his followers received it, and @BrennerMichael received it because his Twitter handle was mentioned.

 Tip

Content makes the tweet. Remember, the more content-rich your tweets become, the more people will read. This is done by linking your blog, your website, and other news sources and engaging in conversations. Remember: Tweeting is what makes Twitter social and builds your personal brand.

Retweeting Your Content

Retweeting is actually an action completed by the members of the Twitter community. Members of the Twitter community who like your post might *retweet* it to their followers—retweeting is the action to share your content. The best way to think about retweeting is an email being forwarded to other individuals by other users. A retweet on Twitter can be seen as a compliment. It means that the content was interesting enough to be passed along.

If you want one goal for Twitter, it is the retweet. There is no function more powerful and more apt to spread your message (and personal brand). It is viral and word-of-mouth marketing at its finest. Retweeting is a way to source content. Just as you would not plagiarize in a research document, you shouldn't on Twitter. The same repercussions could occur. People don't like it when you steal their tweets, comments, content, or sandwich, so retweet them.

By now, you're probably wondering if we're leading you down the retweet rabbit hole, and you're asking where to go from here. Not to worry. Following are some tips to getting your content retweeted:

- **Don't talk about yourself so much**—The more interesting your tweets, the more likely they will be retweeted, especially if you include a link that leads the reader to even more interesting information. Links also give your information more credibility. Most people don't want to hear about your trip to Costco or what you had for dinner. Instead, tweet about things relevant to your industry, a newsworthy story, or a local event coming up, including links to the website or story.

- **Remember who your audience is**—You're not tweeting to 5 year olds, so your tweets can use grown-up language. When you post content that has substance, people may respond to it and retweet it. Try asking for advice or an opinion about something. Questions that evoke conversation will more likely get retweeted.

- **Tweet about how to do something**—Some people are on Twitter to learn, so provide them with your expertise and know-how.

- **Keep your 140-character tweets to between 100–120 characters**—This allows people to retweet your tweet easily and without editing. Twitter adds the name of the individual retweeting to every tweet. After multiple names have been added (a good thing), the tweet is going to exceed 140 characters and be sucked into oblivion.

```
@kyleplacy:    Keep tweets between 100—120 characters so
               people can include your name and give you
               the credit.

@edeckers:     RT @kyleplacy: Keep tweets between 100—120
               characters so people can include your name and
               give you the credit.

@douglaskarr:  RT @edeckers: RT @kyleplacy: Keep tweets
               between 100—120 characters so people can
               include your name and give you the credit.
```

See how that works? Kyle's first tweet was 98 characters. When Erik retweeted it, the entire message was 113 characters because it included Kyle's name. When our good friend, Doug Karr, RTed it (RT is the Twitter abbreviation for retweet), the message had grown to 126.

- **Send a quote**—Twitter users love quotes and will retweet to their little hearts' content. You are actually killing two birds with one stone. Send inspirational quotes to make people smile, and gain followers! Can't get much better than that!

The basics of Twitter are important but there are also advanced features. Now if only there were a way you could manage the account more effectively to fully grow your brand. Oh wait—there totally is. There are also dozens of applications that can help you in your Twitter domination.

Applications for Twitter Domination

So far we have talked about using Twitter.com as your primary source to share and tweet to your little heart's desire. However, the website can be a little hard to navigate if you start getting ungodly amounts of followers (which you'll get, just because you're awesome). We're talking Lady Gaga famous!

```
@edeckers:   Dude, settle down. We don't want to promise that.
@kyleplacy:  What? She's got a few thousand followers. How hard
             can that be?
@edeckers:   No, she's got more than 22.5 million followers.
@kyleplacy:  Oh. Uh, never mind.
```

So, how do we navigate Twitter without opening multiple windows on Internet Explorer or tabs on Firefox?

 Tip

We recommend using Google's Chrome for your Internet browsing. That's because there are all kinds of social media plug-ins that make your personal branding campaign a whole lot easier and more efficient. Plus, it's more stable and less prone to virus and phishing attacks.

Twitter is a great tool on its own because you can engage with readers all over the world and reinforce your personal brand in just a few minutes a day with your brief tweets. But you can get even more out of Twitter with third-party applications designed to make the site even more useful for the professional.

That's because there are hundreds of developers sitting in their basements, offices, and coffee shops tapping away at their computers and creating helpful applications for *you* to use. Applications are tools used to enhance your experience of Twitter and are separate from the actual Twitter.com website. Enhancing *your* Twitter experience should be the top priority of every developer on the face of the planet. (Or at least ours. But we're selfish that way.)

They allow you to manage your time by scheduling tweets, develop niche marketing strategies, organize your followers, and track your success using analytics. Three different types of applications are on Twitter: desktop, mobile, and web-based. Some applications cater to all three types; it is up to you to choose which type is the best fit.

 Tip

A great way to find different applications to use is to surf over to http://www.squidoo.com/twitterapps. This Squidoo lens was created by airabongco and is a massive database of different applications from mobile to desktop that can help you use Twitter as a tool for your personal brand.

In terms of functionality, there isn't much difference between a desktop, mobile, and web-based application. The only difference between the three applications is where they are stored. A desktop application is downloaded and resides on your computer. A mobile application is on your mobile phone and resides on your phone. A web-based application is used online and is never downloaded.

Corporate applications and personal applications are out there for your developmental needs. CoTweet (www.cotweet.com) is a corporate Twitter tool that has been used by everyone from Coca-Cola to Starbucks, and was purchased by Kyle's employer, ExactTarget, in 2010, and is being rebranded under the Social Engage name (http://blog.exacttarget.com/blog/focus-on-social/socialengage-the-next-generation-of-social-media-management). If your personal brand becomes large, you are going to have multiple people managing your Twitter account, CoTweet is a valuable addition to your Twitter arsenal. However, we are talking about individuals using Twitter to develop a personal brand!

First...a couple of disclaimers: The following applications are Kyle and Erik's favorite applications. If you find an application that you find more valuable, by all means, use it. But the following are applications we have used for a couple of years and grown attached to.

Also, you need to understand that the majority of applications (desktop, mobile, and web-based) have the same types of functionality. Try out the different applications to find one that you are comfortable with using.

Desktop Applications

TweetDeck

This is the application we recommend for anyone getting started or for those people who have thrown up their hands and shouted, "I just don't get how Twitter works." Nearly everyone who uses TweetDeck becomes a Twitter ninja. (And trust us, you want to be a Twitter ninja. You just have to buy your own uniform.) TweetDeck helps you by managing multiple Twitter accounts, your Facebook page, and LinkedIn account. You also have the ability to group different Twitter users and have columns for different users. It is also one of the more valuable options because it is owned by Twitter!

Seesmic

Seesmic is an application that you can download on your computer to manage your social media accounts. (It also has a web-based option.) You can post to just one or all your accounts at the same time. A cool feature is the Evernote tool, which enables you to save events, messages, and updates by storing them. You can also share updates and upload pictures by email. It enables you to manage accounts on any platform.

Twitterrific

Twitterrific is a Mac application that sits on your desktop. If you are annoyed by windows cluttering up your desktop, Twitterrific is probably for you. Twitterrific has an excellent user interface and is small enough not to be annoying. It offers the same types of capabilities as TweetDeck but has more keyboard shortcuts for the Mac user. The application is designed to let you view as much or as little information as you prefer when it's on your desktop.

Twitterrific is also available for download on the iPhone as an application. Kyle loves using Twitterrific on his iPhone. Just keep in mind, it costs approximately $9.95 to use this awesome tool, but it is well worth it!

Twhirl

Twhirl is desktop software designed by the people who brought you Seesmic. It can run on both the Windows and Mac platforms. Twhirl allows you connect to multiple accounts on Twitter, Laconi.ca, and Seesmic.

You can let Twhirl run in the background while you work, and it gives you pop-up alerts that tell you when you have new messages (also a feature on TweetDeck). With Twhirl, you can also cross-post messages to multiple profiles on other social networking sites like Facebook and record a video to share on Seesmic.

Web-Based Applications

HootSuite.com

This is a web-based Twitter tool that gathers a lot of the features of different Twitter apps and offers them on one simple web interface. Other apps do similar things, but we haven't found one that does everything HootSuite does. HootSuite is the golden nugget of all Twitter applications. Although TweetDeck can be easier for some to use, HootSuite gives everything you need to dominate in the personal branding world.

You can do the following with HootSuite:

- Using their publishing, you can schedule tweets for preposting throughout the day. HootSuite lets you schedule in 5-minute increments, like 10:15 and 10:20. Their paid version lets you schedule at odd times, like 10:17 or 10:26.

- Manage and monitor different Twitter accounts, like a work account and a personal account. You can manage up to five accounts for free. If you have more than five accounts, it costs you monthly to run six accounts or more.

- Create search columns to monitor a keyword, such as the name of your business or your industry.

- Track links and click-throughs with a URL shortener such as bit.ly, tinyurl, or ow.ly. Hootsuite also enables you to create success reports. Depending on the intensity of your data, you may need to upgrade your account for more reporting features.

- Integrate your Facebook, LinkedIn, and other social accounts in one place.

There are plenty of ways to use HootSuite in the world of promoting yourself through Twitter. Whether you pre-post tweets to be sent out during the day or track clicks for links you have "tweeted," HootSuite is, in our opinion, the best application to use for Twitter management (see Figure 5.2).

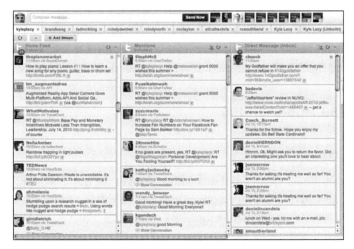

Figure 5.2   *The different columns in the HootSuite database represent different ways to manage and organize your Twitter network.*

Argyle Social

Argyle is a multi-sharing tool, just like HootSuite or TweetDeck. It lets you submit messages to Twitter, LinkedIn, and Facebook pages (but not profiles). You can measure the performance of each message via its analytic services, and even schedule messages to publish at specific times.

Argyle is a paid service, so it has some more bells and whistles on it than the free apps—minute-to-minute scheduling, a hopper that will space out your messages based on the number in the hopper, and a dashboard that lets you send tweets— and a cleaner, more thorough interface.

Argyle Social is geared more toward agencies, social media professionals, and consultants who deal with a lot of clients, but if you're in a position to use it, it can certainly help with scheduled tweeting and sharing of information while you're otherwise engaged.

BufferApp.com

We can't finish the web-based applications without discussing BufferApp. Buffer is one of the newer applications on the market that has revolutionized the way to share and schedule content on Twitter. The application allows you to work out all the tweets you want to send in a given day, and Buffer schedules the tweets for you.

BufferApp is different from Hootsuite because it automates the scheduling process. Simply keep Buffer topped off with tweets, and you can tweet consistently all week! Buffer also offers different plans that range from free to $99 per month. Like Hootsuite, it's dependent on how many accounts you stream through the BufferApp. We're not discounting the other platforms out there, because they have a following as well. You can be sure that there will be many more to come. We'll review some of the other big players we've seen our fellow *tweeple* (Twitter + people = tweeple) use. You should test the different platforms to find the one that best fits your personality and mission statement.

(We're kidding about the mission statement.)

As stated previously, CoTweet is a corporate Twitter application best served when managing multiple people and Twitter. If you have support in managing your personal brand, look at CoTweet as your solution to all things Twitter. It allows you to assign different tasks, manage multiple users on a single Twitter account, and search/track multiple keywords.

Mobile Applications

Mobile applications are important to your Twitter experience because they do one thing: make you mobile. You cannot sit in front of a computer all day. You can network and meet with potential clients, connections, and contacts. You need to include a mobile application on your smart phone. If you do not have a smart phone, upgrade.

Twitter (for Android)

Erik was a regular Android Twitter user on a previous phone (he has since switched to Seesmic). Twitter Mobile is created by Twitter, and is a bare bones app that recreates the Twitter.com experience as closely as possible. The Twitter application tends to be easier to use for the average Twitter user. Try it out to see what you think.

UberSocial (for BlackBerry)

UberSocial delivers an amazing application for BlackBerry users. The basic features of this application consist of the ability to upload pictures, update Google Talk, see who's tweeting near you, update locations, and send embedding videos. It also allows you to use the UberView feature that provides a live preview of linked content including web pages, blog posts, images, and video. If you've been using another Twitter app for BlackBerry, give this one a try.

Many of the applications also support mobile integration. Remember: The choice of your mobile applications depends on the phone you use.

Deciding What's Best

Twitter applications are available to help enhance your Twitter experience. The Twitter website does not offer the functionality that most applications offer. Whether you want to use HootSuite to prepost tweets for effective time management or use TweetDeck to manage multiple social accounts, you can use the tools necessary to use Twitter effectively.

So which one should you choose? It depends on what platform you feel most comfortable with. Don't choose an application based on the name. (They're all goofy names. You just have to get over that you sound like a clown on Ecstasy when you start talking about them.) Test all the applications before you start using them regularly, and remember that the tools aren't as important as what you do with them. One app cannot help you more than another, any more than one kind of pen can make you a better writer than another. Get the app you like best, and then get going.

What Should You Tweet (and What Shouldn't You?)

This is a question many face constantly. They get caught up with trying to figure out what to tweet, how to tweet, and when to tweet—it's exasperating! They start to question and doubt their tweets so much that they stop tweeting altogether. Or they worry that their content is monotonous and lose sight of why they wanted to tweet in the first place (personal branding).

Ultimately, people lose motivation and slowly begin tweeting in circles, sending empty messages that don't mean anything. Or they race around, not sure where to start, so they just start throwing up anything and everything they can think of. Nobody wants to tweet in circles. You'll get dizzy, probably throw up, and embarrass yourself in front of all your friends. You may do it gracefully, but in the long run, you'll still be embarrassed. Following are a few ways to avoid the embarrassment of tweeting in circles:

- **Tweeting for current topics**—How many journals have you started, only to toss them aside after two weeks of struggling to think of something profound to write about? You're trying to write to future generations, in the hopes that someone will think you're interesting 50 years from now. Just write about stuff that's happening to you and stuff that you're thinking about. Just put something, anything, out there on Twitter. Then do it again and again. Learn what is important, and make tweeting a habit.

- **Sharing is caring**—This is crucial for Twitter. If you love reading another user's tweets, chances are someone else will, too. People love following new Twitter users who have excellent tweets (with interesting content), so introduce them. Sharing is more than introducing new people worth following. It's about sharing a variety of great content, too. Content can come in the form of links, retweets, questions, pictures, and more. Share what you know and who you know. When you've hit a rut, find more to share. There's plenty of information worth passing on.

- **Engage and begin a conversation**—Don't have anything to say? Then engage with someone else and begin a conversation. It's amazing how powerful a simple conversation can be if you show someone you're listening! In this weird six-degrees-of-Kevin-Bacon world, one conversation (even on Twitter) can lead to an endless amount of useful resources and information. This is what Twitter is for—networking. And the only way to expand your network is through conversations. No one knows who you are until you've introduced yourself, right? You can't be a wallflower at party, and you can't be a wallflower on Twitter.

  The point here is to share your opinions and ask questions. Use (and grow) your resources and your network just by sitting at your computer or pulling out your mobile phone. Ask and answer new questions, and be a point of reference for someone else.

- **Be consistent**—Remember the times when your head is completely empty and words are escaping you? It has happened to everyone. If you're lacking in ideas for a blog or questions to ask, there are still ways to tweet. Remember, a tweet is only 140 characters long (or short). Rework old ideas, revisit old stories, and send out an "in case you missed this" tweet with links back to the original story. You can repeat yourself. This is how you develop an audience and reach the people who might have missed you earlier. There are rules to be broken in the world of Twitter, and this is one of them. Remember: You can repeat yourself. (See what we did there?)

- **Be active, not annoying**—You know the little kid who talks constantly? That one kid—not your own, to be sure—who chatters, makes a lot of noise, and is a general nuisance? Don't be that little kid. Period! This may be a touchy subject for some, but it is worth talking about. The difference between being active and annoying (which is an important distinction) is powerful. First, you don't need to tweet 100 times a day to be consistent or relevant—tweeting too much can lose followers for you.

  Next, this means don't tweet the same thing over and over. Although we said you can re-send previous tweets, we don't mean 10 times a day. It also means don't tell us what you had for breakfast every morning or that you're sick, healthy, going to lunch, back from lunch, tired, wide awake, going to work, or heading home. You've created all this chatter, and it doesn't do a thing. Remember to focus on your content, and refer to the five principles we talked about in Chapter 1. Your content is what drives your personal brand, and Twitter is one of the main sources of conversation around that brand.

- **Be relevant and surprising**—We don't mean to sound like a "365 Platitudes for a Joy-Filled Life" calendar.

@edeckers:	Is there really a thing?
@kyleplacy:	I don't know. Do you think we could get Pearson to publish it if we wrote it?
@YourDamnEditor:	Boys, just focus on this project. One thing at a time.

So without being all Rebecca of Sunnybrook Farm about this, we do want to say you should post stuff that will make people happy or interested to read stuff from you. Tweet an interesting article you read, a blog post you wrote, a meeting you had with another social media friend, a conference you're attending, a video you uploaded, a video of your latest conference session (see Chapter 13, "Public Speaking: We Promise You Won't Die"), or retweet an interesting blog post from your social media friend. Now that is interesting.

- **Be goal-oriented**—Still driving in circles? Put it in park and breathe. Now is the time to sit back and revisit your goals. Why did you create your Twitter account? Let's go deeper than that. Think back to why you are creating your personal brand. What are the goals and ideas pushing you to becoming more well known in your field or community? Remember: Every goal applies to the overall structure of social media and Twitter, and you should use this with those goals in mind. Figure out which tweets take you a step toward that goal and which kinds keep you in the same place or take you a step backward.

- **Take a break**—When you feel stuck and lose motivation to tweet, don't force it. You're allowed to take a day off. You're allowed to shut down HootSuite and go throw a Frisbee to your dog. You're allowed to have a drink with that special someone. And you are allowed to tweet something personal once in a while (even more than once in a while). Whether your goals are big or small, users want to follow someone they can relate to. They want to know you're a human being, not a self-marketing machine. Twitter (all social media, actually) is not all about constant self-promotion or constant other-promotion. It's not all about "me, me, me," but neither is it all about "you, you, you." Sometimes it's just about "Here's what I like" or "Here's how I have fun." Remember, this is your personal brand, and that includes your identity when you're "off the clock." So your Twitter messages need to be a mix of building your personal image and brand and helping others build theirs.

Personal Branding Case Study : @applegirl

We had been following Suzanne Marlatt on Twitter and witnessed her use the tool to help get a job at Edleman Digital with David Armano. Seriously, she has excellent content. Her story shows us that using Twitter to listen, respond, and use creativity to get noticed simply works.

> *"I had been following David Armano since I saw him speak at Social Media Club Chicago in January 2009. I found his tweets interesting but I never took the time to respond to anything he said until I saw a tweet from him that he was using Yammer. I responded back to him and said that although I like Yammer, it was difficult to implement at my work because people just don't yam.*
>
> *My tweet was different from the other responses he received that evening, and he took the time to look into my social accounts (blogs, twitter, and so on). It just so happened that he was looking for a community manager at Edleman. He decided that I fit the bill after reviewing my online persona and content. A few DMs (direct messages) and an interview later, I accepted the position. Behold the power [of] the @ reply without which I would still be in my current position."*

Do's and Don'ts While Using Twitter

You can use Twitter to effectively further your personal brand in a lot of fun ways. You'll get even more out of it if you keep in mind the rules governing the world of Twitter:

- **Do be yourself; don't be a fake**—Personal branding is about being honest and being real. When it comes to sharing content on the Internet, make sure you're telling the truth. And when you're sharing content, make sure you're sharing both professional and personal information. Remember: Your personal identity is what crafts your professional brand.

- **Do learn the art of following and unfollowing**—When using Twitter, you will have multiple people following your account on a daily basis. This is based on the content you share as well as the people who are retweeting and following your account.

- **Don't automatically follow people just because they followed you**—Check out their profile bio and the content they share. Make the decision on whether they will be valuable to your efforts (or at least aren't a bunch of filthy spammers).

- **Do know the concept of Giver's Gain**—It means you give without expecting anything in return. For Twitter, you're expected to share other users' information more than your own. When you share their content, they're more likely to share yours in return. In the world of personal promotion, you need to have loyal fans who spread your content to others. Remember, it's content that gets other users to notice you. Share content from others, and they'll build your brand for you.

- **Tweet your content on a regular basis**—People have different ideas on how often you should tweet. We have heard everything from 5–20 tweets a day. There's no magic number, but we always tell people to share at least 5 tweets a day. Here is a better rule of thumb: Share one piece of information about yourself, and four pieces of information about other people and your industry.

- **Don't lose track of time**—We could all use a few time-management seminars. Most of us don't have enough time in the day to accomplish everything on our to-do list. That being said, managing your Twitter time is equally important and can be equally as difficult. Use a calendar to track the time you spend on Twitter. Tell yourself you will spend 15 minutes a day using the tool. If you need to, use BufferApp or HootSuite as a way to regulate the time you spend on Twitter.

Twitter applications give you plenty of tools to manage your time, such as notifications and alerts on when individuals reply to your tweets. You can also manage thousands of Twitter users effectively by grouping them in lists and columns in HootSuite, TweetDeck, and CoTweet/Social Engage. There are numerous ways to stay more productive on Twitter; it all stems from your ability to use the applications correctly.

Twitter Tips in 140 Characters or Less

We asked our Twitter friends to give us some tips on using Twitter for personal branding. And our friends came through for us. They gave us a lot of great advice, which we include here.

- Be yourself on Twitter. People will either love you or hate you but at least it's you. —@mooshinindy

- Twitter is a conversation. Take some time to listen to what is going on and respond. —@virtualewit

- Twitter is as good as the people you follow. —@lookwebdesign

- Tweet 80% content your readers will find helpful and 20% self-promotion. —@watsonk2

- Find the perfect balance between the quantity of your tweet versus the quality.

- First—get followers. Second—keep followers. Sounds easy right?

- Pay it forward—giving is as good as getting, and social capital is invaluable. —@jennielees

- Identify. Engage. Respond. Repeat. —@chadrichards

- Simply be genuine and share useful information as in time it will come back to you. —@jillharding

- Don't constantly change your avatar as it's one of the main consistencies in your brand. — @bnyquist

- If you murder someone, don't tweet about it. Bad for the brand. —@brianspaeth

- Focus on building conversations and relationships and the followers will come. —@roundpeg

- Be mindful that your horse precedes your cart. Relationships are key. —@fleurdeleigh

- Content is king. —@taskwum

- Employ a content lure strategy. You point users to helpful content in exchange for influence.

How Does This Chapter Apply to Our Four Heroes?

As discussed throughout the chapter, you can use Twitter to further build your personal brand through content sharing and network building. How do our four heroes use Twitter to further their personal brand in their respective industries and networks?

- **Allen (influencer)** is searching for a job in an advertising firm as an account representative. Twitter is extremely important to Allen because his potential employer uses Twitter because it is a corporate communication platform. It is rare that an ad firm would not use Twitter for communication. Allen needs to be up to date with communication technology. By using Twitter, Allen can connect with influencers in the advertising industry or connect with individuals who work at local ad firms where Allen is trying to get a job. Remember, it is all about building a network and relationships.

- **Beth (climber)** wants to be a CMO at an insurance agency. This is where the use of Twitter can become a little dicey. Beth's main problem is going to be the lack of use of Twitter within the insurance world. Her industry is heavily regulated and does not look on social networking sites such as Twitter favorably. However, Beth can use Twitter for a personal communication platform. By sharing her expertise with the network on all things insurance (not relating to the company but from her personal opinion), she can build her knowledge and personal brand. Beth needs a personal Twitter account to distribute and share information related to her personal opinion of her industry.

- **Carla (neophyte)** is in an interesting situation as well, wanting to switch from a pharmaceutical rep to a nonprofit role. For her, she can use Twitter to start networking within the nonprofit world. Like Allen's advertising prospectives, nonprofit directors and volunteers use Twitter constantly for news, information, and distribution to help further their message. Carla should share information on the nonprofit world and retweet individuals who are already involved.

- **Darrin (free agent)** is also in the situation in which he should use Twitter for development, networking, and content sharing. Individuals within the technology world should use Twitter to (at the very least) understand the system. Darrin should attend networking meetings and connect with individuals he meets on Twitter to further the conversation. Twitter may not lead to many sales leads for Darrin, but it can increase his network size and scope.

6

Facebook: Developing a Community of Friends

Imagine a single lamp lighting a desk deep in the dormi-tories of Harvard University. A scrawny college student types at a computer, working on a computer science project with his roommates. In 2004, Harvard sopho-more Mark Zuckerberg began developing a new kind of website for fellow students to track their social lives. It quickly caught on among students, and membership was first expanded to include Stanford, Yale, and Columbia universities and then to most universities across the United States and Canada. By 2006, the site was called Facebook, and anyone around the world could join this social networking phenomenon.[1] What does 900 mil-lion represent? It's the number of people currently using Facebook to share content and create relationships.

In just six years, Mark's student project transformed into a worldwide social media juggernaut. In September 2011, Facebook announced that it had more than 900 million

---

1. http://en.wikipedia.org/wiki/Facebook.

active users. That is close to a billion individuals using Facebook to create connections with friends and colleagues and further their personal brands and personas.

You're probably already on Facebook, but you may not be getting the most out of it. You could use this incredibly powerful tool for personal branding. The main purpose of using Facebook is to create a community and connect people. Connecting with people and creating community can help fuel the influence behind your brand. Influence creates viral marketing within a community. More on that later.

The average age of a Facebook user is 38.4.[2] Did that number throw you off? You mean to tell me that the average Facebook user is not a college student? It's okay to be shocked. It is normal to assume that Facebook users are much younger. However, they still share content. Facebook users share their thoughts, ideas, and opinions. And each one of them builds some type of identity (whether personal or professional) using Facebook as the tool. The users share about their family, friends, and unique perspectives on life. Why not join in the fun?

Why Should You Use Facebook?

Facebook is a site that exists to help people connect and stay in touch. LinkedIn is an extremely professional site, whereas Facebook is truly the personal tool for your personal brand. Many people use Facebook as a way to share pictures, opinions, and content around their personal lives. Others add a page to their account and a community site around their organization, brand, or personality. There are still some who use it as a community site to gather different groups of people into an online group or fan page. (More on professional pages later.)

---

2. http://royal.pingdom.com/2010/02/16/study-ages-of-social-network-users/.

What we have come to realize is that the essence of your personal life has some impact on your professional brand. Plenty of professionals sell their products and services in direct association with their personal lives. What you do, see, and involve yourself in on a daily basis relates to your job.

An example: An insurance agent could create a Facebook page for her son's little league team and use that group to help promote her business. We're not talking about being awkward and saying, "Hey! Your kid might break an arm with that bat! Are you insured?" We're talking about using the team as the middle ground to create a connection with the other parents. When you create a common association with other people (i.e., the baseball team), they will more than likely join the group. Eventually you can enter into deeper conversations with other parents because of the relationship built from the team.

Facebook is the website to make that connection happen. Are the parents of the other children on the team prospective clients? Probably. Could the insurance broker create a connection with other parents because of her kid's baseball team? Definitely.

We do not condone the use of your children to sell your products. (Well, maybe in a small way. Especially if they're adorable.) We condone the use of similar circumstances to create connections between individuals. The interesting part to using Facebook is to create a greater connection between personal and professional lives. The site enables you to strengthen personal relationships in a way that can turn into professional relationships.

@edeckers:	Do you think @YourDamnEditor would let us use children to market the book?
@kyleplacy:	I don't see why not. We've been acting like children the whole time.
@YourDamnEditor:	Amen!

With more than 900 million people who use Facebook, you are more than likely going to know someone on the site—unless you're a hermit, which gives rise to another question. If you already use Facebook, you're aware of the staggering amount of time most people spend on the site every day. If you haven't yet joined the Facebook revolution, let us assure you that people really, really like to use Facebook. Wrap your head around these statistics:

- Fifty percent of users log on to Facebook in any given day.
- The average Facebook user has 130 friends.

- On average, more than 250 million photos are uploaded per day.[3] (Half of these are of people's feet or what they had for lunch.)

Used correctly, Facebook can be a significant tool for building your personal brand. To be successful, you need to learn how to share information safely and tastefully, and you need to know what the site can do for your personal brand.

What Can Facebook Do for You?

You may be among the millions of people already logging into Facebook every day or every hour, using it to catch up with old friends, reconnect with former classmates, and share your latest baby pictures with your family. Just as you use Facebook as a social support system, you can use it to build professional networks and enhance your personal brand. Facebook has a variety of built-in tools to do all these things.

Reconnect with Old Classmates and Co-Workers

It might be hard to imagine reconnecting with your long-lost friends from high school or college, but they could still be great connections 10 or 20 years later.

@kyleplacy: Or 30 or 40.

@edeckers: I'm not that old. When did you graduate, last week?

Facebook lets you reconnect with them, past co-workers—anyone really. It's just as important to reconnect with people you've lost touch with, like from high school, college, and previous jobs, and expand your network with people who are familiar with you. The more people you connect with, the more opportunity you can have in the future to grow your network and brand.

How can our hero, Allen, use Facebook to reconnect? Allen (influencer) could reconnect with old classmates and co-workers to build his network in the advertising field. He graduated with a double major in design and marketing. His classmates from college are probably involved in other advertising agencies or ad firms. He can connect, network, and build a relationship to further his search for the job.

Use a Facebook Page to Professionally Brand Yourself

The next section talks about the two types of pages in Facebook. You don't need to use your personal profile for your personal brand strategy, especially if you want to

---

3. http://www.facebook.com/press/info.php?statistics.

keep your personal life completely separate from your professional. Instead, use a page (http://www.facebook.com/FacebookPages) for your professional identity and a personal profile for your private life.

How could our hero, Darrin, use this feature? Darrin (free agent) needs to start building a personal brand to build his identity among the IT and corporate professionals in his local area. He must create a page to further his professional brand, gain influence in his industry, and fetch bigger clients.

Help a Cause and Be Philanthropic

What could be a better way to build your personal brand than to support a cause? Facebook Causes is an application that makes it easy for you to support different causes and to persuade your friends to give to each cause. Every brand should have a philanthropic side to it. When you support different causes, you build your personal brand story.

If you were to ask entrepreneur or business professionals how they became successful, the majority of them will say philanthropy. When you give your money and time to an organization, you have the opportunity to network with other individuals associated with the organization.

How might our hero, Beth, use this feature? This is a perfect example of something Beth (our climber) would use to further her network in the corporate ranks at the insurance company. By supporting causes (through Facebook) that the company supports, she can show her commitment to the company and share that commitment with the rest of her Facebook network.

Find and Attend Local Events

Networking is extremely important to building your personal brand. Every aspect of social networking has some type of professional networking system to it. Facebook Events gives you the opportunity to find events in your area to attend and meet new people. The more people you meet, the more opportunity you have to spread your personal brand story (or message).

How can Carla use this feature? This function is for the networker among the heroes. Carla (neophyte) is completely starting over from being a pharmaceutical rep to wanting a job in the world of nonprofits. She needs to start networking with individuals in her industry and attending events to meet those individuals. She can use Facebook to track events, add them to her calendar, and find out who else will be attending each event.

There are plenty of ways to use Facebook for personal branding. Facebook is all about personality, so you can use it as your personal website (but without having to write a single line of code). The first step is to create your own pages within the Facebook community. It's easy to get started.

What You Should Know First About Facebook

Like all social networking sites, Facebook has different elements and uses specific terms to describe its features and functions: the pages and personal profiles (see Table 6.1). Remember from the Twitter and LinkedIn chapters that when you connect with individuals on the sites, they are described in different terms. A Twitter friend is called a *follower*, and a LinkedIn friend is called a *connection*.

On Facebook when someone connects with you on your personal profile, he becomes a friend. When an individual connects with you on your page, she becomes a supporter. You want friends and supporters!

Table 6.1   List of Important Facebook Vocabulary

Personal profile	Your personal page on Facebook.
Professional page	Your professional page on Facebook, which is directly connected to your personal page.
Applications	Fun and interactive elements that can be added to your pages.
Discussion board	Area on the page where fans can engage in topic-based dialogue.
Wall or news feed	Your personal page that logs all activity on Facebook by your friends and your profile.
Poke	An awkward way to say hello.
Status update	A way to let your friends in on your activities and feelings.
Tag	A way to let your friends know they are in a picture posted to your page.
Message	A private message sent between two friends on Facebook.

The professional page is Facebook's way to give businesses Facebook accounts. Facebook calls these professional pages, well, *professional pages* but for clarity, we refer to them only as pages.

To truly take advantage of Facebook as a personal branding tool, you need to build a personal profile and a page to house, store, and create the communication funnel that can nurture your Facebook network.

Professional Page and Personal Profile

There are two types of pages you can create on Facebook: the personal profile and the fan page (see Table 6.2). Facebook personal profiles are meant to represent a single individual and not an overall entity, so personal profiles and professional pages have unique content and offer different Facebook functionality.

What type of page should you create? A Facebook personal profile or a professional page?

Let's make this easy for you: Both.

All pages must have a personal profile connected with them. Personal profiles are the keys to every page you develop. You can have multiple pages associated with one personal profile. Unfortunately, there is no other way around it.

Now see what the official Facebook policy states about Facebook pages and personal profiles:

> *Facebook profiles are meant to represent a single individual. Organizations of any type are not permitted to maintain an account under the name of their organization. We have created Facebook pages to allow organizations to have a presence on Facebook. These pages are distinct presences, separate from user profiles, and optimized for an organization's needs to communicate, distribute information/content, engage their fans, and capture new audiences virally through their fan's recommendations to their friends. Facebook pages are designed to be a media rich, valuable presence for any artist, business, or brand.*

That's just a long, markety way of saying "people have people pages, businesses have business pages." The most important thing to remember is that you must have a personal profile to create a Facebook page. You can't do much on Facebook without a personal profile.

@edeckers: Wait, didn't you get into trouble for having too
                 many friends? :-p
@kyleplacy: Yes, and I think I can solve that by one.

You can use your individual profile for business or for your personal life, but it's usually best to keep them separate; after all, you might not want potential clients seeing pictures of you three drinks into your best friend's wedding. We've all been there. The point is this: There is information that you want to share with your family and friends that you don't necessarily want to share with business associates. If you want to keep a Facebook profile completely private, set it up separately from your profile that you want to use for business and personal branding purposes.

Table 6.2   Differences Between Facebook Pages and Personal Profile

	Personal Profile	Page
Who is allowed to use the page?	Individuals	Businesses and Individuals
Can you invite friends to the page?	You can mass invite people to your personal profile by email.	No. However, you can invite people to join your page from your personal profile page.
Can you update your status?	Yes.	Yes.
Can you mass message your friends?	Yes. You can message multiple friends.	No. You can only send a page update only to your supporters.
Are applications allowed?	Yes.	Yes.
Is there a limit to the number of friends you can connect with?	Yes. 5,000.	No. You can have an unlimited number of friends.
Can you run analytics applications on the page?	No.	Yes. Page has an analytics function to measure effectiveness of content and growing likes or supporters.

After you set up your personal profile, you can set up a page to reflect your business and personal brand. A professional page is particularly useful if you hope to gain thousands of followers because, unlike personal profiles, pages have no caps on the number of friends who can connect to the page. Kyle experienced Facebook's limit when his personal profile hit the 5,000 friend mark and he wasn't allowed to add more friends. He then created a page to manage the friend overflow from his personal account and turned them into supporters of his professional page. Needless to say, having to create a page after spending so much time on his personal profile was a pain. If you plan to grow past 5,000 friends, create a page right after creating your personal profile.

The Basics: Creating a Personal Profile

When you first visit the Facebook home page (Facebook.com), you're asked to register with the massive Facebook database. The straightforward form asks for your name, age, gender, birth date, and email. Next, fill out your personal profile by uploading a picture of yourself; share personal information, including where you've worked and gone to school; and search for people you know in the database (see Figure 6.1).

Like the other wildly popular social networking sites Twitter and LinkedIn, Facebook makes it easy to find your friends in the database. If you use a public email program, such as Google Mail or Yahoo! Mail, to register your Facebook account, Facebook searches for your contacts in your contact list. When you find people you know, send them an invitation to become a Facebook friend and link their profile to yours. (Remember, LinkedIn contacts are called *connections*, and Twitter contacts are called *followers*.)

Fill out additional profile fields on your personal profile. Facebook asks for current and former employers, bio, hometown, likes, and interests. The likes and interests portion of your profile is a great opportunity to build your personal brand. It's up to you to decide how much information you want to share on Facebook. Later in the chapter, we talk about security and different profile filters you can create to block friends from receiving certain pieces of data. We recommend filling out the information you are comfortable sharing.

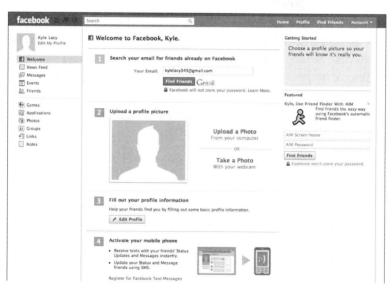

Figure 6.1   *After you create your account, you will be asked to enter in additional information into your personal profile.*

The third step in the process is uploading your profile picture. This is one of the more important steps to the personal branding world and the Facebook account. We have talked about this at length in other chapters, but we'll look at it again.

We have seen way too many '80s glamour shots with permed hair. Come on, people. Permed hair and poofy bangs? Double-popped collar Polo shirts? Keep your professional persona throughout every social site you use for personal brand-ing. Your picture should be current. Following are some tips to uploading a great Facebook profile picture:

- Use great profile pictures for all networks. This is extremely important for your personal brand and your Facebook profile (or professional page). If you have a quality photo...hold that thought. What is a quality photo? It's a picture of your smiling face that is not distorted. It should also be professional and fit your personality. A picture from spring break is probably not your best portrayal, but that depends on your profession. Use the same professional, high-quality photo on each of your social network sites, from LinkedIn to Twitter to Facebook. Use this picture, also, on your page and even your personal profile (if you use your profile for business-only purposes). If you would like to show a more personal side to your profile, use two different photos for your personal and professional pages.

  Leigh Caraccioli from fleur de leigh photography (www.atfleurdeleigh.com) suggests some tips on how to avoid having a terrible picture. A bad picture can repel people, and cause you to miss out on positive online connections. Clear, meaningful, and inviting profile pictures are effectively magnetic.

- Make sure your profile picture is brand-aligned. A good one should tell us at least three relevant things about you in a nanosecond. Know and control your brand.

- Have a professional or someone with a good camera take your photo. Resolution matters.

- Crop in tightly so your face is nicely framed. Having an online conver-sation, as in person, is awkward when you're talking to someone too close and too far away. We recommend you crop your image squarely to 250 pixels (px) by 250 pixels and save it as a jpeg.

- Be approachable. Are you more likely to walk up and have a conver-sation with someone who looks somber and sad, or someone with a genuine smile or welcoming look on their face? We're drawn to happy-looking, professional people.

Caraccioli says that changing your profile picture every six months is healthy to your personal brand. The biggest benefit of that is you'll be known when you are out and about in the real world. People must be able to recognize you from your profile picture.

Staying in Control of Your Profile

After you set up your personal profile, you have some decisions to make about who can access your profile as well as how it appears to the general public. Facebook provides tools that give you specific control. The first issue is the privacy settings and controls of your Facebook profile, and the second issue is your customized URL. Shhhhh. You can use both of these tools to your advantage to further build your personal brand.

Working with Your Personal Page Privacy Settings

Facebook has a ton of work to do regarding its privacy settings and controls. eNews.com reported that users of Facebook had found a loophole in the network that allowed them to view friends' private messages. Talk about a privacy breach! This is not meant to scare you away from using Facebook. We only want to make you aware of why you should use the privacy settings.

You may be thinking, "I am a personal brand. I do not care about my personal privacy. I want to show my brand to all who will look, listen, and be enraptured by my personal branding prowess."

Are you done now? Keep in mind, you are not invincible. You need to understand the potential security problems you could face.

It's hard for Facebook to keep up-to-date with all the hacking and scams happening inside the network. Hackers phish for your information so they can break into your account and steal your information to sell to others.

"Phishing for information" means exactly what it sounds like. Hackers create a code that pulls information from a large number of people. This could include family member names, home addresses, phone numbers, email addresses, and other pertinent information. Everything can be public if you're not careful.

There are ways to keep phishing idiots from getting your data. The first one is self-explanatory. Do not share information you would prefer others not have. The second one is using the Facebook privacy settings to block your information from the bad guys and people you didn't like in high school or your boss and keep it as secret as possible.

Setting Up Your Privacy Settings for Your Personal Account

Phishing scams and hackers aren't the only security threats users face on Facebook. You need to keep your personal brand safe, and that starts with determining how you'll set up the privacy settings for your profile. Remember, all content in your profile is public and open to the Internet community until you lock it down.

When you log in to Facebook, you are taken to your main screen, which shows your stream and other options to interact with the world of Facebook. We discussed some of the tools in Table 6.1. Before you begin exploring the wonders of Facebook, you need to secure your account. To do this, move to the far-right portion of the top blue bar, and click the arrow next to the Home button. When the drop-down menu appears, select the Privacy Setting button. We want you to choose the drop-down option of Privacy Settings. Check out Figure 6.2 for a screen shot of the options.

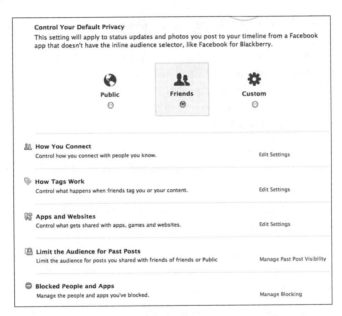

Figure 6.2   *The privacy settings box gives you additional options for personal profile security.*

On the Privacy Settings page, you have several options for choosing who can see your content and what they can see. In the middle of the page is your Default Privacy. This lets you to choose an all-encompassing option for your Facebook profile. Underneath the default options are drop-down menus, which allow you to further customize your settings.

You have three privacy options to choose from: **Everyone**, which makes your profile completely public; **Friends of Friends**, which requires placing a certain amount of trust in the people your friends know; and **Friends Only**, which means that only your Facebook friends can see your content. You can further customize that last setting. Click the Edit Settings button next to the content description to set your privacy details.

Tip

Your privacy options are for your personal preference. There is no absolute rule given for the use of Facebook. Think long and hard about what you would like to share and what you would rather not share to the consuming public.

Part of security is also protection of your name. When you create a website on the Internet, you should choose a URL that exemplifies your brand.

Kyle works for a company called ExactTarget, and his company's website is http://www.exacttarget.com. The company would have never created a URL like http://www.Blahgreatemailmarketing.com. Why?

It has nothing to do with the company brand name. The same concept applies to Facebook URLs and usernames. So, don't pick a name like HotDudez89 as your Facebook name, since that will also be your Facebook URL.

Working with Your Customized URL

When you join Facebook and create your personal profile, you are given an automated URL (http://www.facebook.com/id=20392023/). This ID is your "name" on Facebook.

Needless to say, this URL is overly long, and hard to remember. Your personal name is extremely important to your personal brand. Facebook usernames (or customized URLs) allow you to create a name in your link instead of an ID number. Kyle's company has a Facebook URL that's similar to the company's website: http://www.facebook.com/exacttarget instead of http://www.facebook.com/93820/exacttarget/profile=id. You get the picture.

To set up your Facebook customized URL, go to http://www.facebook.com/username. You'll see a drop-down menu where you can choose a page you have created or your personal profile. Set your customized URLs for each page you have developed under your personal brand. You need to set your name so another user cannot steal it.

Your new customized URL is the personal destination to your brand. Users can enter your Facebook username as a search term on Facebook or Google. This feature makes it much easier for people to find and connect with your personal or professional page.

Now that you have your personal profile set up, you can build a Facebook page that allows you to spread a message virally.

Viral communication is obtaining multiple people (or a network) to share your message to their network. When Erik shares a message on his Facebook page, it is likely going to be reshared by five additional people within his network.

If, out of those five people, an additional five share the content, it will be shared exponentially across the entire Facebook network. This is the definition of viral communication.

Think of it as the cold epidemic but with a positive spin. If you cough on someone and that person coughs on someone else, the cough spreads. Similarly, when others share your content, the content spreads.

How Can I Use a Professional Page for Personal Branding?

Facebook pages are extremely important when creating your personal brand and telling your story. Why? They can reach millions of people in the blink of an eye! The main purpose to use Facebook is to create a community element around your brand. When you have the ability to create the community element, you can experience the beauty of viral communication. Following are four great reasons for using your Facebook page to promote and develop your brand:

- **Facebook reaches millions**—With approximately 900 million users on Facebook, some of them are bound to like your brand, and a professional page makes your brand accessible to them. Unlike your personal profile, your professional page has no limits to the number of Facebook supporters that can be associated with it. The users on Facebook can essentially join your brands page without limit.

- **Facebook pages allow for community-based relationships to develop**—Having your brand on a page is an outlet to post all things about you, but not all things deeply personal to you. A page separates the personal from the professional. It allows you to maintain your professional presence on Facebook. You can share business updates and post videos and pictures for the people who joined your page and want to know the latest news. A page allows professional relationships to develop because people are on the page for professional purposes. A page also lets you grow your professional community in step with your personal community. It gives your audience an outlet to reach you without cluttering up your Inbox.

- **Advertise through Facebook ads**—A professional page gives you plenty of opportunities for paid advertising. You can create ads that appear on Facebook sidebars. You are in complete control of who you want your audience to be. (Target your desired product/service demographic, and verify results with your analytics.) When you set your desired demographics, Facebook tells you how many potential users are available to click your ad. Say you want to run an ad for the Humane Society and reach single females between the ages of 40 and 55 who live within a 10 mile radius of your zip code. Facebook can tell you that 5,403 women meet the criteria and use Facebook. You can test ads you create to see what works best. The ads can promote your page or your website. By using the Like button, you can see how influential your ad is to the Facebook demographic.

  Facebook ads (see Figure 6.3) are based on a pay-per-click and pay-per-impression model of payment. Pay-per-click happens when a Facebook user *clicks* your ad—you pay a price you determined when setting up your ads. Pay-per-impression happens every time your ad is shown, whether it's clicked on or not. We recommend that you not use the pay-per-impression model. The return will not be as high in terms of clicks when you pay per impression. Stick with pay-per-click.

  The best price for pay-per-click is really up in the air. Facebook fluctuates their best cost based on the amount of use in a given 12-hour period. To stay relevant, always look at the amount Facebook asks you to spend. You can find the number in your Settings page. You set the budget and can change it at any time.

  Content has shown a greater clickthrough rate than paid ads within Facebook. Although Facebook ads are amazing for driving users to your pages (fan or personal), do not lose sight of organic (unpaid) content. You need to measure the influence of both types.

- **Facebook analytics provide insight**—Only a professional page gives you the ability to use the Facebook Insights (their analytics package, equivalent to Google Analytics) application (see Figure 6.4). With Facebook Insights, you can gather metrics about your readers, including which wall posts get the most reactions, when users visit your page most often, and what the demographics are for your page's friends. This helps you understand and expand your supporter base. Without a tool like this, you would have to do extensive research for the same information.

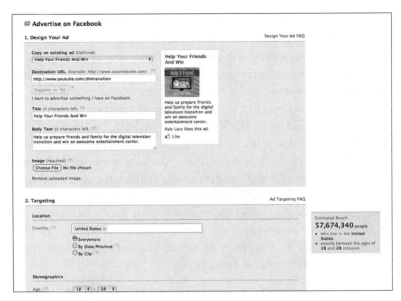

Figure 6.3   *Target your message to your company's key demographic to make your Facebook ad campaign successful.*

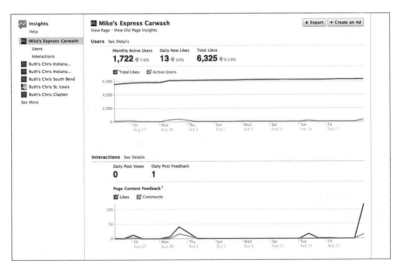

Figure 6.4   *Facebook Insights provides you with qualified information that helps you make content and fan growth decisions.*

Using Insights to Track Your Content Growth

Facebook Insights allow you to gauge who your connections are in terms of gender, age, location, and language. Instead of wasting time on extensive research, these charts show who and where your target audience is. The system is extremely valuable for anyone trying to build a brand on Facebook and is using pages to do so. The Insights data is easy to understand and use in terms of growth of your page and demographic information. Play around with the data a little bit before diving in and try to understand the different aspect of the tool. The Insights application gives you four extremely valuable tools for building your personal brand on Facebook:

- **Measure interactions and engagement**—The Insights tool allows you to measure the interaction of your fans with the content you share on the page. When you post a story to your wall and a supporter likes it and comments on it, that is a form of interaction. The more interaction your page is receiving, the more qualified your content is to the community.

- **Capitalize on content**—Use the interactions numbers from the previous point to determine what content the users find most interesting. Give your audiences what they want in terms of content shared on your page. When you see increased interactions, it means your content has been accessed, viewed, and read by your supporters. You need to share more of that type of content. You also can now see analytics for referral traffic and stream stories in the Insights dashboard, as well as tab views for your page.

- **Save and export data**—Insights allows you to export data into a spreadsheet much like you would export emails from Outlook or an email application. It gives you an enhanced view of the data you see on your monitor. This allows you to save the exported files and research different trends over months at a time.

- **Increased capabilities for further research**—Insights also lets you see some basic metrics relative to the activity for your professional page. You can greatly expand on the analytics capabilities when you integrate them with more robust tracking systems (Webtrends, Omniture, and ExactTarget) that link directly to Facebook, which can provide more robust metrics to answer some of your more direct business questions. The number of likes and the gender of those who visit your business page mean nothing if you cannot do anything with that information.

Setting Up Your Professional Page

When you're ready to set up your page, you'll find that it's not much more difficult than setting up your personal profile. The important thing is to visualize how you want to portray your professional persona, and then build your page with that personal brand vision in mind.

First, go to the create-a-page website (http://www.facebook.com/pages) where you can see the Create a Page button in the top-right corner. After the click, a list of pages with icons appears. On the top-right side of the page is a button that says Create a Page. Facebook gives you six options for pages: Local Business; Brand, Product, or Organization; and Artist, Band, or Public Figure. After you create your page, it's time to add the content.

The Facebook form (as shown in Figure 6.5) includes several fields for filling out company information, including hours of operation, specialties, and upcoming events. You can also post your company logo, pictures of the work you've done (say, if you're a general contractor), videos you've made (maybe you represent a theater company), and links to other sites (especially your company website). The page has much of the same content as a personal profile except it caters to the business aspect of your personal brand.

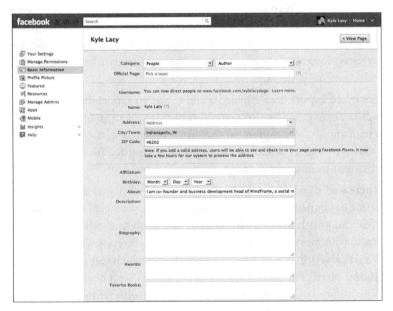

Figure 6.5   *In the same way as the personal page, the fan page gives you additional fields to fill in pertinent information for your business or brand.*

Top Six Tips for Using Facebook

Keep these top six tips in mind every time you log on to your Facebook account:

1. **Realize your brand is public on Facebook**—If you are not using the security settings discussed earlier in this chapter, your profile page is completely public online. More than likely, a Google search of your name will bring up your Facebook account, which anyone in the world can access. Is your mom looking at your profile? How about your boss or ex-spouse? Share content that is reasonable and won't cause you trouble.

2. **Make your Facebook username easy to remember**—Your name should be easy to remember for the people who will be communicating with you daily. The same rules apply to your website URL. Do not create a long username. Usernames are more than likely your name, such as http://www.facebook.com/kylelacy.

3. **Write on your friends' walls**—Remember the wall from Table 6.1? The Facebook wall is a personal feed that records everything your friends do on Facebook. Writing on your friend's Facebook profile wall is a great way to spread your online brand and message. This is especially important when your friend comments on that status update. When a user comments, his entire friend base sees the update on their personal walls. This is a great way to spread your message!

4. **Tag individuals in pictures**—If you have an event or a picture that could be interesting or special for friends and acquaintances, tag their name to the picture. When you upload a photo, Facebook gives you the option to "tag" people who are in the picture as well. Simply click the Tag This Photo button in the bottom right, mouse over, click the person's face, and type in their name. Facebook associates the name to the photo, and those people will be notified that they have been tagged in a picture.

   Remember to tag people only if the picture pertains to them in some way. If they are in the picture, tag them. If they were at the event, tag them then, too. If they have nothing to do with the post or picture, do not tag them. That's annoying. If you want people to see the photo, just share it, or send them a private note.

5. **Create events on Facebook, and invite your friends**—Facebook can create event tags to invite your friends to events hosted by you (your personal brand) or your company. The capabilities of the Events tab is

endless and can help you get more people to events that you host. Just don't invite all your out-of-town friends, because they won't be able to attend anyway.

6. **Join a Facebook group**—Remember the insurance agent who created a Facebook group for her kid's baseball team? We do not talk much about Facebook groups in this chapter, but you should join a Facebook group or two to further your brand message on the site. You can create or join groups on Facebook depending on your subject matter or personal brand story. After you join a group, you can text-message other members, email them, or comment on their profiles.

An example of some groups you could start would be associated around your high school graduating class, fans of an athletic team or college football team, employees of a company, church, and other extracurricular activities.

Ten Do's and Don'ts of Facebook

First things first. Tear out this portion of the book and post it above your computer or on your mobile device. Erik has it posted on his dashboard, and Kyle has made all the mistakes, so it is ingrained in his mind.

```
@edeckers:    Don't have them tear out pages from the book! That's
              destroying books. That's just wrong.
@kyleplacy:   But then they have to buy more books.
@edeckers:    Tear, readers! Tear like the wind!
@kyleplacy:   Or I suppose they could photocopy them.
```

Remember the helpful tips that keep you out of trouble on Facebook.

1. Do Upload a Real Picture.

We talked about this earlier in the book. Upload a picture that is real and has some type of substance to it (i.e., not a photo of you as a baby, your baby, your dog, or a photo with you and friends). Both your personal and professional pages should have the same photo for consistency's sake. After you have established your personal brand and accomplished some goals, you can switch pictures on your personal and professional pages, but for now, stick with your head shot. See Figure 6.6 for an example of Kyle's professional page photo, and Figure 6.7 for his personal page photo.

Figure 6.6 *This shows Kyle's professional page and the professional photo he uses to develop his professional and personal brand.*

Figure 6.7 *Kyle shows the more laid back and human side to his brand on his personal page.*

The two photos show a professional side of Kyle and a personal side. You know what you should have on each site. This is your personality shining through.

2. Do Share Industry-Specific Content.

Post content that highlights your personal interests and your professional areas of expertise on your personal and professional pages. If you are interested in marketing, you might post an interesting link to an article or website on branding or advertising. You clearly want to avoid the content that should have been left on spring break or that weekend party. Keep that content in the filter or away from Facebook.

Don't think too hard about the content you share on Facebook. Remember that you are offering a glimpse into what makes you, *you*. Nothing else. Share interesting and relevant content with your friends on Facebook.

3. Do Use Your Email to Find Friends.

Earlier, we talked about importing your email contact list to find friends on Facebook. If you have not already completed this step, we want you to put down this book and complete it now. Seriously, do it. Importing your contact list is one of the more important things you can do on your personal profile. It helps you connect with users that you already know in the real world.

4. Do Read the Terms of Service.

Your Facebook professional and personal pages have terms of service agreements that you probably agreed to when joining the site. It's okay; we didn't read them at first either. But you need to glance over the terms of service agreements to understand what is right and wrong when using the site. We wouldn't want you to get kicked off for sharing a stupid piece of content or spamming people without "really" knowing. That brings up our next item.

5. Don't Use Inappropriate Language.

"Duh, guys. I would never use bad language in the all-knowing and consuming world of Facebook." Some people do. (We know *you* wouldn't. We were talking to that friend of yours who's thumbing through this book to see what it's all about.)

Keep things clean, and keep the content great. Do not drop the f-bomb on your Facebook wall because you are mad at a service provider or a friend. You'll be a better person for it. Plus, that service provider or friend may see it later.

This does not only apply to curse words. Correct grammar and spelling are extremely important to sharing content on Facebook. Double-check all content you share.

6. Don't Spam People.

What is *spam*? It's when you share content on pages and Facebook that have nothing to do with your goals or objectives. It's when you constantly post promotional or commercial content instead of being a part of the community.

Why do I want to join your page or become your friend when all you do is share about yourself and the stuff you sell? We want to know about your daily routine, and how to become involved in what you are trying to accomplish in the world. If we go to your site and you have all content and no interaction, more than likely you're spamming your followers, or at least annoying them.

This also applies to application and event invites. Most of the time, a friend or follower does not want to help you plant a garden in *Farmville* or be invited to your party 50 times. If you send out an application or event invite, send it once.

7. Don't Poke People.

Facebook has an application that allows you to *poke* your friends. Unless you are poking a friend from college, do not do it. It's extremely creepy to receive a random poke from a person you met on Facebook five minutes before. Instead of poking people, send them a message to connect with them on a more personal level. Besides, you just can't talk about poking without sounding awkward and dirty.

8. Don't Tag Everyone in a Picture.

Everyone loves to be tagged in photos—if they are flattering. Don't tag everyone in a picture that they're not in. The only time this is warranted is when you have a picture of an event and an attendee was present but not noticeable in the photo.

9. Don't Sync Your Twitter Profile with Your Facebook Page.

Facebook updates are completely different from Twitter updates. Twitter users can read hundreds of different updates, and write a few dozen, in one sitting. You do not want to flood a user's wall or feed with your Twitter chatter. Your Facebook friends will become extremely annoyed if you post your tweets to your Facebook account. Imagine making lunch plans on Twitter with friends—we do that kind of thing all the time—and your Facebook friends only seeing half of that conversation. Now you get the picture.

10. Don't Invite People to Your Professional Page Over and Over and Over.

After you set up your professional page on Facebook, you will be asked to invite friends to *like* your page. Some will accept, and some will decline. Don't take it personally if some do not accept your invitation. It is okay to invite users a couple of times over the course of a month in case they accidentally passed it up, but don't request the same friends over and over again. No means no. People become annoyed when they are asked 100 times to become a supporter or like a page. Request more than three times, and you become an awkward stalker. And they will definitely not like you at all.

Facebook Tips in 140 Characters or Less

We asked our Twitter friends to give us some tips on how to use Facebook for personal branding, marketing, and self-promotion. As always, our friends came through for us. They gave us a ton of excellent advice!

- Always make sure your profile pic is of you. —@talk2RyanMitch
- Funny, sports, and food mixed in make you human. Don't be a robot! —@mbj
- Your "elevator pitch" should be 140 characters or less. —@RicardoCazares
- Avoid posting irrelevant pictures in your photo albums. —@SOluwatobi
- Converse. Create and Convert. Converse with people. Create content and then convert people to fans. —@MrDrewLarison
- Share timely information in your market. —@tojosan
- Take a look at the "People You May Know." You may find connections you haven't thought of. —@TimChaize
- Remember to look at your Insights in order to track progress of content. —@aims999
- Export your Facebook status updates using RSS or text messages.
- Read the Facebook TOS. It will benefit you in the long run. —@rachking
- Be sure your profile pic is clear and well-lit. —@fleurdeleigh
- List interests that best differentiate you. Don't overdo the interests section.
- Don't underestimate the importance of your "Favorite Music" section.

- Pay attention to the lists on Facebook. Sort your friends, colleagues, and family. —@igc

- .1% CTR is great for Facebook ads. Anything under that is a mistake. Discontinue and start over. —@edeckers

7

Say Cheese: Sharing Photos and Videos

There's an adage among social media marketers: "Photos do better than plain text; videos do better than photos."

It's also easily provable. Bloggers the world over can tell you that any post where they have a photo has a higher read/visit rate than a post without it. According to Jeremy Williams, interactive marketing manager at the Indiana Office of Tourism Development (where Erik is also a travel blogger), blog posts with photos get 25% more traffic than text-only posts, and posts with video gets 15% more traffic than posts with photos.

Why is that? Because we're largely a visual-oriented society. Because we grew up watching television and seeing photos. Because Google has been pushing toward both video usage and mobile phone usage, and combining the two.

The short of it is this: For your personal branding efforts, you want to embrace this technology and start using photos and videos whenever you can.

This doesn't just mean placing photos of you on every blog post, or that you should create a series of video blog posts. (Although you can if you want to; it wouldn't hurt anything.) Rather, it means you should strategically use photo- and video-sharing sites and consider them part of your personal branding arsenal.

Why Video

Google declared 2010 to be the year of video and made it a big part of their strategic efforts for the year. Because they already owned YouTube, they did everything they could to make videos easy to find, use, and share. Focusing especially on the "find," they started adding YouTube videos to Google search results, so you could watch any videos on the subject. Of course, it doesn't hurt that they own YouTube, having bought it in 2006 for $1.65 billion. So, it's understandable that they include videos in the search results.

In addition, the Pew Research Center's Internet & American Life study showed that 71% of American adults watch videos on video-sharing sites. Split among age groups, 92% of 18–29 year olds watch videos, 80% of 30–49 year olds, and 54% of 50–64%. Even our parents and grandparents watch videos: 31% of 65+ year olds watch videos.

This means that video is so widely acceptable, it's a great tool to build your brand. Your colleagues watch it, hiring managers watch it, and decision makers watch it. Video has become so important, for a number of different reasons, that it's harder to ignore, especially if you want to succeed. (That's not to say you'll fail without it, but you'll certainly have a harder road ahead.) Here are a few reasons why you need to make it a part of your personal branding efforts:

- **YouTube is the #2 search engine in the world:** And Google is #1. Think about the ramifications of that. Not only does YouTube demand more market share than Yahoo! and Bing, it means Google owns first and second place in the search engine market. It also means that if you optimize your videos well, you can easily start showing up in top search results for that video topic.

- **Google declared 2011 to be the year of mobile:** What does that have to do with video? Ask any 20-something with a smartphone. Google made sure that the videos they promoted so heavily in 2010 were easily viewed and shared on mobile phones in 2011. The long and short of it is this: If you produce an awesome video, you're likely to get some significant views from people on mobile phones. Figure 7.1 shows the popularity of mobile viewing on Erik's YouTube channel.

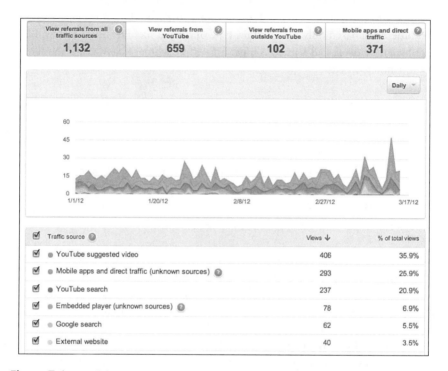

Figure 7.1   *Mobile views on Erik's YouTube channel is more than 25% of the total views on his channel. This can be much higher on other channels.*

- **Videos are easily and quickly viewed:** With mobile phones, embedded videos in a blog post, or even on the movie viewer, you can watch a quick video, get the information you need, and move on. Short videos are especially important for this reason. Three minutes seems to be the magic number that people will watch, but 2 minutes is better. Anything longer, and people won't watch the entire video, or may not watch it at all.

- **Videos have a positive effect on search engine optimization (SEO):** If you use videos on your blog or website, it helps your site to be found more easily on the search engines. Chapter 9, "Finding Yourself on Search Engines," discusses this more, but for now you should consider using videos whenever possible.

Where to Put Your Video

Where you actually host your video is up to you. There are at least 80 different video-sharing sites around the world, some serving as a general video-sharing site, like YouTube and Daily Motion. Others are specific to a certain type of use, like Viddler for business or FunnyOrDie.com for comedy and humorous videos, while still others are based only on a certain type of format like HD Share (www.hdshare. net) for HD videos, and Vimeo is ideal for people who are passionate about creating top-notch videos.

@edeckers: Have you checked out FunnyOrDie? They've got some awesome videos up there.

@kyleplacy: Is that why you were late getting your part of this chapter in?

@edeckers: I was researching! I had to make sure they had comedy videos on there.

@kyleplacy: But 8 days late?!

@edeckers: I had to be really sure.

Although there are more than 80 video-sharing sites, you only need to focus on one or two sites that you prefer. Some people think you can and should upload some of your best videos to more than one sharing site. After all, these are sites that people visit and peruse, just like any other massive content site, like reading Google News or browsing StumbleUpon. People browse these video sites to see what they can find, so you can be a big fish in a small pond, or you can be a small fish in one of the most popular ponds in the world. There are benefits to either approach, and there are even tools like TubeMogul that let you share videos across multiple platforms. However, we'll focus on the two most well-known video sites.

YouTube

Believe it or not, YouTube was originally envisioned as a video dating site, but when it went online in 2005, users uploaded every kind of video so they could share them on MySpace. Since then, it has become the number one video-sharing site in the world, with more than 60 hours of video uploaded to YouTube every hour (that's one hour for every second), and more than 4 billion videos viewed per day.

That should tell you a few things:

- It's easy to shoot a video. All you need is a smartphone, a cell phone with video capabilities, a digital video camera, a digital camera with capabilities, or a laptop with a built-in video camera.

- It's even easier to upload a video. YouTube wouldn't have that many videos uploaded if it wasn't that easy.

- YouTube is everywhere. Basically, if you have a Google account of some sort—Gmail, Google Docs, even iGoogle—you have a YouTube account. Just sign in with your Gmail account, and click the Upload link in the upper-right corner. Figure 7.2 shows you the YouTube upload window, and the different upload options, including a drag-and-drop feature. Just drag a video from somewhere on your computer to anywhere on your YouTube window, and it does the rest.

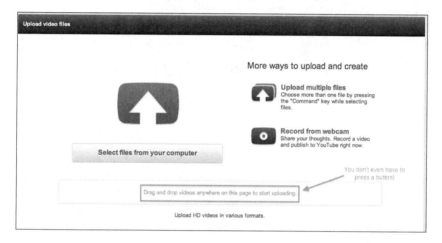

Figure 7.2   *Uploading videos to YouTube is one of the easiest things you can do on the Internet. It has several different options you can choose from to fit whatever technology you use.*

After you upload a video or two, you can start sharing your video on your different social networks. You can even set up YouTube to automatically notify Facebook and Twitter that you uploaded a new video. Go to the Settings tab in your account, and then choose the accounts you want to connect to. Figure 7.3 shows the Sharing Settings screen.

Vimeo

Vimeo is a video-sharing site for people who are serious about their videos. According to the website, Vimeo is "a respectful community of creative people who are passionate about sharing the videos they make." These aren't just people shooting videos with a cell phone camera of a guy getting hit in the groin with a football. These are professional and enthusiastic amateur videographers who have great gear, great editing skills, and an interesting subject. There are channels for people interested in the arts, nonprofits, comedy, nature, and sports. Rand Fishkin of SEOMoz uploads videos of his talks and his Whiteboard Fridays. The rock band Modest Mouse has released several videos here; indie movie producers and documentary filmmakers post their movies; and even The White House (yes, that White House) has an official video channel on Vimeo.

Figure 7.3   *On YouTube, you can share videos, favorite them, add them to a playlist, and even edit them online. You can subscribe to others' channels, leave comments on their videos, and embed their videos, and yours, in your own blog posts or website. (We'll discuss copyright issues in the "Copyright: Permission, Creative Comments, and Licensing" section.)*

One of the reasons we mention Vimeo is because if you can shoot and edit some great video, you will be in some august company.

Flickr

Flickr is normally a photo-sharing site, and we'll talk more about it later. But we want to mention it here because it does allow short videos—no more than 90 seconds or 150 MB in size. And unless you have a Pro account, you can upload only two every month. You can also upload HD videos, but they are viewable only as HD videos to Pro account holders.

Flickr sees videos as "long photos," which is why it limits them to 90 seconds. But as Rocky Walls and Zach Downs, owners of 12 Stars Media remind both of us constantly, most people don't watch a video past 3 minutes anyway, and they insist that any of our video projects they do are close to 2 minutes in length.

Uploading to Flickr is done the same way that you would upload to YouTube, but without as many options.

It's worth mentioning that Picasa also has video sharing, up to 15 minutes in length, but it's part of the YouTube family, so it's no surprise they offer this functionality.

Shooting Video

You can shoot videos with just about any type of camera, whether it's your smart phone or video-enabled cell phone. It can be a $150 digital video camera you plug in to your computer, a $3,000 professional digital camera, or the little camera that came with your laptop. You can even record what's happening on your computer monitor with screen recording software.

Because there are so many different camera options, we won't go into them all. But here are a few things you'll want to look for if you decide to get your own camera:

- **High-definition capability**—The current maximum resolution of HD TV is 1080p (pixels), although 720p is also good. Make sure your camera is at least 720p and can shoot 30 and 60 fps (frames per second). Some phones, like the iPhone 4S, comes with 1080p already built in.

- **USB connectivity**—You'd be hard pressed to find a digital camera that doesn't have a way to plug into a computer, but they're probably out there. When you look for a camera, just make sure you can easily plug it in. Erik has always preferred the Flip camera, with its built-in USB connector, but the manufacturer has stopped making them. There are alternatives to the Flip though, and you can find them at most electronics stores or on Amazon.

- **Read the customer reviews**—While we were researching this chapter, we found a lot of inexpensive cameras online. You can get an HD video camera for as little as $50, but the quality of the camera is rather dubious. One $60 camera was so ferociously panned by different buyers that we would hesitate ever buying it. As you research a camera, visit different sites that sell that camera and read the reviews. They'll tell you more than any marketing brochure ever will.

- **Look for built-in lighting**—This isn't a deal breaker, but if you can find a camera with a built-in light, or even a slot to add your own, that's always going to be a better option than a camera that doesn't have any lighting. It adds some cost to the camera, but if you can get it, it is worth it.

- **Get a microphone jack**—Again, this isn't a deal breaker, but if you get a camera with a mic jack, you can plug a cheap microphone into it for better sound than the built-in microphone. Because the audio is nearly as important as the video, make sure the camera at least has a decent built-in mic. Read the customer reviews for this information.

Video Do's and Don'ts

Here are a few things to remember when you shoot videos. These are true if you do an interview, shoot an event, or just take a video of yourself:

- **Remember you're shooting for different machines**—People who watch your videos are not just watching on laptops anymore. They're watching on iPads, Galaxy Tabs, and Kindle Fires. They're watching on their mobile phones. And sometimes, they're watching on an Apple TV box and HD TV. Don't output only small videos for mobile viewing thinking you're saving space or making things easier for other people. And don't create the largest video possible because it will get bogged down trying to load over a slower Internet connection.

- **Make sure you have adequate light**—If you're in the dark when you shoot the video, it's going to be hard to see you. Make sure you're well lit but not washed out. Some basic lamps or strong overhead lights are enough, but shooting outside on a sunny day will give you a great effect.

- **Avoid ambient noise**—Shooting a video in a noisy coffee shop or outside may make it hard to be heard. This is where a mic jack in your camera and a good mic will come in handy. If you don't have either of those, find a more quiet setting. Or shout.

- **Master the basics of video editing**—Both Apple's iMovie and Windows Movie Maker have basic video editing capabilities, as does YouTube, and unless you're going to be a professional video producer, that's all you need. All you need to focus on is editing out bloopers and long, awkward pauses. It also helps if you can drop in a caption, like your name and URL. Don't worry about producing professional video-level editing.

- **Don't worry about whether you stumble over words**—What do you do when you're speaking in public, or talking to a friend, and you stumble over your words? Do you start the entire talk or conversation over? No. The same is with a video. Unless you actually say the wrong thing, or stumble so badly that people will think you've been hit in the head, just keep going. A misspoken word or misstep doesn't mean you have to start over. If you make a mistake, pause for a second, and then start over from the previous thought. Delete the mistake and the pause in your video editor, and it will run the two broken segments together.

- **Remember your personal brand**—Videos are a great way to express yourself, goof around, and record memories and things that you think are hilarious. However, not everyone may share your sense of humor, so if you take videos of things that might damage your personal brand, keep them to yourself. Don't share them with friends online.

Recording Screen Capture Videos

You can also use Camtasia to record screen captures—record the things you're doing on your computer screen so that you can show people later how it looks, and you talk through what you're doing. (Use a decent microphone for better sound quality, too.) This is great for sharing presentations and giving demonstrations on something you want other people to see. We recorded the videos in the enhanced ebook version of this book using Camtasia and a Blue Snowball microphone.

If you need a free screen capture program, Jing is available for both Windows and Mac and can record up to five minutes of your screen. It's great for short videos, like showing someone how to start a new blog post, how to use an online tool, or even give a short presentation with a slide deck. You could even record in five minute segments and edit them together. Other free and shareware video recorders are out there, too.

Case Study: Gary Vaynerchuk

Gary Vaynerchuk is possibly the most famous wine taster of the last five years. That's because he's hosted his own wine show at WineLibraryTV.com, recording 1,000 episodes of different wine sampling, turning that into two books, a speaking career where he gets to swear like a sailor, a new social media consulting company, and now a twice-weekly show on SiriusXM satellite radio. He has gotten Conan O'Brien to lick salted rocks, and Ellen Degeneres to try different samples of dirt and grass, and been on ABC News and "Mad Money with Jim Cramer."

But it all started with learning as much as he could about wine, as a way to help sell wine at his father's liquor store in Springfield, New Jersey. He basically trained his palate "backward" by tasting everything he could—unusual fruits and vegetables, grass, dirt (you have to know what "earthy" wine tastes like, right?), wood, even sweatsocks—so he could tell people what certain wine tasted like. Because he did this, people believed him when he said a wine tasted earthy, oaky, like artichokes, or reminded him of dirty socks.

As a result, he became a widely sought wine expert to his customers. As he grew his father's store in popularity, he wondered how to reach even more people. When he discovered video being used on the Internet, he knew this would be an earth-shattering way to reach wider audiences, educate more people, and ultimately, to sell more wine. He started WineLibraryTV.com, recording episodes to review wine and to answer questions, like whether cold affected the taste of wine, or what wines went well with breakfast cereal. He even started leaving comments on other people's blogs whenever they wrote or asked questions about wine, spending hours a day building his network of people interested in WineLibraryTV. This netted him speaking gigs to a wide variety of groups and settings, and the chance to write two different books: *Crush It* and *The Thank You Economy*, both of which have been best sellers.

In five years of doing videos, speaking, writing, and being "the" wine guy, he turned his father's liquor store from a $4 million a year business to $45 million. And while Gary spent his high school years educating his palate with grass, vegetables, and socks, it actually all started for him because he thought that video on the Internet might be something worth looking at.

What Should I Make Videos Of?

That's the great thing about personal branding and videos. You can make videos of anything you want. Rand Fishkin of SEOMoz.org makes Whiteboard Friday videos, where he shares the latest SEO research his organization has done. Gary Vaynerchuk built his personal brand making wine-tasting videos. And both Mike Hanner and the Poynter Institute use Vimeo to create citizen journalism videos and documentaries.

You can record videos of book reviews for your industry. Have a friend shoot a video of you giving a talk at a conference. Give a three-minute presentation on a piece of knowledge or information. Turn one of your blog posts into a video presentation.

Whatever you choose, a video can be one of the most powerful ways to grow your personal brand. It lets people see and hear you; it can help you get speaking engagements; it can put you in touch with new people who have never met you; and in some cases, it can even help you find a job, or build a personal empire centered around one thing that you love to do.

The best way to figure out what to make a video of is to go back and reread Chapter 3, "Blogging: Telling Your Story," about finding your niche. Whatever you write about on your blog should also be the subject of your videos. This way, you can share some of your ideas in an entirely different format, and they may even lead you to a whole new audience.

Why Photos

Photos are one of the first things that come to mind when people think about sharing. And it's so easy now. Even the most rudimentary phones—unless you're rocking the giant phones from the 1990s—can take pictures, which you can then text to an email service like TwitPic.com to post on Twitter.

Photos are sort of the "proof" that you've done something or seen something. It's a way to share interesting stuff with friends. Or show yourself in action giving a demonstration or a talk at a conference. You can provide a visual element to anything you're working on, like a blog post, website, or even a single Tweet.

Thanks to sites like Facebook, Picasa, and Flickr, people are sharing millions of photos every day with their friends, family, and even complete strangers. It's the ultimate in sharing and community building.

Where to Post Your Photos

The places where you post your photos almost dictate who's allowed to see them, and who you want to see them. Using regular photo-sharing sites like Photobucket, Picasa, and Flickr are great for a general catch-all place to put your photos. Instagram is more of a community of sharing. And remember, we said not to use Facebook for a job search (see Chapter 6, "Facebook: Developing a Community of Friends"). So don't place photos there if you *don't* want potential employers to see them.

Picasa

Picasa is a photo-sharing site owned by Google, with more than 8 million photos uploaded to it. Because it's owned by Google, it's tied in to every other Google property available—Blogger, Gmail, Google+, and YouTube. Post a photo to your Blogger blog, and it's uploaded to Picasa. Share a photo on Google+, and it's uploaded to Picasa. Take a photo with your Android phone, and it will be on Picasa within a couple minutes.

Picasa gives users 1024 MB of storage, which can take a while to fill up if you don't take extremely large photos. It has unlimited photo storage if you're a Google+ member.

There is even a desktop organizer and uploader you can use to sort photos into libraries before you ever upload them. Erik uses that instead of iPhoto to download photos from his camera and then uploads them to his Picasa site. With Picasa, you can make photos public, share them only with people who have the URL, or keep them completely private.

Other cool Picasa features include embedding photos in your blog posts; creating slide shows and image timelines; a few basic photo-editing functions like red-eye reduction and cropping; adding text, tags, and captions to photos; and, even facial recognition. This last one is either especially cool or a little scary—when you use Picasa, especially the desktop organizer, you can tag a person's face and tie it into your Gmail Contacts/Google+ list. Then, when a photo is uploaded, you can ask it to automatically notify that friend that there's a photo of them out there on the Internet. This is the same thing you can do with photos on Facebook.

Flickr

The Flickr sharing site is owned by Yahoo and has approximately 6 billion images. It's a global online community of photo sharers who want to share photos of anything and everything. We've found photos of festivals in Germany, palaces in India, buildings in Poland, sheep shearing in New Zealand, fishermen in China, and all kinds of things in North and South America. This, like most general photo sharing sites, is truly global.

Flickr has a great search function that, if photos are tagged properly, can bring them up in search, which you can use in blog posts and presentations. (See the section on Copyright before you just start borrowing photos willy-nilly, though.)

You can access photos and videos on the Flickr site without having an account, but you need an account to upload anything. There is also a desktop uploader and a mobile uploader for iPhone, Android, and Windows Phone.

Photobucket

We can't talk about Picasa and Flickr without talking about Photobucket, which has more than 9.6 billion photos stored on it, making it the biggest of the three. It works just like the other two sites, with photo-sharing capabilities, filters and editing capabilities, and even an uploading tool for iPhoto (Apple's photo organizer), as well as uploading mobile apps for iPhone, Android, Windows, and Blackberry. You can also easily share your Photobucket photos to Facebook and Twitter. It doesn't allow videos, however.

Instagram

Instagram is a photo tool that applies special filters—at this time, it has 11 different filters—to the photos you take on your iPhone to give them an interesting, professional, sometimes retro look and share them on the Instagram site, as well as Facebook, Twitter, Flickr, and your blog.

@edeckers: Instagram: Making today's technology look 50 years old.

@kyleplacy: *sigh* You can always tell an Android user. You just can't tell them much.

Instagram, despite what *some* curmudgeons might say, is more than just a series of filters to make photos look old. It's a sharing community where people get to share their experiences and likes and dislikes. It tries to raise awareness of public issues, share things that are important, and celebrate special events.

Instagram is such a welcoming, sharing community, users report having never seen a negative comment on someone's photos. There are users from all over the world sharing photos from their own corner of it. In some ways, it has become more of a strong, friendly, sharing community than Flickr and Picasa, which are great communities themselves.

Instagram recently made an Android app available, much to Erik's delight, allowing him to make his own photos to make fun of. Also, it was recently announced that Instagram was acquired by Facebook for $1 billion, which adds to the overall value of the photo-sharing mobile app, which makes Erik's criticism of the tool seem pretty silly (especially since he downloaded the Android version the day it became available).

Facebook

Facebook is the ultimate photo-sharing site because it's all about being social and sharing memories and good times with your friends. That, and it has 100 billion photos on it. This is the place to post your fun photos, of you and your colleagues, you and your friends, or just things you find interesting. While Picasa and Flickr are devoted to photo sharing, Facebook is more about social networking. It's also the place where more people are going to see your photos. You can drive people to your Picasa or Flickr albums, or your blog site, where they can see the rest of your photos.

Just remember that you're playing on Facebook's playground. If they, or you, ever decide to delete your account, those photos are gone forever. And because Facebook is well known for changing the way they do things, this is more likely than you might think.

Copyright: Permission, Creative Commons, and Licensing

So we've talked about sharing photos with people, which implies that people are willing to share photos with you. They are. They want you to see them, admire them, and comment on them. But borrow them and use them in your own blog posts and presentations? That's a whole different thing.

Basically, copyright means this: If you created it, you own it. If you own it, you get to say what other people do with it. The "default setting" for copyrighted material is *you can't use it without express written permission.* That means that unless someone sends you an email or letter that says, "Sure, you can use my photo/video/audio file/written text!" you can't use it. Ever. Not ever.

Even if they're a friend of yours. Even if you're giving them "exposure." Even if you're really famous. Even if you think their photo/video/audio file/written text is wonderful, and it gives you a warm feeling all over, and you want to share it with the world. Not even then.

However, there are some instances where you can use someone's content without their express written permission. You don't even have to ask them because they gave it to you in advance. This is called Creative Commons.

Creative Commons

Creative Commons basically says that *some* rights are reserved, but not *all* rights are reserved. If you see "all rights reserved" on an image or story, that means that every right you can think of is reserved by the content owner to do with it what they will. But *some* rights reserved means that the owner is letting you, the user, use it in certain instances. Maybe it's to share with people, maybe it's to remix and add your own flair, or maybe it's to build upon and combine with something else, like reading all your poetry to a great music track.

Regardless of what it is, Creative Commons gives you, the creative individual, a chance to share your content with people and a chance to use other people's content legally and with their blessing. Table 7.1 shows some of the different licenses available from CreativeCommons.org. If you create and upload a work to a CC-compliant site, like Flickr, you can choose which license you want to grant. If you use someone else's work, you need to make sure you abide by their creators' licenses. A few Creative Commons license buttons including Attribution, Non Commercial, Share Alike, and NoDerivatives. Creative Commons buttons and images are used in strict compliance with its licensing policies, which you can find at CreativeCommons.org. (See how we did that?)

Table 7.1 A few Creative Commons license buttons which you can find at CreativeCommons.org

Symbol	License
(cc)	**Creative Commons:** This is the CC logo. If you see it, you may be able to use the content you find. If you don't, assume you can't.
(i)	**Attribution:** Give credit to the creators, including their website.
(⊘)	**NonCommercial:** You can use the creator's content in any manner except a commercial manner (i.e., you can't make money from it).
(↻)	**ShareAlike:** You can use the creator's content in any manner, but you have to grant the same rights to anyone else with this creation.
(=)	**NoDerivatives:** You can copy, perform, or exhibit only original copies of the work. No modifications or editing.
(cc)(i)(⊘)(↻) BY NC SA	A sample of a Creative Commons button you might see on a website. This one gives Attribution, NonCommercial, and ShareAlike permissions.

We had to ask permission from the Creative Commons people to use this. Ironic, no?

Creative Commons was created as a way to help copyright law keep up with the rapid growth of the Internet. Let's face it; copyright laws are being created by people who are still having a tough time understanding the nuances of the fax machine. There's no way they can keep up with the rapid changes things like Flickr, Picasa, Google+, and Pinterest are throwing at us. Creative Commons enables people to use online content with permission, and without fear of getting into legal trouble.

Basically, unless you have the creators' written permission, or are complying with their Creative Commons wishes, don't do it.

When you use someone else's content, be sure to give credit in your blog posts or on your website whenever possible. Either include their name in the caption, or put something at the bottom of the page or post. For example, write something like "Photo credit: Kyle Lacy (Flickr, Creative Commons)" and then link to the person's page where you got the content.

Embedding Videos and Photos in Your Blog

Embedding videos and photos is easy after you understand that, in nearly every case, you can embed photos and videos in your blog. The only place that you can't easily do it is on a WordPress.com blog, and even then, as long as you pay the $60 annual upgrade, you can do that. Unfortunately, that's the only way to add videos to a WordPress blog, so you're kind of stuck with it. (Believe us, we've tried. There's no way to trick the system, even if you add streaming windows instead of actually embedding the video.) Still, it is much cheaper than paying for server space for a self-hosted WordPress blog, even though we still think that's the best way to go for an advanced personal branding and blogging campaign.

We'll show you a couple different options for adding photos to WordPress and Blogger. If you can figure either of these out, you can figure out how to add photos to any other blog platform as well. We'll also show you the only way you need to know to add YouTube and other videos to your blog platforms.

Adding Photos

The technique is nearly always the same from platform to platform. Every blogging platform has an Add Image or Add Media button on the main formatting bar. Figures 7.4 and 7.5 show the WordPress and Blogger buttons for adding videos and photos to your blog. Click the appropriate button and follow the instructions. You either need a photo saved to your computer—WordPress lets you even drag and drop the photo to your browser window—or have the URL of a photo on another website.

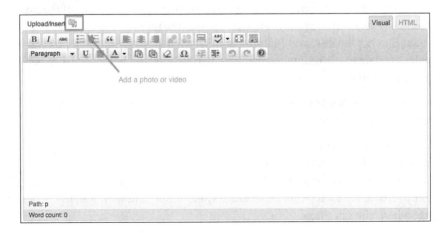

Figure 7.4 *The WordPress Add Media button is just a single button, unlike other blogging platforms, which has both an Add Photo and Add Video button.*

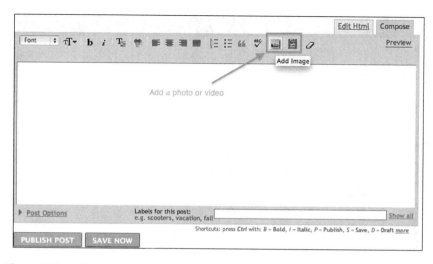

Figure 7.5 *The Blogger Add Photo/Add Video buttons. You have to choose between file formats. That's easy.*

After you open the Add Media dialog window, you will see several fields of information to fill in. Figures 7.6 and 7.7 show the WordPress Add Media window. To add a photo from another site, you just have to right-click the photo, Copy Link, and then paste it into the URL box in the appropriate place.

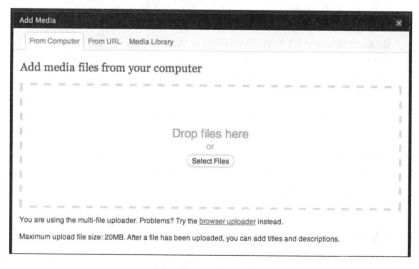

Figure 7.6 *To add a photo or video to WordPress, you can just drag and drop from your computer desktop to this window in your web browser. WordPress takes care of the rest.*

Figure 7.7   *If you would rather keep the photo or video in its original site, just get the URL (right-click, and then select Copy Link), and paste it into the URL field.*

- **You must fill in the URL and Title box**—That tells the blog and the search engines what the photo is called. That's especially useful for SEO.

- **Be sure to use ALT text**—We discuss that further in the section on SEO, but that's something that people who are blind use to understand what an image is. The more descriptive it is, the better they can "see" it with their screen reader.

- **Write a caption**—Sometimes a caption is useful to explain why the photo is relevant. You can also give credit to the photographer.

- **Set the alignment of the photo**—Erik always likes using Align Right for the first photo in a blog post and Align Left for the second photo. If you don't set the alignment here, it can screw up the body of the text.

Adding Videos

Adding videos from YouTube and other video-sharing sites is easy. That's because they usually provide the code from their site and let you copy it and paste it to wherever you want. Figure 7.8 shows the YouTube embed code box. You get to it by hitting the Share button underneath the video, and then hitting the Embed button. Select the size of video you want, then copy the code, and paste it into your blog window. (Make sure you use the HTML interface, not the Visual interface, on your blog when you paste it. Otherwise, your post will just show a string of code.)

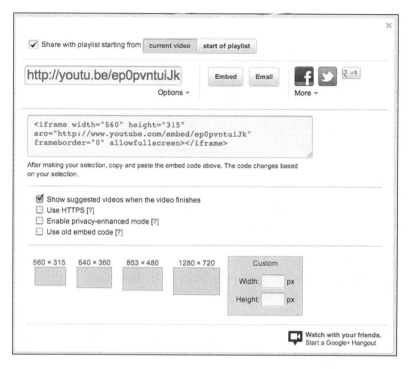

Figure 7.8 *Adding videos to your blog posts are easy. Just grab this code, and paste it into the post. Make sure you use the HTML interface on your blog, and not the Visual interface, when you paste it. You can switch back to Visual to keep working.*

One exception is a self-hosted WordPress page, which lets you paste in the URL of a video you want to use and give it a title. Click the Insert Into Post button and you're done. You can see how simple it is in Figure 7.9. This method lets you save space on your own server, although it can be risky if your video is ever taken down by the original creator. Then you're left with nothing but a big empty box where something cool used to be.

SEO for Videos and Photos

Your photos and videos—especially your videos—are great for boosting the SEO for your blog or website. After you finish Chapter 9, come back and read this section because if you're new to SEO, this will make more sense after you've read that.

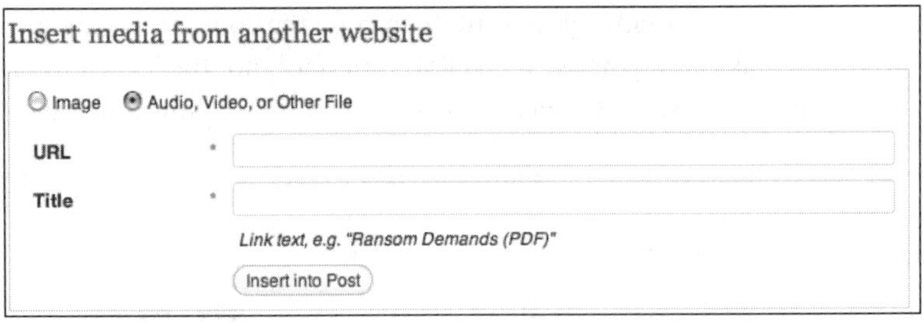

Figure 7.9 *The only thing easier than adding a YouTube video is adding it with the WordPress Add Media box. Paste in the URL, give it a title, and press the button, and you're done.*

YouTube SEO

While we're talking primarily about YouTube here, the rules are the same for Vimeo. However, keep in mind that as the second biggest search engine in the world, it's the 800-pound gorilla. If you want to win video search, you need to do what YouTube wants first, and then worry about other video-sharing sites later. But the rules are pretty much the same throughout. Everything we discuss here is applicable on other video-sharing sites.

Doing SEO on a YouTube video is easy. After you upload your video, go to your Video Manager, find your new video, and then click the Edit button. There, you can do some basic SEO steps to your videos. But while they may seem easy and obvious, few people do it, so by optimizing your video, you can make it stand out from the rest of the crowd. Following are the basic video SEO steps you should take. Figure 7.10 shows different examples.

- **Use keywords in the title**—Pick one central keyword that you want your video to be known for. In this video, Erik picked "Hot Wheels," "Yellow Driver," "Tanner Foust," and "Indianapolis 500." This way, if anyone searches for one of those terms, the video is more likely to be found. We discuss keywords more thoroughly in Chapter 9.

- **Use keywords in the description**—Make sure to write a 1–3 sentence description that uses the keywords from the title.

- **Keywords are tags**—You should actually start in the Tag field to start figuring out your keywords. What do you want the video to be known for? Pick 2–5 keywords, and then use the most important ones in your title and description. Leave the ones you didn't use in the tag field. Don't try to force them into the description or title.

- **Specify the date**—Make sure you fill out the date the video was taken, not the date you upload it.

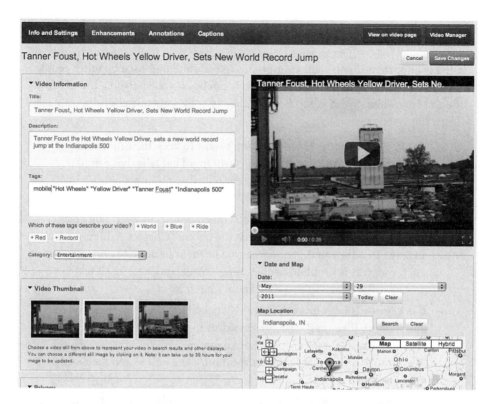

Figure 7.10 *Video SEO can help a video be more easily found on YouTube or Google. Erik captured this video at the 2011 Indianapolis 500 after Tanner Foust set a new world record jump as the Hot Wheels Yellow Driver.*

- **Specify the location**—As Google's search results are more locally focused (see Chapter 9), this can be important because your video could show up in someone's localized search results.

- **Choose the best video thumbnail**—It doesn't have much to do with SEO, but it does affect the click rates on the video. Pick a thumbnail that is representative of the entire video and not just the first frame of the video. That could be the opening credits, or a blank screen, which doesn't look interesting enough to watch.

Photo SEO

SEO for photos is just as important as it is for video. For one thing, Google occasionally drops images into their search results. For another, photo sharing sites like Picasa and Flickr are also search engines. People visit the sites to look for interesting photos, and to find photos they can use in their blog posts and presentations.

(If you do this, be sure to read the section on Creative Commons and Copyright first.)

SEO is important if you want your photos to be found and used by other people. While it may not help your SEO directly, it can boost your personal brand. You don't know when one of your photos will be seen by someone else who wants to learn more about you.

- **Use keywords in the title**—You don't want to keep the original file-name from your camera, like IMG_0017.jpg. That tells the searcher nothing about what the image is, and so it will absolutely never be found.

- **Use a keyword-rich alt text**—If you embed photos in your blog posts, you can use alt text to describe what the photo. (Chapter 3 discusses alt text.) Be sure you describe what the image is because the primary use for alt text is for blind people using screen readers. The alt text describes the image so that they know what it is.

- **Use keywords in your anchor text**—Anchor text are the words you put in a link (like that). Use the keywords in the links that point to your photos. If you took a photo of an orange, you could write, "Here is a photo of an orange I took on vacation." The link would then lead to your photo.

- **Use keywords as tags**—When you upload your photos to Flickr and Picasa, add tags about the subjects of the photos. These are important because if you don't have them your photos aren't searchable. Maybe you renamed the photo, but if you used only one keyword, no one can find it for any of the others. Both Picasa and Flickr use *space-separated keywords*, instead of *comma-separated*. That means that every space you put between a word makes it its own keyword. So I*ndianapolis 500* would be "Indianapolis" and "500" for keywords. To use a multiword key phrase, put quotes around the phrase, such as "Indianapolis 500."

- **Use date and location on photo-sharing sites**—If you remember what we said about optimizing videos on YouTube, you'll want to do the same for Flickr and Picasa. Put in the location of where you took the photo and the date you took it.

- **Remember not to stuff keywords**—We talked a lot about keywords in this section, but it's important that you don't stuff your keywords. Calling a photo "Orange on an orange tree in an orange grove in Florida" or writing "here is a photo of an orange that I took while we were at an orange grove in Florida" could mean that Google thinks you're spamming them, and they will act accordingly, either dropping your site's rank, or even dropping it completely from the index.

- **Make sure your images are small**—Well, smallish. We're not saying they should be a half-inch in size. Then, no one would see it. But make sure you edit the photos so they're smaller in file size. The problem most people have is when they take a photo, they have it on the highest possible setting. The end result is sometimes photos that are 44 inches wide and 300-dots-per-inch resolution (which is laser printer quality). A photo like that could be 100 MB in size easily. But if you put that on your blog, it will take several seconds or even a minute to load. Google has said that one of the SEO signals is how quickly a site loads. A huge picture takes longer and lowers your rankings. So use a photo editor—either Preview for Mac or Photo Viewer for Windows—and reduce the size of the photo to no more than 1,200 pixels wide and the resolution to no more than 150 dpi. When you embed the photo in your blog or website, set the size of the photo between 240–400 pixels wide.

The Video Resume

Video resumes are becoming more popular, especially among 20-somethings in creative roles, because it gives them a chance to stand out from everyone else they may be competing against for a job. Wow the hiring manager with your video resume, and you'll get invited to come in for a real interview. Just remember though, your video resume is like a real resume. It's not supposed to get you the *job*; it gets you the *interview*. The interview gets you the job.

@edeckers:	Slipping them 50 bucks doesn't hurt either.
@kyleplacy:	$50? Are you serious? I had to give my intern director $100 before she'd hire me!
@YourDamnEditor:	Guys, we are NOT advocating that people bribe their potential employers in ANY way. Got it?!
@edeckers:	Yes, ma'am.
@kyleplacy:	RT @edeckers: Yes, ma'am.

- **Look like a professional**—Your video resume needs to look as professional as you would if you were going in for a real interview. Put on a suit or work appropriate attire, and have a simple, clean background for the shoot. Not in your kitchen, not in your bedroom with dim lighting. Make it look great. If you need to go to a friend's place, or borrow an office, do it. Don't do what one so-called "professional" did, and use a flowered bedsheet for a backdrop.

- **Use good equipment**—Use a decent digital camera with a video setting, or get a Flip camera or similar model. Shoot this in high-definition, if at all possible, and use a tripod or set the camera on a stable surface. Don't record this with your laptop camera or your cell phone camera (unless you have a smartphone with high-definition resolution).

- **Sound is important**—This is essential. The sound must be clean and clear, so it sounds appealing. Although the video quality is important, you can't use your laptop camera, so don't use your laptop microphone either. Get a mic with a decent sound quality. Even a $10 microphone from an electronics store can do the trick.

- **Lighting is also important**—Make sure you're well lit. If you can shoot this during the day when you have great ambient light, that's the best. If not, use some desk lamps as spotlights. Be sure to check and adjust your settings as you need to. You don't want to be in the dark or so brightly lit that you appear washed out.

- **Speak clearly**—Speak slowly, and enunciate. Just speak in a conversational tone, like you would on the phone. Don't mumble; don't speak too quickly; don't shout. Also, speak conversationally, rather than reading from a script. Be sure to practice several times, so you can get it just right.

- **Use the right format**—You can upload videos to YouTube as mp4s, which will be your best bet. It works on YouTube directly, it can work on mobile smartphones, and it can be downloaded and opened with a regular video browser. If you have a choice about format, choose mp4. If you don't, you should be okay, but do a test run first before you start sending out your resumes.

- **Answer anticipated questions**—Rather than run through a laundry list of all your accomplishments and experiences—that's what your paper resume is for—use the video resume to answer any questions you're likely to be asked: Why do you want to work at that company? What's the biggest challenge you've ever faced? What's a success you've had? If you need to, list one or two major accomplishments, such as organizing a major conference.

- **Keep it short**—Keep your video to 2–3 minutes long. The closer to 2 minutes, the better. If you have so much stuff that you're going over 3 minutes, you have too much information. Remember, the purpose of the video resume is the same as the paper resume: to get you an interview. You won't get a job based on your video resume, so don't try to win the job in 180 seconds.

You can host your video resume on YouTube, and then embed it in your blog's About Me page, or host it on a video resume site, and point potential hiring managers to it.

Many hiring managers express a positive interest in video resumes and like to see them. If you're in the right kind of industry or applying to a more forward thinking company, by all means, give a video resume a try. Just know that some companies aren't as progressive as others and may be a little wary of video resumes.

A Cautionary Note About Video Resumes

While we like the creativity and boldness of video resumes—correctly created, they can show passion, energy, and vibrancy—and we think they can be used to great effect, we also want to urge extreme caution about using them. Here are a couple of reasons:

- There are still federal EEOC laws and rules in this country. They say that it is against the law that makes it illegal to not hire someone based on age, sex, race, color, national origin, religion, military status, and physical or mental disabilities. Companies can be sued if a job candidate thinks they weren't hired for any of those reasons. And unless an employer writes a letter that says, "let's not hire this person because he/she is _____," you're going to have a hard time proving that you were discriminated against.

  @kyleplacy: Can I be not-hired for being too attractive?
  @edeckers: Uhh....
  @kyleplacy: What? You're not saying anything.
  @edeckers: I honestly don't know what to say without hurting your feelings.

  But that doesn't stop nonhired candidates from trying. To prevent that, many companies and government agencies will not look at personally identifying information on your resume. Some administrative assistants have been instructed to mark out any information, such as group memberships, that can identify a candidate's race, religion, national origin, and age. If your resume is too laden with that information, it can be tossed. For that reason alone, we're a bit iffy on video resumes especially in larger companies.

- Video resumes are still not widely accepted as a practice. If you're in a creative industry where people expect, and condone, this kind of behavior, you'll have some luck. But if you want to work in a more traditional industry, you're better off showing restraint. While the business we're in—technology, startups, and entrepreneurial ventures—loves the wild creativity and daring of a video resume, we don't know a lot of bankers, government managers, or insurance executives who love wild and daring anything, let alone when it comes packaged as a potential lawsuit waiting to happen. Again, if you're applying for a job in a traditionally buttoned-down market, you may want to hold off on the video resume.

Photos and Video Tips in 140 Characters

- Lesson #1: Learn about framing your subject. —@mmercenary
- A blank wall does not make a good background for your video. Pick something with more visual interest. —@RockyWalls
- If you're using your smartphone for videos and photos, use an app that will automatically upload them to your favorite sharing site. —@edeckers
- Say your name and give a URL in your video for when it gets separated from your description, when shared. —@SteveGarfield (Steve is the author of *Get Seen: Online Video Secrets*.)
- You are producing web video to convince your audience to convert on your call to action, not to win an Oscar. —@RockyWalls
- For video.... If your subject doesn't move, don't make it move. —@DaddysInCharge
- It's okay to break some of the rules you learned in journalism school. —@LeilanMcNally
- When interviewing w/ a handheld camera or smart phone, the closer your subject, the better the audio. —@RockyWalls
- Learn the camera, by shooting with the manual at hand. "Why is this shot so dark?"...look it up, experiment w/ settings. —@mmercenary
- Learn the rules of design (composition, etc) so you know when & how to break them, because you will break them and it will be good. —@dezrad

8

Other Social Networking Tools

According to Wikipedia, there are more than 200 notable social networks in the world. And when they say notable, they mean it. A notable social network has more than one million users and is growing at an extremely fast rate over the past 6 to 12 months. For authors in the technology world (like us), it is an absolute pain to keep up with all the changes in technology from social networking to mobile phones. We can only imagine what it is like for the normal (non-nerd) individual to keep up to date.

When we first wrote this book in 2010, we wanted to give you a brief overview of the main social networks of the time like LinkedIn, Facebook, and Twitter. They are still extremely important, however, we have witnessed an uptick in smaller sites that could also build your personal brand. It is literally every day when a new social networking site explodes onto the scene. And many of them tend to promise untold amounts of fortune pertaining to content and personal branding development. There are some sites that are valuable and others you would be better off ignoring.

After reading at least halfway through this book, we hope that you fully understand that value of top sites like Twitter and Facebook, but how do you sort through the rest of the story? Thanks Paul Harvey. How do you figure out which of the NEW sites are best for your personal branding quest? Fear not, young personal branding warrior! We are here to lead you through the new social networking mire as new networking tools pop up on a regular basis. This chapter is meant to define the top five social networking sites that may be new to you but are building the social networking and personal branding scene by the minute.

Google+

Alright, the basics. And yes, you guessed it, it is the search engine giant's attempt to rival Facebook, and it might actually succeed. The site was launched on June 28, 2011, with a private beta to some of the tech luminaries and top marketers throughout the world and has since grown to staggering proportions.

There are a few features and social products that make the social network unique and some that are similar to that of Facebook or Twitter.

- **Circles**—This feature is essential to building a personal brand mastery of the site. It is the center point of everything that happens throughout Google+. Circles enable you (the user) to drag-and-drop friends into different groups (known as Circles). You have the ability to create a Co-Workers circle, a Friends circle, and a Co-Authors circle. You have the ability to create as many circles as you like! Think of Twitter lists but with more power! Circles enable you to group friends, co-workers, family, and the miscellaneous for easy sharing in the future.

```
@edeckers:   What circles do you have me in?
@kyleplacy:  Uh. You have your own circle.
@edeckers:   Special circle?
@kyleplacy:  Actually, it's more like a square.
```

- **Stream**—This is what you see first when using Google+. This is the area of your page that shows what your friends (circles) have updated. It's sort of like your Facebook wall, but more, well, Google-y. You have the ability to switch your Stream between all the different circles you have created.

  Want to know how to update your Google+ status? Look at the top of the stream in Figure 8.1. Kyle's stream starts at the top. If Kyle wants to share something new with his network, he types into the box that says, "Share What's New." Type content into the share box, and choose which Circles to share the content with. You can share text, photos, videos, and links—all the juicy content you want to produce to build your personal brand story.

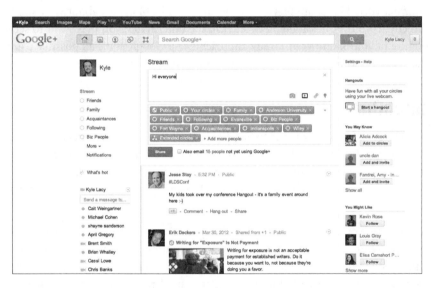

Figure 8.1   *You have the ability to send messages to one circle or multiple circles.*

- **Sparks**—Google wants you to have the most interesting experience possible while you use Google+, so they created Sparks. Sparks is a feature that finds the most interesting news content related to a specific search topic. It helps you organize and build massive amounts of data to further your knowledge in a given subject.

- **Hangouts**—This is by far the coolest tool in the Google+ arsenal. Turn on your web camera, grab some friends, and click Start a Hangout to start streaming live video between your friends. Clicking the button opens a chat window where you check your levels, and you can invite different people to join the hangout. There is a maximum of ten people who can join the hangout. The video can switch from person to person based on who talks into the microphone. This is a great way to network with individuals across the world while never leaving your home or office!

There are many in the software world today who extol the virtues of personalized messaging. At ExactTarget (Kyle's employer), it builds its brand around the software's capability to deliver one-to-one communication with potentially millions of people in a database. Google+ allows you to deliver the same thing via your social network. When you create circles of people within the social networking, you have the ability to send a message to only those users in the circle. This is unlike any other social network out there like Facebook and Twitter where one message is sent to all your friends. This gives you the ability for targeted messaging within your network. For example, you may want to send a blog post about your skills directly to your professional network. On the other hand, you may want to send a picture of your kid to your family and friends via Google+. It's all possible using the social network, which may be the next answer to Facebook.

BranchOut

If Google+ is Google's answer to Facebook, then BranchOut is Facebook's answer to LinkedIn. It uses your Facebook connections to explore any possible professional connections you might have. Although we have preached elsewhere in the book not to use Facebook for job searching, we can recommend it if you use BranchOut.

BranchOut works on the assumption that your Facebook friends may have professional connections for you, as well as the assumption that many of you have ignored our previous warning and are currently besties with people from work or your professional network. But if you want to use BranchOut, here are a few basics you need to know as you start:

- **Log in through Facebook**—You can reach BranchOut at BranchOut.com, but it pops you back to Facebook whenever it needs to. Just stay on the BranchOut app for everything you need. You may not be able to access this in the workplace because it is built on the Facebook interface. If you're blocked from Facebook at the office, you'll be blocked from BranchOut, too.

- **Don't add all your contacts**—Remember, some of these people are family, friends, and people you friended playing *Farmville*. They aren't necessarily interested in connecting with you on a professional level. You'll have to do a lot of clicking of boxes, but connect only with the people who are truly going to impact your personal brand. Tharg the Bloodthirsty from Viking Clan is probably not.

- **Import your résumé**—If you already have one, make sure it's up to date. If you don't have one, export your LinkedIn resumé. There doesn't seem to be any way to get LinkedIn and BranchOut to work together—why would they because they're competing networks?—so you'll have to do everything manually.

- **Be professional and thorough**—Be sure to check your profile thoroughly. Don't think that just because this is Facebook that you can get away with doing slipshod work or have typos in your résumé. Treat this just like any other professional presence online. Figure 8.2 shows you what a completed profile looks like.

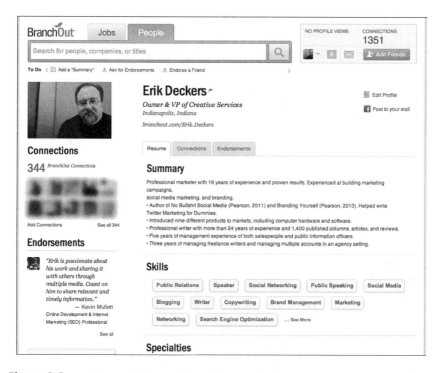

Figure 8.2   *Erik's completed profile on BranchOut. You need to make sure this is as perfect as your LinkedIn profile and any other online resumes you have.*

- **Select several skills, but don't overload**—There are so many skills you can choose from, but some of them are sort of repetitive. Writer and Writing, Speaker and Speaking, Branding and Brand Management. These are nearly the same, so you need to decide whether you want to have them all listed. People can search for these skills, and it's almost like choosing the best keyword for a particular skill. All these skills won't show up on your front page, but they will be present in your BranchOut profile. Just don't go nuts and choose every one that's sort of related to what you do.

- **Get and give endorsements**—These are just like LinkedIn testimonials, only much shorter. You have a limited number of characters to sing someone's praises. Give before you ask. But don't give over to hyperbole and overinflation. Yes, the other person will see this, but that doesn't mean you need to gush inappropriately.

@kyleplacy: Is that why you said I would be an adequate marketing manager?

@edeckers: Er, did I? I meant aqueduct. I think you should sell aqueducts.

@kyleplacy: Oh. That's okay then. I thought you were saying I was just average.

@edeckers: No, not at all! Hold on, I have to do something on Facebook completely unrelated to this.

BranchOut works a lot like LinkedIn for connecting with people, getting and receiving endorsements, and even searching for jobs. Although it doesn't have groups and Questions and Answers, it does let you connect with people who may have a unique path to new opportunities for you.

Twylah

In Chapter 3, "Blogging: Telling Your Story," we talk a lot about telling your story using blogging. We also talk about how to apply that story across all channels of communication from Facebook to Twitter. What if we told you that there was a website that takes all your tweets and displays them as a website?

Enter Twylah.

As of this writing, Twylah is officially in beta-mode, which means that it is open by invitation only. Kelly Kim (co-founder) was gracious enough to give Kyle and Erik each an account to test out the features and plain awesomeness of the site. It is time to get excited.

Instead of spending hours trying to break down the pieces of Twylah, let's take the definition straight from the source. Twylah "allows you to extract maximum value from your tweets. By using proven branding and marketing strategies, Twylah creates an optimized experience out of your tweets, which highlights the value you provide and attracts new and more targeted followers."

From a personal branding perspective, it is completely possible to use your Twylah page as you would any other website you own (like your blog). When you create and send content through Twitter, it displays on the Twylah site for all to see and consume in one place! You can see in Figure 8.3 that Kyle's Twylah site has displayed many stories surrounding social media and digital marketing. Why? They are the center point of his brand. This also allows Kyle to display multiple thoughts and ideas on Twylah when they disappear so quickly on Twitter.

Figure 8.3 *Kyle's Twylah profile shows all the relevant content Kyle has shared through Twitter.*

There are a few things you should probably know before diving into the world of Twylah and asking for an invite. If you want to use Twylah to build your personal brand, here are a couple tips to keep in mind:

- **Remember the power tweets**—The Twylah service gives you the ability to send a power tweet. A power tweet is defined as a single tweet sent through Twylah that creates a custom landing page for the tweet, complete with an automatic back-link to your page, the text of your tweet, any linked content, and other related tweets from your account.

- **Increase engagement**—According to Twylah, the power tweets increase engagement by 4,000%. Technically, that is 40x. That is a huge increase in engagement! Also, the viewers who tend to click the power tweet spend a total of 3–5 minutes on your landing page. Remember, that while the tool is powerful, it is always the ability to share content that is valuable.

- **Link Twylah to Twitter**—Be sure that you create a custom tag for your Twylah profile within your Twitter profile. This can help increase engagement with your Twylah page and build. Be sure to check Chapter 5, "Twitter: Sharing in the Conversation," if you need a refresher on Twitter profiles and tags.

- **Show focus and commitment**—If you have read this book in its entirety, you know that we find education and professional development to be keys to success. If you are building your educational prowess and using Twitter to share that development, you can use Twylah to show that commitment. If you are a job-seeker or even a busy professional, you should show feature the content that demonstrates your expertise and skills. It shows that you are focused and committed to the task at hand.

- **You want to be a part of a community**—The great thing about sharing your passion is that people who share that passion will soon find you. If you write about marble collecting, other marble collectors will find you on the search engines and any networks where marble collectors hang out. You can share information via your blogs, talk about upcoming events, and eventually meet face to face at the Marble Collecting Convention. (Yes, there really is one.)

Another thing to keep in mind, we're asking you to spend a lot of time time building our stories and constructing the perfect bio statement. Do you want all this hard work to just disappear through one Tweet on Twitter?

Twitter is a fast-moving communication platform in which one tweet can disappear in a nanosecond. Yes, the tweet is still there, but it has probably been missed by thousands of people. Twylah enables you to give your tweet a long life—yes, even *that* tweet—and build the content portal that can truly take you to the next level in your personal and professional brand, or destroy it. Please be careful with your tweets, because Twylah will give them a much longer life.

Pinterest

This site came seemingly out of nowhere and hit the social-networking scene with a bang, and it keeps building momentum as millions of people start pinning and developing their own personal brands. We believe it is one of the top new ways to build your personal brand in a creative and thoughtful way.

Pinterest is a sharing site where you basically tell people, "I like this. I think it's cool/cute/neat/interesting/funny." You "pin" photos you find online to your board, and those pinned photos get shared with your friends. Take a picture of something you made, something you'd like to buy, something you want to make, a restaurant you want to visit, or even something that made you laugh. If a picture is worth a thousand words, then Pinterest is speaking volumes every second.

Pinterest (like Twylah) is currently in beta mode, so you must request an invite to join the site. Be sure to ask for an invite as soon as possible. Heck, put down this book right now and go request an invite at www.pinterest.com. We'll wait.

(You may chant if you'd like during the moment of silence for the Pinterest invitation gathering. Erik did.)

Pinterest enables you to organize and share everything you find on the web. And yes, we mean everything.

 Note

> If you know someone who is already using Pinterest, ask for a beta invite!
> It is much easier than waiting for the Pinterest staff to approve your
> request. You can also gain access by linking your Facebook and Twitter
> account.

When your invite is approved, you are given a virtual pinboard that can be used to create collections of things you love from all over the web. You also have the ability to follow and be followed when sharing content. This means you can follow the pinboards of other friends and users. Think of it as following a Twitter account or friending someone on Facebook. Whenever an individual pins an object to their pinboard, you are alerted and you then have the opportunity to also share that object. People collect a ton of things. Kyle's wife used Pinterest to plan their wedding, and Erik uses it to track his Jelly Belly obsession.

```
@edeckers:   How did we not catch that in editing? Such a lie!
@kyleplacy:  You know you love Jelly Bellys!
@edeckers:   Hmm. Well, I do love a good Jelly Belly. Alright, I
             WILL start a Jelly Belly board! First up, coconut and
             rum make Piña Colada.
```

Collecting and pinning pieces of imagery can be extremely influential in building your personal brand. The main value of Pinterest is the users' ability to share who they are and share it in a visually appealing way. More on that later. Let's look at the simple vocabulary you need to know to be successful on Pinterest.

- **Pins**—The pin is an image that you want to share with your followers. It could be anything from a photograph to a video! It could also be something you created or something you found while surfing the Internet. What is extremely valuable about a pin is that it usually has a link paired with it. The link gives you the opportunity to share with people where you found the image. More on the value of that later.

- **Boards (or pinboards)**—This is a grouping of pins that you have designated as belonging to the same interest like interior design or marketing ideas. You may pin objects that are important to your personal brand and lend to your credibility as a graphic design or interior designer.

- **Pin It button**—This browser button makes it extremely easy to pin any image in your web browser just by clicking the button. When you accept your invitation and sign up, Pinterest will ask if you want to install the button and guide you down the path of pin-lightenment.

- **Repin**—Think of a repin as a retweet on Twitter of a share on Facebook. Repinning is the act of pinning an image to one of your pinboards that was previously pinned by another user. It's your way of saying, "I, too, think this is awesome."

The beauty of Pinterest is that anything pinned or shared within the site is easily transferred to Facebook or Twitter. Imagine the potential to share your passions with people who could potentially become employers or clients.

(Also, imagine the dangers of you sharing your passions with people who could potentially become employers or clients. Seriously. Practice safe pinning, people.)

We know, we know. You're probably about to jump out of your seat with excitement.

@kyleplacy: They're on "pins and needles," get it?

@edeckers: No! NO! Bad Kyle. Bad! Puns are the lowest form of humor. Next time, I'll rub your nose in it.

However, Pinterest can be deadly and exciting at the same time. We have all said at one time or another that Facebook is extremely addicting. It doesn't come anywhere close to Pinterest. So, before we jump into the world, let's look at some tips so you don't waste your valuable time:

- **Authentic pinning**—Pinterest should be an ultimate expression of who you are using images from all over the web. Be sure to follow your brand story when pinning and sharing content via Pinterest. Pin the images, videos, and illustrations that tell the story of how *you* are and what *you* like, not what other people think.

- **Showcase your work**—This applies to everyone but is extremely important to those people who make a living and a brand out of the stimulation of the senses, whether you're a cook, an artist, or a graphic designer. Pinterest is an ideal website to showcase your best work. Pin up that logo design and share it with your followers. Figure 8.4 is a great example of showcasing your work for the benefit of a personal brand. Kyle repinned infographics from his company ExactTarget, which he helped design and worked on. This shows his expertise in the world of social media and data management.

Figure 8.4   *Kyle's Pinterest profile showcases his work and projects from his company ExactTarget.*

- **Keep up to date**—All credit goes to Oscar Del Santo (@OscarDS on Twitter) for this tip. Using Pinterest is another way to build your credibility and personal brand. According to his article on the Personal Branding Blog, Oscar breaks it down for us, "Being part of the Pinterest success story in any way proves that you keep up-to-date with the latest trends and development in the digital world. Being part of the fastest site to go beyond the ten million unique visits mark in history sends the right signals about you in more ways than one."

- **Credit your sources**—We stated this previously but felt it is better said again. Always link back to your pinned images. According to Pinterest, "Pins are the most useful when they have links back to the original source. If you notice that a pin is not sourced correctly, leave a comment so the original pinner can update the source. Finding the original source is always preferable to a secondary source such as Image Search or a blog entry." Basically, give credit where credit is due. Stealing is bad for personal brands.

With the amount of data on the web, you can realize the true brilliance of Pinterest in the personal branding world. People are visual and with visualization comes a level of understanding that doesn't happen through the written word. Find imagery, video, and pictures that drive the understanding of your personal brand. Take the thoughts from the first part of this book and find the images associated with your story. Go forth! Pin away, build boards, and speak to your passions whether personal or professional.

Quora

We talk a lot about using social networks to display your expertise and tell your story. There is no better site on the net to display your intellect than Quora, a social forum that enables users to ask and answer questions on varying topics that are appealing to their professional or personal lives. It is truly a knowledge engine. Frankly, it is one of the easier places to write new content and share that content with like-minded individuals. Think of it as a higher-level question and answer section like on LinkedIn (LinkedIn Answers), which we talk about in Chapter 4, "LinkedIn: Networking on Steroids."

We also recommend checking out Yahoo! Answers and Focus.com. The sites give you the ability to organize people and interests so that you can find, collect, and share information most valuable to you and your personal brand!

You have three ways to gain entry into the world of Quora: Sign up through Facebook, Twitter, or by email. Kyle and Erik decided to connect via Twitter because it allows them to share their answers and questions with the outside world. You could use Facebook, but Twitter is the better choice for a professional setting. Facebook should be used to foster your closer network of connections instead of the entire outside world. Here are some things to keep in mind when jumping into the world of Quora:

- **Build thought leadership**—Any question and answer site (like LinkedIn) gives you the ability to ask insightful questions that pertain to industry trends or new topics entering the minds of your network. When asking or answering a thoughtful question, it shows that you are building your knowledge and staying on top of industry trends, which is extremely valuable when building your personal brand.

- **Building your network's knowledge**—By answering the questions of others, you are building the knowledge base of your personal network, which creates a foundation of trust. When you answer questions thoroughly, you become the go-to person for that individual, which increases your visibility and personal brand in the market.

- **Stay in touch**—Quora enables you to follow certain individuals and topics related to your industry and passions. By keeping in touch with people in your network, you will be the first to hear and respond to trends relating to your industry and personal brand.

- **Link everything**—Like many social networking sites, Quora gives you the ability to link your blog, company website, and other social networks. Be sure to link all networks to share your knowledge with every point of your network. One word of caution: Be sure you are not oversharing. It could be damaging to your brand.

- **Vote up often**—The site gives you the ability to vote on answers and questions relating to your niche. If you agree with someone's answer to a question, you can vote it up so that it appears higher on the list of answers. This will increase the visibility of you and the person you voted up; your name appears next to the Vote Up button and their name appears higher in the list of answers. This builds your credibility with key players in the Quora world.

We're not sure we would categorize Quora as the next big thing because we know it doesn't want to be the next huge social network. And that is the beauty of the network. Quora is still large but is extremely focused on one thing: answering and asking questions that further the knowledge of the educated world. This allows you, the user, to network and build your knowledge with people who truly care about a specific topic. Unfortunately, that is where some sites like Yahoo! Answers and LinkedIn Answers fail. Quora is truly the site to gain credibility and focus within a given trend or industry.

How Does This Apply to Our Four Heroes?

Now that we have given you multiple new social networks to use, let's look at how our four heroes would use this new information and what sites would they utilize.

- **Allen (influencer)** spent 14 years as an account manager in a marketing agency, so he has a lot of expertise in account management, marketing campaigns, and ad creation. He's also looking for a job. Allen wants to look trendy and has a ton of creative content that can be shared to show his ability in the creative space. Allen is going to start using Pinterest to build boards with images that influence him as well as sharing his own work throughout the years. He is more than likely going to come across an interactive or creative manager who may love the work that he has completed at his previous job. He can also use Quora to help answer questions for other marketers, which will boost his credibility for potential networking targets.

- **Beth (climber)** wants to be the chief marketing officer at her current company. Insurance marketing is a specialized niche, which makes it ideal for Quora. Beth can answer questions and build her reputation with professionals like herself. This can give her more opportunity to showcase her knowledge in the industry. She can also use BranchOut as a way to continue networking with any work colleagues she happens to be friends with on Facebook.

- **Carla (neophyte)** has left a career in pharmaceutical sales and wants to become a program director or development director at a nonprofit. Although the for-profit and nonprofit worlds are different, some of the ideas are the same, like getting people to give you money in exchange for something. Carla can use Pinterest to drive more interaction with individuals in the nonprofit space, as she shares ideas and images that could be helpful/useful to her network. Pinterest has been used extensively by the nonprofit world and will be used further as the site grows. This can also give Carla a good look into the minds and creative appetites of the nonprofit industry.

- **Darrin (free agent)** is an IT professional who spends his days troubleshooting computers, and he moves from employer to employer every two or three years. He's almost a commodity in the IT field, so he needs to distinguish himself from every other IT professional. Google+ is one of those sites that is currently used more by the technical elite. It would be a perfect site for Darrin to start networking with individuals within his space, and sharing cutting-edge information. Quora is another good choice, because he can share knowledge with people who are looking for answers to questions he's able to answer.

9

Googling Yourself: Finding Yourself on Search Engines

Some people call it ego surfing, others call it reputation management. Whatever you want to call it, and no matter how egotistical you think it makes you sound, you need to search for yourself on the search engines.

Why?

Because your potential employers, clients, and even former classmates are searching for you. People who are deciding whether to hire you (or want to reconnect after "that awkward way we left things back in high school") are going to search for your name to see what they can find out about you.

Do you know what they'll find? Are you confident enough that they won't find anything to make you look bad?

More important, are you confident enough that they'll find things that make you look good?

In 2010, CareerBuilder released a study that said more than 75% of HR professionals and hiring managers reported making hiring decisions that were positively influenced by a candidate's online reputation. At the same time, 60% of recruiters and managers rejected a candidate for negative information they found online.

Silly Facebook pictures, an offensive tweet, and even a rarely seen blog post where you used some colorful language—any of these can get you rejected quickly, and you'd never know why.

Similarly, well-written blog posts, interesting videos, and a clean online footprint can move you along in the hiring or sales process.

But if nobody can find anything—if you haven't done anything to catch Google's attention—then you'll go unnoticed, un-contacted, unhired.

The only thing worse than being found on Google for something bad is not being found on Google at all.

Have You Ever Googled Yourself?

Take a few minutes. Google yourself. Type your name in the search engines to see what you can find.

@kyleplacy: Heh. Google yourself.

@edeckers: Man, grow up. That's just—oh, I get it! Ha! Good one!

What did you find? Did you find the websites and profiles you hoped to find? Or did you find some embarrassing information? Or did you find someone else with the same name and no mention of you at all?

How deeply did you dig? While the average Google user typically only looks at the first results page, you need to click the Next link and look at more results. Better yet, go into your Google Settings, and set the number of results on one page to 100. This will save you a lot of clicking. Turn off Google Instant, too.

@kyleplacy: Why would you tell people to do that?

@edeckers: I don't like it.

@kyleplacy: So people have to change their search engine habits
to suit you?

@edeckers: I don't see a problem with that.

Keep digging until you've seen at least 100 results and make sure that at least nothing bad has been said about or by you. (If there has been, don't worry. We'll discuss how to fix that shortly.)

Next, sign out of Google and try it again. Or set your browser to Private Browser (Firefox) or Icognito Browsing (Chrome), which makes your browser and Google think you have signed out, and are an unregistered anonymous user.

 Note

> If you have any kind of Google account—Google Docs, Gmail, Picasa,
> and so on—you have a Google identity. Chances are, when you go to
> Google.com, you're actually looking at iGoogle, a customized Google page
> just for you. What happens is that Google tries to deliver search results
> they think you want to see. These are not the same results as everyone
> else gets, especially if they are not connected to you in any way whatsoever
> (more on that later). If you want to see what everyone else sees, sign out of
> Google, and then do your search again.

Did you get different results? Did you appear more or less prominently on the pages? The results you see when you're not signed in are closer to the results that people see when they're not connected to you. These are the hiring managers at other companies, conference organizers who want to invite you to speak, potential clients who check to see if you're worth calling. Because they have never met you and aren't connected to you online, these "objective results" are the ones they're likely to see.

The people who are already connected to you, through Google+ or Gmail, are more likely to see the results you see when you're signed in to Google (although not completely accurately).

This distinction is important because we don't want you to do a basic Google search, see the things you want to see, and think everything is just fine. It's what other people see that you need to be most concerned about.

What Do You Want Others to Find?

For now, we're going to approach this as a job candidate. Whether you're looking for a job, trying to book a speaking engagement get hired as a consultant, or just to impress an old high school friend, we want you to put yourself in the shoes of someone who is trying to get hired for a new job. In some ways, every other situation we named is a job search of sorts. Your job is to speak at a conference, or work for a new client. And impressing the high school friend thing? Just a bonus.

@kyleplacy: Do you have issues about your high school days?

@edeckers: "Most likely to live at home" my ass! I'll show them!

The whole point of your résumé, and your countless phone and in-person interviews, is to demonstrate how qualified you are for the position. You want to demonstrate that you know your stuff—that you're up on the important topics, worked on those issues before, and have some brilliant ideas on how to deal with it.

In this way, your social media footprint is an extension of your résumé, and a glimpse of how much you know about the issues, what your personality is like, and how well you'll fit within the organization. Think about what your different social networks say about you:

- **Blogging**—Your deepest, biggest, most profound thoughts on the areas that affect your industry.
- **Twitter**—Your sense of humor, your willingness to share information, and a look at what you think is important and valuable.
- **Facebook**—What you like and don't like, support, and even your decision-making abilities. (Did you put up a "Spring Break" photo? Could demonstrate poor decision making.)
- **LinkedIn**—A bigger, more robust version of your résumé, as well as your networking connectivity.
- **YouTube**—Your ability to speak in public, or at least communicate with others.

Why do we talk about these tools in the chapter on search engines? Because it's all findable on Google and other search engines. If someone searches for your name, these results can show up, whether it's the good stuff you want them to find, or the bad stuff you hope no one ever sees.

Basically, you want people to find the good stuff. You want them to see your brilliant thoughts on a particular topic, see that you're witty, and see that you can get along with others. And the reason we've been talking about all these networks in this book is the whole reason for this chapter: being found on the search engines.

Because if people can find you on the search engines, it makes your job search (Chapter 15, "Personal Branding: Using What You've Learned to Land Your Dream Job") or getting speaking engagements (Chapter 13, "Public Speaking: We Promise You Won't Die") so much easier. Our editor, Katherine, even checked us out online before she signed us up to write this book.

@kyleplacy: I think she was impressed by my LinkedIn pro-
                   file.

@edeckers: I'll bet it was my humor blog that sold her.

@YourDamnEditor: Boys, don't flatter yourselves. I just needed to
                   make sure you weren't felons.

@kyleplacy: Uh, yeah, not felons.

@edeckers: Yes, not felons at all. Especially not felons.

(Don't worry; we talk about reputation management and hiding negative informa-tion later in "The Value of Reputation Management.")

Search Engine Optimization

Search engine optimization, or SEO, is the art and science of getting your website or blog ranked at the top of the search engines. It uses a variety of techniques, drawn from a variety of sources and tools, and opinions vary about what works, what doesn't, how much of something works or doesn't, and so on.

The reason no one knows for sure is because Google isn't telling. And Google is the king of this particular hill because they currently own 70—75% of the search engine traffic. That is, nearly 3 out of every 4 searches performed on the Internet come from Google. So, people look to Google for the barometer of what's accept-able and what isn't.

But not only is Google not telling us, the end user, what works, they don't even tell each other. According to industry legend, Google employees who work on their algorithms are not allowed to share what it is they're working on, for fear that someone has too big of the Google piece.

So people—SEO professionals, mainly—try things on different websites. They tweak the copy a tiny bit, or they move the keywords in the headline, or they use certain keywords in a hyperlink, or anything else they can think of, and watch what happens to the search engine results page (SERP).

There are enough people doing this, and sharing what they find, that people have put together what works and what doesn't on the search giant.

What SEO USED to Be

To tell you about SEO, we need to take you back to March 2011, when it seemed like every SEO professional had everything figured out. We read all the right blogs, we knew all the right moves, and we used all the right techniques. Some of our colleagues—the ones whose names we never mentioned in polite society, or spoke about in hushed tones, as if we were speaking of the Devil himself—had even developed techniques that, if they were ever confirmed or proven, would bring a screaming mob of Google employees to their doors with torches and pitchforks.

@kyleplacy: Chill out. It's search engine optimization, not freaking Frankenstein.

@edeckers: That's the last time I read Mary Shelley before a writing session.

But SEO had some basic rules that most people knew about. It wasn't cheating; it was the way Google had asked people to create and lay out their pages, so Google's bots and spiders could properly index a page and know exactly what it was about. But some people had figured out how to make Google's spiders know a page better than they knew other pages. Some of these techniques were still allowed, while others were teetering on the line of what was considered "black hat SEO." (SEO done by the bad guys; good guy SEO is called "white hat.")

We need to look at what SEO was in 2010 and early 2011. It's important to know, but it's no longer enough to guarantee a top ranking on Google for a particular keyword.

Keywords

Keywords and key phrases are the topic of a website, a blog, or even a single blog post. The keyword or phrase for this book is *personal branding*. Everything we wrote about, spoke about, did videos about, would all be about personal branding. And everything we talk about hereafter is centered on the keywords. If you can identify your keyword or key phrase, that's where you'll start.

Titles

The title of a single web page or a blog post needs to have the keyword in it. That's what tells the search engines what that page/post is about. We would title a single blog post, "5 Personal Branding Secrets You Can Use Right Now." The search engine bots would come along and find the words "personal branding" in the title and then check to see if they're used elsewhere within the blog post. It will look for other clues that says these are the best words to describe the post.

Body Copy

Whatever keywords you use in the headline, you have to use them in the body copy, and vice versa. Don't make the mistake of using them in one and not the other. For example, if "personal branding" is in the headline, you need to use it a few times in the body copy; otherwise, the bots won't know that your post is actually about personal branding.

The general rule of thumb, depending on who you ask, is to use the keywords roughly 2% of the time. That is, out of every 100 words, don't use the keyword more than two times. If you have a 350-word post, use it about seven times.

Keep in mind that this is not a hard and fast rule. Don't tear your hair out trying to get exactly 2% keyword density. The truth of the matter is that no one actually knows what the correct number is, or should be, so you don't need to fret and worry, counting all the words and doing the math on the back of an envelope trying to get just the right ratio.

All we're saying is, don't go nuts and try to cram your keyword in as many times as you can, thinking more means better. Let it all flow naturally and you'll be fine.

Anchor Text

Anchor text refers to the words you use inside a hyperlink. In other words, if you link to another website about a particular topic, you should use the keyword in the headline as your anchor text and make sure the link points to the thing the keyword is about. That is, if personal branding is your anchor text, make sure the link points to a web page or blog post about personal branding and not, say, women's shoes.

Here are some other hints about proper anchor text:

- Link only to the actual keywords, not an entire sentence. For example, "I found a recent article about **personal branding**," not "I found a recent article about personal branding." Otherwise, Google thinks the link is about how you discovered a written piece online about personal branding.

- Never, ever use "**here**" as your anchor text. That is, "You can find the article about personal branding **here**." Okay, almost never. There are a few cases where you might want to do that. Like, "**I found a recent article about personal branding**. And **here** is another one. And **here**, **here**, and **here**."

- If you do this, make sure you use the Title tag within the link. Sometimes when you create a link in a blog post, you can specify a title. For instance, some blog platforms use a dialog box where you can give a title to the link (see Figure 9.1). Just highlight your anchor text, click the link button on the formatting bar, and type in your keywords.

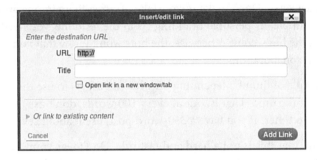

Figure 9.1   *A link-making dialog box sometimes enables you to specify the title of a hyperlink. You get to this by highlighting your anchor text and then clicking the link button.*

- Or if you know how to do some basic HTML formatting, pop in the title tag inside the <a href> tag, like this:

```
<a href="http://www.brandingyourselfblog.com"
title="personal branding">here</a>
```

Backlinks

Backlinks are links on other websites and blogs that link to your site. Google and other search engines count these as votes or a thumbs up. Basically, it means the user has said, "I think this post over here is worth reading." The more backlinks a site has, the more popular Google thinks it is.

You can get backlinks from a number of ways, such as when a blogger writes a blog post about you and your blog. You write a guest post for another blogger. You write an article for an online publication and include the link in your bio. Or people link to your website whenever they mention your name.

What SEO Looks at Now

So we told you about all of that, and you're probably thinking, "Hey, this SEO stuff sounds easy. I could do all of that." Sorry, but we're going to burst the balloon and say all of that is no longer as important as it used to be—significantly less important. So much less important that if this is all you're relying on, you'll quickly be outranked by someone who's barely doing the new way correctly, even when you're doing the old way perfectly. You can still get some juice out of these methods, but you can't rely on them alone anymore.

In April 2011, Google rolled out their new Google Panda updates, finalizing it by October of that year. They were no longer as concerned about the backlinks and keywords because people had figured out how to game the system and create hundreds, and even thousands, of backlinks for a single article with automated software. So to eliminate all that cheating, they basically said, "We no longer care about that stuff. We're more concerned about the user experience and whether they like and can use your website."

According to some experts in the SEO industry, there are three important factors Google looks at to determine whether a site will rank higher in their index for a particular keyword or key phrase, and how they think those factors are evaluated.

In short, if your site/blog is good looking, well designed, and most importantly, well written, Google will rank it higher than the sites still relying solely on keywords and backlinks.

These are not 100% absolute factors—remember, no one knows for sure, and Google's not telling—but based on the research of several SEO professionals including our favorite, Rand Fishkin of SEOMoz.org, these are some of the new factors that Google seem to be considering.

Time on Site

In essence, the more time a person spends on your site, the more interesting it must be. If visitors stick around for a few seconds and leave again, the assumption is that the site must have been poorly designed or poorly written. If they stay for a while, then the assumption is the page must be well done. Or your visitor passed out before they could leave. You can see your Time on Site on your Google Analytics page (see Chapter 11, "Measuring Success: You Like Me, You Really Like Me").

Bounce Rate

You have a "bounce" on your site if people come to a single page and then leave again. Basically, they hit it once and are gone, just like bouncing a ball. But if people visit a second page on your site, there's no bounce. (The bounce rate on your analytics measures the people who came and left without visiting a second page.)

Click-Through Rate

What happens when a particular blog post or page appears near the top of the Google results and no one clicks it? Google assumes that the site is actually so awful or unrelated to the search—usually because of the description on the search results page—that no one even wanted to go there. This is the equivalent of having a store in the mall that no one visits because they don't like what they can see from the outside, even if they can only see a small portion of the store.

Having a high click-through rate tells Google that people were interested enough in your site to visit it in the first place, which means other people will also find it interesting, so they keep it high on the results page.

Click-through rates are not measured on Google Analytics.

All these factors affect each other—they're the three legs on a stool, and shortening one makes the whole stool crooked. For example, when people click through to your page, did they click the Back button instead (leads to short time on site and higher bounce rate)? Or did they stick around for a minute, read the post, and then read something else (higher time on site, lower bounce rate)?

Page Load Speed

A fourth factor of SEO is your page load speed. Does your page load quickly, or does it take a lo-o-o-o-ong time to load, causing your readers to die of sheer boredom as 37 pictures of your cat load in your latest blog post?

Your users will be tired of waiting for your pages. The Internet and broadband has made us impatient. In a world where the microwave takes too long, users don't want to wait for your pictures to appear, your Flash content to load, or your entire web page to warm up so they can start reading it. Nothing is more frustrating than to see the little rainbow wheel or hourglass while waiting for a page to load on your computer.

But fast-loading sites benefit the visitors because they don't want to wait. And because Google is dedicated to serving up search results that appeal to their visitors, they want to deliver page results that the users will like, which means giving a slight preference to pages that load faster than others.

No one is exactly sure how much of a factor page load speed is because it's one of 200 indicators that Google uses, and Google's face of SEO, Matt Cutts, has said that page relevance is more important than load speed. But still, enough is being said about page load speed that a lot of SEO professionals are paying close attention to it. Basically, if your page takes a long time to load, it could be outranked by a page that loads much more quickly, assuming the other 199 factors are equal.

We like tools like Pingdom's Full Page Test (http://tools.pingdom.com) to measure whether a website or blog page loads quickly. Just enter the URL, and it will give you a grade and areas that you can fix. If you're a Google Chrome user, Google has even released the Page Speed plug-in that you can use to get a full report on your—what else?—page speed to see what you need to fix.

How Can You Influence These Factors?

When Google released Panda, it caused a chill in the hearts of the SEO profession-als—especially the black-hat ones—who had perfected their link-building software system to give them thousands of links with the click of a mouse. Although that didn't make them go away, it certainly reduced their effectiveness.

Instead, it put the focus on the quality of the blog and website, whether people would actually want to read it and interact with it. It started to look at how *good* a website was, rather than how *popular* it was.

This means that if you want to have a high-ranking website, you need to focus on the quality of what's on there, and whether it's something people want to read or watch. Get them to stick around, and your site will begin to outrank the bigger, more-backlink-owning sites that produce low-value crappy work.

Here are five areas you need to focus on to help improve your search engine rankings.

Quality of Content

Basically, this means you have to write well. Or at least not write crappily.

@kyleplacy: Is that even a real word?

@edeckers: I didn't think they'd let us say "like $#!%."

What was happening is that a lot of these SEO people were using article spinners to take a piece of content—in our industry, we call everything "content," rather than "written text," "videos," or "photos." It usually means written text, but we're never satisfied with calling things by what they really are—and run it through a piece of software called an article spinner. The spinner would then rewrite the text so it was different enough from the original text that Google wouldn't think it was the same thing. Then you'd get something like this:

> The rotator would then recast the words, so it was unusual from the primary words that Google wouldn't deduce they were the identical objects. Later you'd receive an item such as this.

It's just awful. Not only is it unreadable, it's annoying to anyone who stumbles across one of these in their searches. You'd think it was written by someone who translated it from English to French to Mandarin to Pig Latin and back to English.

So Google decided they were going to penalize sites like this. One way they do this is by looking at the Time on Site factor. Because no one would read bad copy, if enough people came to this page and left quickly, they would know the site wasn't very good and it could drop in the search rankings.

But this also means that if you write well—if you focus on the quality of your writing, avoid misspellings, and actually string some coherent thoughts together without rambling—you can keep people around longer.

This also means the length of a single piece of content is also important. A 30-word blog post is probably not going to win a lot of searches, but then again, neither is a 5,000-word piece. Not only will someone read the 30-word post in a few seconds (low Time on Site), but it also means they're going to take one look at the long 5,000-word piece and leave again if they're not ready for it. This is why we still recommend between 300–500 words for an acceptable post length. If you need more time, break everything up into readable chunks using subheads like we've done throughout this book, and use a lot of short words, short sentences, and paragraphs to keep propelling people forward.

This means that if you want to win search, earn readers, and ultimately show people how well you know your subject area, pay particular attention to the quality of your writing and other content.

Quality of Design

You need a good-looking website. Don't spend thousands, or even hundreds, of dollars on a cool-looking website. Good design doesn't bring people in, but bad design will make people leave. That will affect your time on site, and can even play into your bounce rate. That is, if they come to your site, see how awful it looks, and leave again a few seconds later, you can negatively affect both those factors.

Using some of the blogging tools we described, you can create a good-looking website for a few dollars, or even for free. The point is, you don't want to have a site that looks like it was built in 2003. Set up a blog, get a good-looking theme, and that's it. It may not bring people in, but it won't make them run screaming from the room whenever your site shows up.

For WordPress.org users (see Chapter 3, "Blogging: Telling Your Story"), we recommend a theme from Genesis, Woo Themes, or Elegant Themes. All these are paid theme sites (approximately $20 for a single theme), although there are thousands of good-looking free themes as well. Find one, make sure it works on your blog, and use it. Don't swap it out whenever you think you want a new look. Not all the themes available are stable or work the way they're supposed to. When you find one you like and it works, stick with it for a couple years at least.

For WordPress.com, Blogger.com, and other hosted blog platforms (again, see Chapter 3), all these sites have themes already available. You don't need to search for any or download anything. In most cases, they have been fully tested and optimized to work with your blog platform. Some of them cost money, but most of them are free. They're also not going to have the same stability and functionality problems that WordPress.org users might face. That means that, if you'd like, you can swap out your theme a little more frequently than the WordPress.org folks. It may affect some of your blog's functionality, but only in minor ways. So it's still best to test out a theme before you settle on it full time.

Ease of Navigation

How easy is it to get around your site? You don't want to make it difficult for people to get around, and you certainly don't want them to follow a series of links down a rabbit hole only to have to hit the Back button several times to get to where they were going. Make the navigation easy to use, not only so they can find their way around, but also so they're encouraged to stay longer.

Remember what we said about bounce rate? If you want to reduce bounce rate, make it easy for someone to find another piece of content on your site they would like to read. Include an Other Articles You Might Like link at the bottom of every post, or Newer/Older Posts links. These can help get people to click to a second page on your site, thus lowering your bounce rate. Depending on the blog platform or website platform you use, you can get plug-ins to put these kinds of links at the bottom of each blog post. Otherwise, you have to hand code it.

While we're on the subject of ease of navigation, consider page load speed again. You want to be sure to do a few things that can affect your speed:

- **Use low-resolution photos**—When a lot of people take photos, they have them set for high resolution and large sizes. You could basically print a poster with some of the sizes people upload for pictures. We've seen photos that are 22 inches across and 300 dpi (dots per inch). And people unknowingly load those onto their blog. A photo this size can take several seconds, if not minutes, to load. Open your computer's photo viewer, and reduce that to 6 inches wide and 150 dpi.

- **Host your videos elsewhere**—Don't upload videos to your blog or website; host them on a video-sharing site like YouTube, and use the embed code to place them in your blog. That saves all the load time of the video and puts the bulk of the work elsewhere. Chapter 7, "Say Cheese: Sharing Photos and Videos," talks more about embedding videos.

- **Avoid using a lot of Javascript**—You may find these interesting scripts to add to your blog, but many of them use Javascript to run. These all take time to load, plus they chew up a user's processing speed. If you can, avoid them completely. If you can't, see if there are any non-Javascript alternatives, or see if you can place the scripts into an external file, not within your regular html code. (If you don't know what this means, ask a knowledgeable friend to help you out; if your site is big enough, consider hiring someone to help with this. It could be worth the effort and expense.)

- **Eliminate unnecessary plug-ins**—If you're a self-hosted WordPress user, and you've loaded several plug-ins to try out, be sure to delete them when you're done. You can't just deactivate them and leave them in place. WordPress basically checks every plug-in to see if it's running, including the deactivated ones. Save yourself a little time by getting rid of the unused ones.

- **Avoid Flash**—Flash is not a good user experience for many reasons. It takes up a lot of computer resources to run; it's unreadable by search engines (which means they have no idea what's in it); and it takes quite a while to load, which hurts your page load speed.

A Quick Note About Backlinks

We've just gotten done bagging backlinks, but we don't want you to think they're completely unnecessary. We wanted to show you what was now important, so you get an idea of how serious Google is about your SEO. They *do* consider backlinks, but not as much as they used to, especially if those links are on a link farm that has thousands of unrelated links that have nothing to do with the sites they link to.

But what they are paying attention to are backlinks from *related* sites. If Kyle writes a blog post about camping gear, and Erik has a camping blog, a link from Erik's blog to Kyle's post is going to carry a lot more weight than a link from a website about fountain pens.

Video

Don't let the fact that this is a subsubsection of one chapter fool you. Video may be one of the most important factors of SEO you can use. Entire books have been written about videos, video SEO, and video marketing. There are entire companies that specialize just in making Internet videos. And these videos have a huge impact on SEO.

That's because a couple years ago, Google declared 2010 to be the year of video. They put a lot of attention and energy into getting people to use and promote videos on YouTube, their video-sharing site. (It's also no coincidence that they called 2011 the year of mobile, and making the whole Internet experience—including videos—something worth doing on mobile phones.)

To help things along, they included videos in their search results. So, when you search for certain topics, you occasionally see videos pop up from YouTube. Search for a particular TV show or movie, and you'll find web pages, but you'll find trailers and clips on YouTube. Search for an actor, and you'll see the same thing. Do a search for something like lawn mower repair, and videos show up in the SERP, in addition to the "how to" and "where to" pages.

And, we also mentioned it in Chapter 7, "Say Cheese: Sharing Photos and Videos," that YouTube is the #2 search engine in the world, right behind the #1 search engine in the world—you guessed it—Google. That means that if people want to learn how to do something, like clean a computer keyboard or replace a key on their keyboard, they'll go to YouTube to see a video on how it's done.

So, what does all this mean for your personal branding efforts? These two pieces of information have major implications for your SEO efforts.

- **You need to make some videos**—Videos are more important than ever, period. And people will view them. Make some videos of yourself doing whatever it is you're passionate about. Maybe it's about how to repair a lawn mower, or it's a product review and demonstration, but shoot the video.

- **You need to optimize your videos**—Be sure to use the keywords in your title and description of your video. Also include a backlink to your blog or website, especially if it's also embedded at the site, and point a couple backlinks to the video from other locations (not the same blog post where you embedded it).

- **Don't try to win search on Google, win it on YouTube**—Only a few videos on YouTube are properly optimized, usually by video professionals and SEO geeks. If you take the time to optimize your videos, you can more easily win a YouTube search. And because Google pulls search results from YouTube, your top video there will show up here in Google.

Personal Connections/Social Media

Google+ (Google Plus) is making a big splash in both social networking and SEO. That's because Google uses our personal connections to start giving us the kinds of search results they think we would be interested in. They call it My World, and it features all the people you know and the related content they share.

Let's say Erik is searching for information on skiing vacations in Colorado. Kyle has just returned from a skiing vacation in Colorado, and has shared some photos of his vacation on Picasa, blogged about it, and even shared the website of the ski lodge where he stayed.

Because Erik and Kyle are connected on Google+, Kyle's results will most likely show up near the top of the regular search results. Why? Because Google assumes that if Erik and Kyle are connected, then Erik is probably interested in what Kyle has to say on a certain subject.

Remember, Google's goal is to give its users the best possible experience it can, so the users will come back again and again. One way to give us a good experience is to show us the things that our friends might have shared with us, if only we had asked them.

What this means for you and your personal brand is, if you want to be known for a particular topic by particular people, connect with them on Google+. If you're connected with them, and they search for something you have shared or written about in the past, your results show up on their results page. Connect with potential hiring managers. Connect with conference organizers. Connect with publishers. Be sure to use Google+ while you're at it.

Reverse Search Engine Optimization

Reverse SEO is basically regular SEO but with a different intention. With regular SEO, we want to push something to the top of Google's search rankings, like a blog or a LinkedIn profile. But with reverse SEO, we want to push a top result down off the results—usually something negative about us, whether as a result of our own doing, or someone else's. We do this by ranking other content higher than the negative content.

Say you have a blog post that ranks high on the search engines for something you didn't want to be known for.

@kyleplacy: Oh, wait! Is this that blog post that you—

@edeckers: No.

@kyleplacy: Or was it that time that you forgot to—

@edeckers: No!

@kyleplacy: I know! I know! It was that time when that woman slapped—

@edeckers: NO!

@kyleplacy: You're no fun.

For whatever reason, because that's how these things work out, you can't remove the blog post. And that blog post keeps showing up whenever anyone searches for your name. You need to replace that blog post by getting other, better content online as much as you can.

By doing reverse SEO, and focusing on getting other pieces of content to the top of the search results, you can begin to push that one negative piece off of the results. Try a few of these tactics to get the reverse SEO working for you to protect your reputation.

- **Start a blog**—If you completely ignored Chapter 3, now is the time to start one. Go back and reread the chapter, and don't continue until you start a blog. No, seriously! Do it now! We'll wait for you.

- **Focus on more than one property**—If you focus all your energy on one property, like your blog, you may get that to the top of the search results, but the offending post will be second.

- **Use videos**—We already talked about the power of YouTube. Be sure to create a few videos and upload those. Embed a few on your blog to see if you can get other bloggers to pick up other videos.

- **Write guest posts**—Write guest blog posts for other people. Try to pick some high-traffic blogs with people who will help promote your work.

- **Purchase your name as a domain name**—Pick your favorite domain registrar, like GoDaddy or Network Solutions, and purchase your own name. Forward it to your blog, or at least set up a free website with Google (http://sites.google.com), and point the domain there. Make sure you properly optimize that page. Set outbound links to other social properties discussed in the book.

- **Optimize your LinkedIn profile**—LinkedIn shows up high on Google results. See Chapter 4, "LinkedIn: Networking on Steroids," for more information on how to do that.

- **Use another online résumé**—There are résumé sites all over the Internet, especially visual résumés that look like infographics. Recently, Erik was testing out Revu (www.re.vu) as a visual résumé, although there are other infographic résumé tools. Again, these can be found via search engines, so it's worth trying at least one of them.

What if You Share a Common Name?

Erik considers himself lucky. He's the only one with his name in the entire country. There are three Erik Deckers in Belgium, but, as he says, "I totally own those guys on Google." Kyle's rather fortunate, too. There are only a handful of Kyle Lacy's in the United States, and certainly only one Kyle P. Lacy, which is why @kyleplacy is still a good Twitter handle.

And most of the people we know have a somewhat uncommon name that few people have. But what do you do if you have a fairly common name, share your name with a celebrity or athlete (Douglas Karr shares a name with a movie director named Doug Karr, and Erik has a near-match with Eric Decker, wide receiver for the Denver Broncos)...

@edeckers: I had that guy on my fantasy football team.

@kyleplacy: How'd he do for you?

@edeckers: I don't know. I was losing so badly, I quit paying attention by week 13.

...or you're already known for something you'd rather not be known for—then you may have a problem.

When someone searches for your name—say they look for "Doug Karr," hoping to find the owner of the Marketing Tech blog—what they'll see instead is a results page filled with movies that the other Doug Karr has made, and nothing about our friend. And it can get kind of confusing, especially when you want people to know who you actually are.

Erik once pitched a campaign to a possible client who had a rather uncommon name; although he had a couple of "name twins." One guy, who lived in the same state as the client, was convicted of real estate fraud, which is a felony. The felon and Erik's client, a respected businessman and former sports reporter, shared the same name, but had a different initial.

This is when you need to consider renaming yourself, at least professionally.

We're not talking about changing your name like Chad Ochocinco (the former Cincinnati Bengals wide receiver who legally changed his name from Chad Johnson to match his jersey number, #85). Rather, we're talking about how you use the name you have.

We already mentioned Douglas Karr versus Doug Karr. Even though our Doug—Douglas Karr—is known as "Doug" to those people around him, he needs to use the name "Douglas" online so people don't confuse him with the other guy. Similarly, Christopher S. Penn of the Marketing Over Coffee podcast goes by "Christopher S." so he's not confused with the movie actor and brother of Sean Penn, Chris Penn, or the NFL player of the same name.

You have several options:

- **Use your middle initial**—It worked for Christopher S. Penn.
- **Use your middle name**—The odds of someone having your same first, middle, and last name are quite remote.

- **Use your full name**—Both Douglas Karr and Christopher Penn use their full first name, even though they go by their nicknames—Doug, Chris—when they're around friends.

- **Do the first initial, middle name thing**—This is what a lot of lawyers do. Actually, this is one of the only places you tend to see it. Of course, it's a little confusing because you never know whether to use that first initial when addressing the person.

- **Change your name**—This is a huge pain, and something we don't recommend lightly. But noted blogger and consultant (and fellow Que author) Penelope Trunk changed her name several years ago.

Of course, once you do this, you need to make this change as public and permanent as you can. It means changing the name on all your different social networks, or even starting new ones. For example, Douglas Karr has @douglaskarr as his Twitter handle. He's Douglas Karr on LinkedIn and Facebook. He even uses it for his domain name, douglaskarr.com. Rather than fighting a constant battle with the movie director, our Doug is taking the path of least resistance and changing what people call him. After they meet him, they can call him whatever they want. But when it comes to online usage, he can be found only by the name he wants to be known by.

This tactic can also serve as a reverse SEO tool. As we previously discussed, you can "reverse SEO" your old name down the search engine rankings by creating a variation of your name and using that everywhere you can—new Twitter handle, new Facebook name, new LinkedIn name, and even new blog site and domain name. Eventually, your old name will be pushed down the search engines as its replaced by newer, better content associated with that new name.

Search Engine Tools

We've used "Google" and "search engines" almost interchangeably in this chapter, and although that's not to downplay other search engines, it *is* worth noting that Google has more than 75% of the search engine market, which means most of the people who search for you are going to use Google. Here are a few Google tools you can use to find your name on the search giant.

Google Alerts

One of the greatest discoveries we ever made was when we learned you can save Google searches and have the results emailed to yourself on a regular basis. Rather than visiting Google day after day and doing the same searches, hoping to find something new, you can now save your search and have it emailed to you once a day, once a week, once a month, or even as it happens.

Since you're monitoring your own name, which is the most important facet of your brand, you ought to do this every day. While you're at it, you should also create Google Alerts for your company, key names and phrases from your industry, and if you're looking for a job, for the names of people and companies you want to work for.

Visit www.google.com/alerts and set up your alerts. We recommend you have the service return "All Results" rather than "Best Results" when you first start. Then, if/when you start getting too many results to keep track of, switch back to "Best Results."

Similarly, use tools like Twilert to look for Twitter mentions of your name or Twitter handle.

Google Image Search

You can search Google Images at images.google.com to see what kinds of pictures are out there with your name attached to it. Normally, this would show you only the photos where you have had your name attached. However, you occasionally get results that have a photo on a page that has your name on it but is not you. Sometimes it's a photo you took and is on your blog or website; sometimes it's a photo of you on someone else's site; and occasionally it's a photo that's not you and it's not on your website. We're not entirely sure why this happens because the photo hasn't been tagged with your name, you're not in the alt text (the text descriptions of photos that screen readers use to help people who are blind "see" what the photo is), and there is nothing to make anyone think the photo is of you. But there it is.

So, you need to check your Google Image Search once in a while to make sure the photos out there are the ones you approve of.

Conduct this search with the Safe Search turned to Off. Not because we want you to see dirty pictures, but because if there are pictures associated with your name on R-Rated and X-Rated websites, you need to know it. Warning: This may be a problem, especially at the office, so you may want to do that at home.

Google Blog Search

This is one of Google's hidden treasures that the average Google user doesn't even know about. When you do a basic Google search, click the More link at the top of the window, and then click Blogs to search only blogs for your keyword. Figure 9.2

shows a Google search window with the More drop-down menu, and Figure 9.3 shows what kind of results this could turn up.

Figure 9.2 *A Google search window looking for results for Kyle Lacy, and the blog window. Erik especially likes that bottom center photo of Kyle.*

Bing

Bing uses a system similar to Google's My World by incorporating sharing with your Facebook friends. Bing and Facebook team up to provide you with a social search, showing you what it is your friends have shared, liked, and are interested in. A quick search of a few book titles we know our social media friends might like shows us that they do "like" them.

Most results that showed up on Bing made it to the top because our Facebook friends thumbed them up either on Facebook or on the onsite Like This Page button many websites sport these days. Even searching for large, extremely competitive keywords like "jewelry" showed whether our friends liked a particular page.

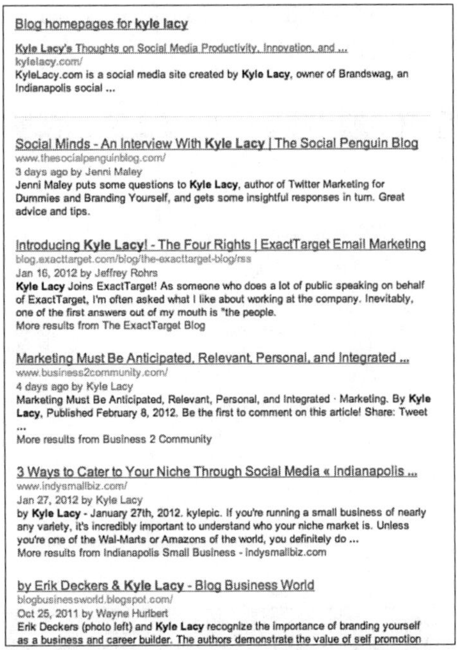
Blog homepages for kyle lacy

Kyle Lacy's Thoughts on Social Media Productivity, Innovation, and ...
kylelacy.com/
KyleLacy.com is a social media site created by Kyle Lacy, owner of Brandswag, an Indianapolis social ...

Social Minds - An Interview With Kyle Lacy | The Social Penguin Blog
www.thesocialpenguinblog.com/
3 days ago by Jenni Maley
Jenni Maley puts some questions to Kyle Lacy, author of Twitter Marketing for Dummies and Branding Yourself, and gets some insightful responses in turn. Great advice and tips.

Introducing Kyle Lacy! - The Four Rights | ExactTarget Email Marketing
blog.exacttarget.com/blog/the-exacttarget-blog/rss
Jan 16, 2012 by Jeffrey Rohrs
Kyle Lacy Joins ExactTarget! As someone who does a lot of public speaking on behalf of ExactTarget, I'm often asked what I like about working at the company. Inevitably, one of the first answers out of my mouth is "the people.
More results from The ExactTarget Blog

Marketing Must Be Anticipated, Relevant, Personal, and Integrated ...
www.business2community.com/
4 days ago by Kyle Lacy
Marketing Must Be Anticipated, Relevant, Personal, and Integrated · Marketing. By Kyle Lacy, Published February 8, 2012. Be the first to comment on this article! Share: Tweet ...
More results from Business 2 Community

3 Ways to Cater to Your Niche Through Social Media « Indianapolis ...
www.indysmallbiz.com/
Jan 27, 2012 by Kyle Lacy
by Kyle Lacy - January 27th, 2012. kylepic. If you're running a small business of nearly any variety, it's incredibly important to understand who your niche market is. Unless you're one of the Wal-Marts or Amazons of the world, you definitely do ...
More results from Indianapolis Small Business - indysmallbiz.com

by Erik Deckers & Kyle Lacy - Blog Business World
blogbusinessworld.blogspot.com/
Oct 25, 2011 by Wayne Hurlbert
Erik Deckers (photo left) and Kyle Lacy recognize the importance of branding yourself as a business and career builder. The authors demonstrate the value of self promotion

Figure 9.3 *Search results after looking for Kyle's name. Most of these are because Erik was signed in to Google when we did this search. If he had signed out, the results would have been different.*

(If nothing else, this shows why you should include a Like button on your website and blog. Check out the Facebook page for information, or download a WordPress plug-in to make this work.)

Our one caveat is that because you shouldn't build your professional brand on Facebook, don't rely on Facebook to deliver the professional results you're looking for. In other words, don't be Facebook friends with potential bosses, hiring managers, HR recruiters, and even potential co-workers (unless you're already real-life friends). Most of your professional networking needs to come from LinkedIn and Google+, not Facebook.

Yahoo!

Yahoo! started out as the premier search directory on the planet. It was one of the first, and eventually turned into an entire portal, offering all kinds of news, content, and other services. Although it was originally known only for search, that quickly became one of the smallest services it offered. Yahoo!'s search results (and analytics) have now been incorporated into Bing so that if you search one or the other, you get (mostly) the same results, with one or two variations. Together, the two control approximately 25%–30% of the search market, while Google still owns the rest of it. There are a few other search engines, but they barely make any difference to figure into the total market share. (This is an interesting and massive change from the late 1990s and early 2000s, when most of them were on equal footing, and Google was only starting to make its presence known.)

Other Search Engines

While Google, Bing, and Yahoo! own approximately 99% of the entire North American search engine market, there are a few other search engines that take up the other 1%. You may want to play with these to see what you can find for occurrences of your name and identity.

- **Infospace**—A meta search engine, this pulls in results from Google, Bing, and Yahoo!. It doesn't use any social search, so you get pure, unfiltered, objective results. It's a great way for HR recruiters and hiring managers to do a comprehensive people search.

- **SpokeO**—A name search, sort of like the Internet's white pages. You can search for a person's name, username, email address, or even physical address. You can access some information for free, but if you're interested in finding out who lives at a certain physical address, or find information about the house at that location, you have to pay a fee. It's not completely accurate, but it's a great place to start a search if you want to find some social networks where a particular person might be found.

- **Technorati**—This is more of a blogging directory than a real search engine. You can search for particular blogs or even posts by looking for a topic, category, or author. Blogs have authority based on links within the blog. They also have topic authority based on a particular keyword or category.

- **IceRocket**—This is a search engine that scours blogs, tweets, and Facebook messages all over the world. It's billed as a real-time search engine, so it finds the latest in search results. Figure 9.4 shows a typical set of results from IceRocket.

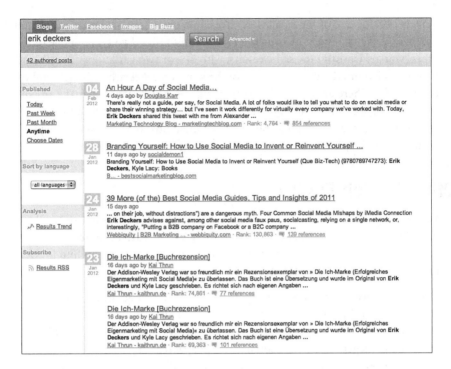

Figure 9.4 *IceRocket looks at blogs, Twitter, and Facebook. This is what the blog search results look like. Note the German entry at the bottom of the page. This book was translated into German while we were working on the second edition.*

The Value of Reputation Management

Occasionally we get pulled into the "I'm a person, not a brand!" discussion with people.

"Get over it," we say. "You're a brand." We've already discussed what makes you a brand in Chapter 1, "Welcome to the Party," but we'll amend that a tiny bit here.

If you don't want to call yourself a brand, then talk about your reputation. Even the most dogmatic "I'm not a brand!" advocates agree they have a reputation. And in all actuality, a brand and a reputation are actually the same thing. We just call it a brand because that's the most common term these days.

So that's where *reputation management* comes into play. For whatever reason, we're still calling managing your brand reputation management. Why? Because *brand management* is the new fancy-schmancy business term for *marketing*.

Reputation management is basically just making sure your online brand—your reputation—is a positive one, that people see you in the best possible light, which is the whole point of this entire book. But it's important to discuss reputation management as an area of practice because you may need it one of these days.

Reputation Management Tools

There are tools online that let you do everything we've talked about up to this point. A couple of them are free, or have freemium models (free + premium = freemium). Others let you try out their system for a short amount of time, usually 30 days, before they start charging you. If you have a particularly sticky situation or a spotted reputation, you may want to consider trying one of these tools.

 Note

A *freemium* service means there is a *free* component and a *premium* component. You can use the network for free, but you can't take advantage of everything the network has to offer. Some sites have a limited free offering—can only import three links; can only monitor three accounts—while others have robust free offerings but charge for the elite usage—being able to view everyone outside your network; having unlimited messages.

BrandYourself.com

BrandYourself is a reverse SEO/reputation management tool that basically looks at your Google ranking for your own name and shows you where and how to add positive content that will then bury the unwanted results. You are assigned a grade, A–F, for your search results; a percentage score based on how much you have "boosted" your best links; a progress line to show you how well you're moving up the search rankings; and you can even earn badges based on your reputation management accomplishments. For example, you can achieve the Spotless badge for having no negative content about you in the first page of results, or the Love at First Sight badge for having the first four search results about you. Figure 9.5 shows the BrandYourself Score screen.

Reputation.com

Reputation.com is another freemium reputation management tool, similar to BrandYourself. You enter data into the required fields—more is better, so it can find the right you—and it returns your results after checking sites like Google, Bing, Yahoo!, SpokeO, RapLeaf, Facebook, and LinkedIn.

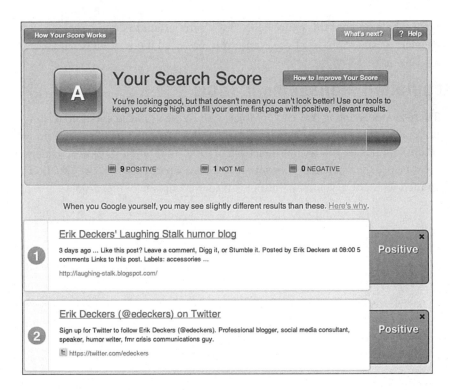

Figure 9.5 *Erik's score on BrandYourself.com. He owns the first nine out of the top ten positions. He'd have all ten if it weren't for Eric Decker, the Denver Broncos' wide receiver.*

Basically, if you use and monitor all these sites already, and work diligently at managing your reputation, you may not need Reputation.com. But it's still a good idea to check it out to make sure you're firing on all cylinders. You need to tweak all the information and results you find to ensure you get accurate information.

It's still worth checking out, especially if you want to grow your personal brand for the first time or repair a damaged reputation. We especially liked the Assessment screen under the MyReputation tab, which looks at the overall sentiment it's finding about your results; the Discoveries screen, which looks at all the different sites and properties it finds about you; and especially the Search Results page, which shows how often people have searched for your name this month (not you, but your name) and then gives you a percentage score of how likely you are to be found on that search.

Reputation.com also offers a MyPrivacy service, which can help you seek and destroy any public information about you, making sure your privacy is as safe as it can possibly be in a world where every little detail of your life is already known and stored in giant databanks in secret bunkers, where it can be accessed by the government, large corporations, and worst of all, direct marketing professionals.

@edeckers: Or at least is willing to admit they know. MWAHAHAHA!
@kyleplacy: Knock it off.

You can also tell Reputation.com about any negative content you want to suppress by entering the URLs where that content may appear. The ReputationDefender product helps bury that negative content on the search engines. This is a paid product.

Google's Me on the Web

Google knows a lot about you. And if you use any Google properties, or have in the past, you may want to know what they track and to see how much they know. Go to www.google.com/dashboard and log in with your Google credentials (Gmail, YouTube, Blogger, or whatever you use to access any Google properties; probably your Gmail address). This is your Google dashboard and shows everything that Google knows about you.

@edeckers: MWAHAHAHA!
@kyleplacy: I said knock it off!

It knows your websites, your Google Analytics profile, your Gmail contacts, and any Google properties that you have claimed, like Picasa and YouTube. You can access your saved Google Alerts, see your Android phone information (if you use an Android phone), and even check out your Google Voice number.

Unlike the other two products, this one does not give you a score based on your visibility or sentiment. (You can get a basic idea of your visibility if you use Google Analytics but no percentage scores, grades, or badges, or anything cool like that. But if you're a regular Google product user, it's an interesting look to see how tied in you are to all their search products.)

Me on the Web can tell you when your personal data is released on the web, like your phone number or email address, and then even lets you remove unwanted content about you online, whether it's an embarrassing photo or your phone number. Just click the Remove Unwanted Content link on your dashboard, in the Me on the Web section, and follow the directions. Also, be sure to read the Manage Your Online Reputation article in this section of your Dashboard. Unlike the other two products, this is a free product.

How Do Our Heroes Use SEO?

All our heroes monitor and manage their online reputation in the same way, keeping their profiles clean, monitoring what is found/said about them through Google Alerts, and making sure they put out good content to help them be found on Google, Bing, and Yahoo!. They also start participating more thoroughly on Google+, including adding people from their professional networks into Google+ to boost their search engine rankings. Of course, they want to make sure they put out the stuff that's related to their next job or industry, as well as sharing that kind of information on Google+, Twitter, and LinkedIn.

If they happen to make a mistake and there's something they wish wasn't up there, they can use Reputation.com or BrandYourself.com, as well as practice some solid reverse SEO, to remove the negative information from the front pages of the search results.

Reputation Management Tips in 140 Characters

- I try to keep Flickr current with recent photos that are tagged. —@VirtualJason
- Use the same photos w/filename across social accounts. —@BTutterow
- Use rel=author as appropriate. —@BTutterow
- Just live right and then it is easy to be authentic and then the reputation follows. —@TahiraCreates
- Establish, curate, and promote profiles i.e., @résumévu and others to help establish a presence and story. —@Mah1
- (For businesses) have policy for responding in place; set up industry alerts because your biz is affected by industry news. —@CharleneBurke

 Note

The rel="author" tag should be used whenever you can link your own name to your Google+ profile. It basically tells Google anything you write (i.e., a guest blog post) is yours, and should be associated with your Google+ profile and any search results with your name on it. It would look something like this:

```
<a href="http://bit.ly/xyLk6s" rel="author">Erik Deckers</a>
```

(We shortened the Google+ link with Bitly, because the original URL is about a mile long.)

When you do this, you're not only creating a *backlink* back to your Google+ profile (remember backlinks?), you're also telling Google you're the *author* of that particular piece, and that the *keyword* of the link is you.

If you didn't write the piece, and you're just linking your name, remove the rel="author" piece, and then that link can point to wherever you want.

10

Bringing It All Together: Launching Your Brand

Some people have called it the campaign of the century. Others have called it the best campaign ever run in the political arena. Still others proclaimed that the use of the Internet was absolutely genius and won the presidency. President Barack Obama and his team created and launched a personal brand that redefined the idea of a campaign. They planned and developed a story and then built that story into a campaign centered on change.

The campaign redefined the idea of using traditional and grassroots promotions. The Internet, blogging, Facebook, and the creation of content were used to win the hearts and minds of the American public. Obama's people accomplished all this by planning and launching the best personal brand campaign on the face of the planet. And they used the tools and strategies talked about in this book! Whether you're running for President of the United States, or just want to get a new job, the same strategies and principles apply. Social media isn't just a matter of politics. It's strategy, planning, measurement, and imple-

mentation.

This book is about planning to launch your personal brand into the market and make the most out of your skills and attributes. President Obama's presidential campaign is the most famous case study for you to use in planning and launching your own campaign, but there have been many more.

Ever since we published the first edition of this book, countless people have used it to launch their own personal branding campaigns, and found new jobs, gotten new speaking engagements, gained more readers, and even landed publishing deals.

Everything launched into the world, whether it is product or business, has one common characteristic: The creator has a plan, and with the plan comes a campaign. President Obama certainly did not launch his bid for presidency (his personal branding campaign, if you will) without a plan.

It's not a good idea to launch anything new without a plan—"If you fail to plan, you plan to fail" goes the old saying. To successfully launch your personal brand, you must build a campaign. We have given you the ideas and tools to create, test, and promote your personal brand. And in this chapter, we've given you a roadmap to help launch your personal brand into the market.

Launching a successful personal brand requires more than creating online profiles, posting regular updates to your blog, and keeping track of your site's analytics; you also need a solid campaign to launch your personal brand.

What Is a Personal Brand Campaign?

What does it mean to create a personal brand campaign? We know how to define our personal brand story, and we understand we need to have some sort of campaign to launch that brand. That's like what President Obama did, right? Not necessarily, but the two are fairly similar in their own right. To fully build your personal branding campaign, you need to understand what we mean by the term.

A personal branding campaign is simple: You make the consumers—customers, readers, organizers, and hiring managers—aware of your personal brand and gain their trust to transact with you. You use a positive message (your personal brand story) to make the consumers (your network) want to go to you when they are ready to make a transaction. Your personal brand campaign is the succinct planning and implementation of your promotional vehicles that lead to exposure for your personal brand. In this way, your personal brand is positioned for the right transaction.

What do we mean by positioning and transaction? Positioning is where you fit in your overall marketplace (depending on the product you sell). It is determined by what you offer to the individual interacting with your personal brand. (See Chapter 2, "How Do You Fit in the Mix?.") This includes your benefits as an individual. You are also positioning yourself against the competition. How are you different? How are you similar? A transaction is the acceptance of your personal brand by other people: reaching the goal. It can be defined as multiple things depending on your story. You get hired. You get booked to speak. You get the publishing deal. People click the link to read your blog.

The final outcome of defining your position and transaction is what we call the positioning and transaction statement. This "statement" is basically your tagline as an individual. Remember the short personal biography you wrote at the beginning of the book? Same concept but more succinct. You may even use your short personal brand bio as your positioning and transaction statement. It is a catchy or memorable phrase or sentence that expands on the uniqueness of your personal brand. What questions should you ask yourself about positioning and transaction?

We want you to get a piece of paper and outline the following questions. Yes, right now. Write down Table 10.1.

Table 10.1   Setting Up Your Positioning and Transaction Statements

Positioning

Who is your competition? (List three individuals or companies.)

How are you different from your competition? (Three reasons for each competitor.)

How are you similar to your competition? (Three reasons for each competitor).

Transaction

What does the transaction look like?

What is the end goal?

Positioning and Transaction Statement

Write down one sentence about what makes you different.

It is important to fill out the preceding information to get a better idea of how you are going to launch your personal brand campaign to make the most impact. How do you apply these ideas to your campaign?

Kyle uses his positioning and transaction statement as a way to keep focused while building his personal brand. In answering the positioning question, Kyle would list other authors, speakers, and thought leaders at competing marketing companies. After doing research on the competition, he would understand what makes him similar and different. Kyle would probably say that his location and age, being a published author, and working for a company like ExactTarget set him apart. However, the things that make him different to one group could also be similarities to another group.

In answering the transaction question, Kyle would look back to Chapter 2 and define his goals. The end goal for Kyle would be focused on his personal goals as well as the goals of his employer, ExactTarget. The transaction would be the fulfilling of the goals.

After much hard work, sweat, and tears (kidding. Sort of. Kyle's a bit of a crier.)—

@kyleplacy: C'mon man! It was dusty.

@edeckers: Curious how it's always dusty when ESPN's 30 for 30 stories are on.

—Kyle's positioning and transaction statement would look something like this:

I'm a young, interactive marketer focused on positioning my personal and company brand as the premiere thought leader in channel marketing.

It covers his aspirations to write, teach, and consult on ideas that change business (social media and technology). His main differentiation is being a young and successful author in the interactive space.

@edeckers: Who cries at the drop of a hat.
@kyleplacy: Knock it off!

How Do Our Heroes Build Their P&T Statement?

- **Allen (influencer)** was an account manager for a marketing and advertising agency for 14 years but is looking for a new job. Remember Allen's short personal brand bio?

  I'm a creative professional in high-level marketing and advertising, and I used to work for one of the top agencies in the country.

  Allen will be positioning himself as a high-level account manager who is also creative and has plenty of work experience. He is probably going to be trendy and exude the creative passion that makes advertising firms great. Allen must build a positioning statement that is different from his competitors. A transaction in Allen's world would be a new job. He is building his personal brand story to get in front of the right people (hiring managers—usually the principals—at advertising firms) to get a job. His networking and ability to spread his message will be fundamental in him getting a job in the near future.

  Unfortunately, Allen's personal brand bio does not fully represent a P&T statement. Allen needs to do the research on his competition and then define himself differently. By filling out the information from Table 10.1, Allen has further solidified what makes him different from the competition. By taking that information, he can build a positioning and transaction statement.

  I'm a creative marketing professional building successful campaigns for Fortune 500 clients.

  How did Allen change his personal brand bio? He showed a success statement. What makes Allen different from his competition is the level and size of clients he has successfully helped.

- **Beth (climber)** is a marketing manager for a large insurance company and wants to move up the ladder in the firm. Beth's positive transaction is going to be her ability to meet, network, and move up the ladder in her company. What was Beth's short personal brand bio?

I am a marketing manager for Inverness Insurance and have been ranked as one of the top marketing professionals in my industry for the past three years by Insurance Marketing Magazine.

From a positioning standpoint, Beth does a good job at explaining why she is qualified for the position, but she is going to have a harder time because she has to navigate the politics of the corporate world. However, she can still define what makes her different from her competitors. The majority of Beth's competitors might be her co-workers, so it's important that she note that she stands out within her industry. Her entire launch campaign is going to be designed around the transaction of getting a better job in the company. With that transaction in mind, she knows exactly what she has to build her positioning and transaction statement on and eventually her brand launch campaign.

Beth's personal brand bio fits quite well with her P&T statement. However, she needs to tighten the statement to make more impact.

I am ranked one of the top insurance marketing professionals by Insurance Marketing Magazine.

This is a simple and succinct statement. What makes Beth different from her peers? She is ranked one of the top in her industry by an objective third party—a trade magazine dedicated to her industry.

- **Carla (neophyte)** is a former pharmaceutical sales rep who was laid off after eight years with her company and is interested in working for a nonprofit. Remember Carla's personal brand bio:

  I'm a former pharmaceutical salesperson trying to make the leap to the nonprofit world.

  Carla is similar to Allen except she has to completely reinvent herself. It is going to be harder for her to define her competitors because the world of nonprofits is completely new to her. She has to do some major research to define her competition. Her transaction is twofold: She wants to get a job, but she also wants to completely change her personal brand story. Carla's positioning and transaction statement would be designed around how to change to become competitive in a brand new environment.

  Carla's is going to be the more extreme change between her personal brand bio and P&T statement. It is going to take more research and creative thinking to define what makes her different from the competition.

  I'm a former business professional who wants to make a difference using the skills learned in the corporate environment.

How did Carla change her statement? She is now defining what makes her different from other nonprofit professionals. She worked in the corporate sales environment and understands how to sell and build a successful product. Notice that she also dropped the "former pharmaceutical salesperson" because she found that the term "salesperson" could have a negative effect when pitching herself to an organization. She also appeals to the emotional side of the reader by saying "wants to make a difference," which makes her P&T statement even more powerful.

- **Darrin (free agent)** is an IT professional who leaves his job every two or three years in pursuit of more money. Darrin's short personal brand bio was great for his P&T statement:

I'm an IT professional who is trusted by 10 of the top corporations in the city.

Darrin's positive transaction is going to be his ability to get better-paying jobs over the course of his personal brand launch campaign. What does he have to do to build out his ability to sell? He has to define his positioning and transaction to fully understand how to launch his personal brand story. He is trusted by 10 of the top corporations in the city.

Darrin's competitors are going to be extremely active in the space because of the fast-changing world of technology. He is going to have to be extremely comprehensive in defining what makes him similar to and different from his competitors. The transaction for Darrin is going to be a better-paying job. What he has to do to accomplish this goal is going to lead his personal brand campaign as well as what his competitors are doing to beat him up. His personal brand bio actually works quite well for his P&T statement, but he would be adding one thing to the mix:

I'm an IT professional who implements technology solutions that create success for the top 10 corporations in the city.

What did Darrin do differently? He added why the top 10 corporations in the city actually trust him. When you create something that makes another individual (or organization) successful, it needs to be built into your P&T statement.

You now have a better idea of how to build the beginning of your campaign. It is important to figure out your P&T statement. Remember, you can use your personal brand bio as a positioning and transaction statement, but it is important to fill out the information in Table 10.1 to fully understand what makes you different. You can't launch your personal brand campaign without defining your P&T statement.

Why Is a Personal Brand Campaign Important?

Did you read the first section of this chapter and nod your head in agreement? (Or at least want to?) It is easy to understand that you have to plan to be successful. We have heard it from every success guru on the face of the planet. However, there is more to planning than just building a system to accomplish a goal. It is about designing a system to launch your personal brand story, the key word being launch.

The importance of launching your personal brand story into the world should not be taken for granted. You don't simply want to create another promotional campaign. The world is overrun with promotional campaigns. You want to build something that will launch onto the world and create personal change. The term launch is significant in itself. Let's look at its definition:

> To send forth, catapult, or release, as a self-propelled vehicle or weapon: Rockets were launched midway in the battle. The submarine launched its torpedoes and dived rapidly.

You are the submarine. Chills, we know.

@edeckers:	I am the walrus, goo goo g'joob.
@kyleplacy:	What the hell are you talking about?
@edeckers:	It's a Beatles song.
@kyleplacy:	Oh yeah, my dad listened to those guys.
@edeckers:	Shut up.

The concept of launching something into the world is a powerful proposition, especially for your personal brand. The launching of you is more significant than the launching of any Snuggie or Reverse Flush Toilet campaign could ever muster. This is the personal brand story that will build your life from here on out.

Before you get into the planning details, you need to understand a few issues that should guide your branding campaign:

- **People are overloaded**—You know exactly what we are talking about. People are constantly bombarded with an onslaught of branding messages. Make sure yours is new, personal, and compelling, or your personal brand won't get much attention. Your P&T statement and campaign help define what will make your campaign compelling.

- **You want to be different**—Developing your personal brand story helps you understand exactly what makes you different in the marketplace. Your campaign plan should share this with the world creatively and interestingly.

- **You want to create a professional demeanor**—When you create a plan to deliver your personal brand story, you are setting yourself up for not only sounding and looking professional but also being professional. When you plan for something, you are becoming the professional you need to be to achieve your goals in life.

- **You want to be constant and consistent**—You can't just launch once and wait for something to happen. People are busy, so they're not going to see your messages the first time. You need to publish your message regularly. (This is where luck comes in.) You also don't want to be a pest, so professionalism is important. Don't send the same messages over and over every 10 minutes.

We know you have invested a ton of time already in developing your personal brand and learning about the tools to share your brand story. We want to further solidify your desire to champion your personal brand by creating the launch campaign. You are now spending time developing a plan to help you completely understand your personal brand story. When you build a campaign to champion the work you have completed so far in this chapter, you are creating more meaning in your work than ever before.

Building Your Personal Brand Campaign

Now that you understand the "why" of a personal branding campaign, it is time for the implementation. You can launch a campaign in hundreds of different ways. A Nike product may have a completely different launch campaign compared to a Reebok product. We are going to design your launch in three phases: developing, implementing, and automating.

Developing Your Personal Brand Campaign

You have built your positioning and transaction statement that will lead you down the development of your personal brand campaign. Your personal brand campaign is truly defined as how to use the tools described in this book. Remember, you should have set up your different social networks with the help of the corresponding chapters. You have been taught how to differentiate yourself (P&T and personal brand bio) and which tools to use to differentiate (networking and social media). Now is the time to show the world what you have built! Your campaign calendar is the center point of your campaign.

We are going to assume that everyone reading this book uses some type of calendar. Whether we are talking about Google Calendar, Outlook, or a paper day planner, it is important to get a calendar if you are not already using one to help track your day. (We like Google Calendar because we're both Gmail users, but any calendar will do.) If you do not have a planner, you may want to read a few articles and blog posts first about how to plan your day. The calendar is going to be extremely important to managing your personal brand campaign.

An important area of campaign management is blocking out certain parts of every day to accomplish tasks associated with your personal brand campaign. You can apply the following time blocks to any area of your business or personal life. Time blocks help you manage your time effectively. The most important thing to remember is to stick to what you have planned.

Think of your typical work day. What is going on throughout the day? You need to pick the kids up, you have a report to file somewhere, you need to do some shopping, the boss is breathing down your neck, or you have a business to run. It is important to block out time in your day to accomplish your personal branding campaign. You've already spent so much time building and tweaking the system you might as well stick to it, right?

You can set up between 30 and 60 minutes every day when you use the social networking tools described in the previous chapters to further launch your personal brand campaign.

 Tip

Block out at least 30-minute units of time, but don't make them more than 60 minutes. You want to develop a habit, not overwhelm yourself with things to do.

The whole point of the calendar is to keep you productive so that you can accomplish your goals. What does it mean to be productive?

- **Set your time**—Find two 15- to 30-minute time blocks. You can choose to place the time blocks at the beginning and the end of your day or during your lunch break. It is up to your extreme management skills to decide.
- **Respect your time**—Would you call a prospective client to reschedule a meeting because you needed to run to the store or pick up office supplies? No. The same rule applies for your time block. Do not schedule other things during your personal branding promotion.
- **Adjust your time**—If certain times of the day do not feel productive, move the time block. You do not have to keep your time block in the same place. It is meant to be adjusted and changed depending on how and when you do your best work.

You are probably wondering, "Kyle and Erik, I understand this entire blocking out of my time thing for productivity, but what do I put in the time block?" The promotional activities during your promotional time are just as important as setting up your calendar.

Implementing Your Personal Brand Campaign

Take the tools learned throughout this book and apply them to your daily routine. This routine can launch your personal brand campaign. It is the promotional piece that helps push the message (your personal brand story) you have been building throughout this book. You should build a campaign launch daily task sheet to fully understand what you need to accomplish during your time blocks. Table 10.2 gives you an example of a campaign launch task sheet. Accomplish this task sheet on a daily basis, and you will be successful in launching your personal brand.

Table 10.2 An Example of a Campaign Launch Task Sheet

Daily Activity Sheet

The following activities will be completed on a daily basis:

Facebook

- Post one status update.
- Answer messages and postings on your wall.
- Friend at least five people from your locale.
- Send one message to a friend with personal content.

Twitter

- Follow 10 people.
- Pre-post five tweets daily using Hootsuite or another Twitter platform.
- Respond to @ replies.
- Respond to direct messages.
- Send one tweet telling your followers to follow a friend.

LinkedIn

- Connect with two people, or ask for a connection.
- Answer one question from a LinkedIn group.

Blogging

- Comment on two blogs.
- Write one blog post.

Weekly Activity Sheet

Weekly Facebook

- Tell a success story.
- Share a funny story.
- Announce good news. Tell about awards the company has won, welcome a new client, share presentations, or post on a blog.
- Upload a picture.
- Run a promotion campaign.

Weekly LinkedIn

- Post one question to a LinkedIn group.
- Connect with one person for a face-to-face networking meeting.

Weekly Twitter

- Send out five #followfriday tweets.

Aim to do this every day, and using social media extensively every day will become a habit. That's what we've learned. We're online promoting our personal brands at least an hour every day because we've discovered how effective these tools are for furthering our brand campaigns.

Automating Your Personal Brand Campaign

You may have built your campaign launch task sheet and realized that (based on what you have learned) it will be easy to automate some of the tasks in the list. Good for you! We are happy.

You have learned in different parts of this book the capability of tools like HootSuite to preschedule content. Also, the tools can help with distributing content from your blog to different social media sites. This is what we call automating a portion of your campaign. You want to automate the posting of some of your content so that you can focus fully on defining and redefining your personal brand. Creating content is key to the distribution of your personal branding campaign.

When you create content, you must understand what content can be automated and what shouldn't be automated. When using social media, you have the right to automate the posting of blogs or other articles, which is called informational content. If you look at Figure 10.1, you can see that Kyle's blog post was posted automatically to Facebook. This is an example of informational content. The content that should not be automated is conversational content that is in the moment or live. Figure 10.2 shows a type of conversational content that Kyle had sent through

Twitter to another user. However, you shouldn't automate content that is "live" or "active." Live and active content has to do with the moment. Do not automate conversational content.

Figure 10.1   *This content post was sent to Facebook from TweetDeck, which Kyle had prescheduled to go out the morning before.*

Figure 10.2   *Don't automate the conversation. Use conversational tweets like this one.*

We have discussed different tools in this book to automate the posting of blogs to different social networks. The best are HootSuite, Ping.fm, and TweetDeck. It may be worth it to you to go back through earlier chapters of this book and apply the tools we have discussed to free up more of your time on your campaign calendar and daily task sheet.

Unique Ways to Launch Your Branding Campaign

Okay, you now understand the specific steps you need to take to successfully promote your personal brand. Keep in mind your daily tasks, and implement some fun ways to make the day more enjoyable. The more you enjoy launching and promoting your brand, the better the launch.

- **"Thank you for meeting with me" note**—This step is in more of the traditional sense. It may be surprising that we are actually recommending this tool. Yes, we understand we are asking you to use a pen and handwrite a note, but the power behind the note is extremely beneficial to your personal brand. It is rare that an individual writes a note after meeting or talking to someone. It is extremely important to utilize the art of a handwritten note. Go buy some thank-you cards and some stamps. It will help. Erik even knows a graphic designer who created her own 1/3 sheet cards—the size of 1/3 of a sheet of a paper—with her face and contact information. It fits inside a #10 envelope. After a meeting, she writes a note, sticks it in an envelope, and mails it.

- **Use video**—Video (whether you upload through YouTube or Facebook) is an extremely powerful tool to promote yourself. When you use video, you establish a form of trust. People have the tendency to experience a deeper connection when the majority of their senses are stimulated. You want to create one simple video per week, sitting in your office/studio/garden to talk about your latest success, to go over a tutorial, or something else. However, remember to be professional!

- **Hire a dancer with a sign**—You know who we mean, right? Hire the person who dances around with the pizza sign on the side of the road. The ability to dance for hours and not get hit by a car is an extremely valuable asset to a personal branding campaign. Okay, don't really do this. We just wanted to see if you were paying attention. But, you need to stay creative in your search for the ultimate promotions vehicle.

- **Write for smaller publications**—Smaller publications are easier to land a byline in because they have fewer writers you're competing with. If you write well, you will have an easier time getting published and promoting your brand.

- **Use an email newsletter to connect on a different level**—Sites like Constant Contact (www.constantcontact.com), Emma (www.myemma.com), and ExactTarget (www.exacttarget.com) are great tools for email marketing, especially if you have an email newsletter. Use one of these systems to keep in contact your database. Email is used daily by nearly everyone but isn't used as effectively to market content. Remember, do not spam! Your email provider can help with understanding what constitutes spam. You can even measure open rates and click-through rates to see what content is most interesting to your readers.

- **Give something away for free**—People always love free. Give away a special report or whitepaper to gain some traction for your personal brand. We have seen people give away entire books just for an email address. Give away something valuable to gain something valuable in return. Use the email addresses to start an email marketing campaign. You can then send a newsletter or marketing material to the readers who sign up.

- **Write guest blog posts**—This is an extremely powerful step to getting your personal brand in front of other people. Kyle writes for sites like Jay Baer's "Convince and Convert" and Douglas Karr's "Marketing

Tech Blog"; Erik writes for Dan Schawbel's "Personal Branding" blog. When you share content, you receive links (remember the importance of backlinks to build search authority) and new eyeballs to read your own content. There are a few ways to guest post on other blogs: Email the writer of the blog, write a quick post for an online publication and send it to the editor, or ask the person to swap blog posts for publishing. We suggest writing at least three guest posts per month.

- **Hire someone to design a business card**—Most people go to a third-rate printer to get the same business card that 100,000 other people have printed. Spend some money and hire a graphic designer to design a fashionable and memorable business card with a logo. Print 500 cards, and use these to give to contacts at networking events. (See Chapter 12, "How to Network: Hello, My Name Is...," for the best ways to network with other people, and hand out your business cards sparingly.)

- **Use your email signature**—Your email signature is shared and sent more often than any other form of marketing. Include your name, preferably both first and last, a title, and your social media links (Twitter, Facebook, LinkedIn, and your blog). Put your signature at the bottom of every email you send. Most email programs like Gmail and Outlook allow you to add an email signature at the end of every email sent with a program like WiseStamp. Find the Settings option in your email program and add a signature to automate the process.

- **Get involved in your local community**—Join organizations such as the Chamber of Commerce or a development alliance. We have talked extensively about marketing your personal brand through networking. A strong local community network can help in your search for a successful personal branding campaign. Join the Rotary Club, volunteer your time and expertise to a charitable organization, or coach a sports team. Any form of helping others in your community can build and help launch your personal brand campaign.

- **Always have a smile on your face**—Make sure there is a smile on your face. This makes you approachable and can give you confidence. Keep your energy levels high, without bouncing off the walls. Someone who is energetic, interested, and enthusiastic always stands out.

Maybe we went a little Pollyanna with that last tip, but it is extremely important to keep a positive attitude while launching your personal brand campaign.

How Should Our Heroes Launch Their Brands?

- **Allen (influencer)** needs a more creative promotional strategy than the rest of the heroes. His industry is harder to make a splash in because *everyone* makes a splash in the advertising world. Allen needs to spend more time on developing a different communication strategy with more consistency, more reaching out to influential people, and creating some great ideas and messages.

  Allen may design and send different mailing pieces to hiring managers at advertising firms around the country. He may follow up with a phone call and tweet after the package is sent to the individual. Allen wants to connect to people on multiple levels (phone, mail, Twitter, and LinkedIn) to be sure the hiring manager remembers his name.

- **Beth (climber)** needs to stay in line with the corporate structure of her company. Her tactics are going to be more in the form of networking and being involved in her community. She will spend more time sharing and writing content on LinkedIn. Beth will also frequent (maybe even plan) community events related to her company. Anything she can possibly attend to rub elbows with the executive team would be beneficial to her.

  Beth could start a personal/professional blog to talk about her industry without representing her corporate company. By creating content outside of the office, she starts to establish herself as a thought leader. And thought leaders tend to get better jobs within the walls of corporate America.

- **Carla (neophyte)** is going to be like Beth in the world of networking. Because Carla is completely switching industries, she must start networking to rebuild her platform. She needs to start a blog to write content centered around the nonprofit industry. By writing this content, Carla is learning, defining, and implementing what will make her successful in the long run.

  Ideally, Carla would attend every networking and seminar event because it is important for her to learn and meet nonprofit professionals. Volunteering is another way Carla can establish her personal brand story in the nonprofit world.

- **Darrin (free agent)** is established in his industry, which means he doesn't need to build a personal brand story as much as developing his already-strong reputation. Darrin should be carrying around a digital video camera to record and distribute videos of his expertise and his interviews of happy clients, as well as screencasts. (Use video recordings of your computer screen; use special software like Camtasia to record this; we used Camtasia to record the videos in the e-version of this book.) Video content should be a key marketing tool for Darrin in the world of information technology. The more content that Darrin distributes through this medium, the higher the probability he will be recognized among the firms that will be a new employer for him.

Do's and Don'ts of Launching Your Personal Brand

Certain rules and regulations must guide your use of social media, networking, and other tools when launching your brand. Read carefully, and be sure you adhere to each "law."

- **Do accomplish your campaign launch task sheet (daily)**—An important section of this chapter is the buildout of your daily campaign task sheet. This system is the driver of your promotional activities for your personal brand launch campaign. If you adhere to your task sheet, your promotional activities will come easier over time.

- **Do send out conversational content**—We talked about conversational content earlier in this chapter. The content that is live, real, and involves other individuals is the true content that will drive your personal brand campaign. Be involved in the process of creating content, and join in the development of other people in the process.

- **Do give more than you receive**—Sharing, retweeting, and forwarding content from others is one of the more important rules in the promotional campaign on social media. Many people send more content about themselves than anything else. It is not all about you. In truth, it is about the development of relationships online. Share and retweet more content from others than you send about yourself.

- **Do be aware of criticism; just ignore most of it**—You are going to be the top dog in your sphere of influence because of the strategies in this book. Be aware that you will face some criticism no matter what you do in the socially driven Internet world. Don't be offended by criticism when launching and promoting your personal brand campaign. More than likely, the people criticizing you are jealous of your success. Be aware of the criticism, but ignore it when it gets personal and petty.

- **Do be consistent**—Think of your personal brand campaign as a relationship. If you are in a relationship and are not consistent with spending time with that individual and conversing, it is safe to say the relationship will not be strong. Consistency of content and conversation help drive your overall influence in the social media world. Also, the strength of your personal brand depends on the consistency of your content.

- **Don't be socially awkward**—Imagine having a conversation with an individual who changes the topic of conversation every second. After the third switcheroo, the conversation becomes highly annoying because you cannot follow anything the person is saying. The same concept applies to social media. Create a list of what you are going to say and talk about on the social networking sites. If you talk about a ton of different topics, it is going to be hard for people to pinpoint what your personal brand story is all about.

  @kyleplacy: This is what it's like talking to you when you've had too many lattes.

  @edeckers: I don't jump around. I just have a lot to talk about.

- **Don't expect quick results**—The campaign launch is a process. Building a brand takes time and energy that (over time) will build a strong and healthy personal brand. Unless you are sponsored by Coke or are featured on *Good Morning America*, your personal brand is going to take some time to build. If you expect quick results, you will become frustrated, and frustration negatively affects a personal brand launch campaign.

- **Don't use only one tool**—If you are building a workbench, do you use only a hammer? No. It takes a mitre saw, a tape measure, and a drill. The same concept applies to your launch campaign. Don't use only Twitter or only Facebook to build your personal brand.

- **Don't share unworthy content**—There are times when you shouldn't send a tweet or share a picture on Facebook. Usually we would say you shouldn't send any type of message between the times of 11 p.m. and 5 a.m., especially if alcohol is involved, but we are going to leave that for you to decide. We all know what content is worthy and what is not. If you are a pastor of a church, a decade-old spring break photo is probably not the best piece of content to share online, or ever. If you're trying to portray a professional image, tweets about what you're having for lunch for three months running are not worthy of you.

- **Don't hard-sell people**—This is the more important thing not to do on social media and while promoting your brand in the public sphere. Imagine walking into a networking event, and the first thing you hear from a person is about his product or service. Individuals want to build relationships before being sold a type of product or service. Start with a conversation and work into the sales funnel.

11

Measuring Success: You Like Me, You Really Like Me!

So far we have dealt with building your personal brand and understanding the intricacies of telling your personal brand story, through blogging, Facebook, LinkedIn, Twitter, and a number of other tools. You're now busily building your personal brand online, taking advantage of everything these tools have to offer your professional growth. But how do you know if it's working? You need to measure the overall effectiveness of your personal brand on the consuming public. This is called metrics, analytics, and return on investment (ROI).

In short, you need to know the numbers.

The "numbers" define the success of a brand. In any company (large or small), the numbers drive strategy, creative thinking, marketing development, and goal orientation toward the company brand. Think of numbers in any sporting event. A score defines the winner of the event. The score must be defined and measured to reach a given outcome. In sports, the winner is the individual who scores the most points. The more you score, the better your chances of winning an event (unless you're a golfer). The same concepts apply to personal branding.

A score in a personal branding campaign can be defined as numbers, followers, friends on Facebook, blog posts, engagement with fans, and so on. The more engagement you have with your followers and peers, the more success you will have with your personal brand strategy. Everything in life needs to be measured, scrutinized, and changed to be successful. As people, we lean on the concept of change to define how and where to focus our energy. If we are not changing or adapting to the world, it is harder to make waves in the consuming public.

We don't want to go all "live your best life now" prosperity guru on you, but measuring your personal brand is crucial to its success. If you are involved in any type of business role, you understand the importance of measurement. You measure a balance sheet. You track the shipping routes of a transportation company to adjust timing and ship packages on time. You develop measurable systems to track your close rate through the sales funnel.

Your personal branding campaign is another marketing campaign. The training, planning, and development lead to a set of results about the success of your campaign. The measurement system you use helps you identify whether you're winning or losing in the world of personal branding.

Why Should You Measure

Say you have a huge week on your blog, Facebook, and Twitter pages. Your traffic is through the roof. Congratulations! Your follower and friend counts are growing, and people are congratulating you on your awesomeness.

@edeckers: People never congratulate me on being awesome.

@kyleplacy: Fine. Congratulations on being awesome.

You think, "They're right. I *am* awesome. My personal brand is going to be the deciding factor in my ability to accomplish my dreams."

Good for you. You deserve it. We definitely pat you on the back. But let's back up for a minute. Do you know what the trigger was for that growth? Do you have any idea what action you took to direct the type of response that helped build your brand? If you do, you might want to repeat the action and get that boost in social media and Internet traffic again.

Finding that nugget of info that spiked traffic or that one post that sparked your readers' interest can be tricky. When you understand what works and what doesn't, you can build on multiple measures of influence and promotion to supercharge the growth of your personal brand.

What Should You Measure?

There are plenty of metrics you should measure in accordance with your personal blog. We could expound upon our ideas of what you should measure, but we decided to consult another personal branding expert, Chad Levitt, author of the popular "New Sales Economy" blog (http://newsaleseconomy.com). Chad's blog focuses on how Sales 2.0 and Social Media can help you connect, create more opportunities, and increase your business. Levitt writes regularly for the "Personal Branding" blog (www.personalbrandingblog.com) and shared his expertise on what to measure when building your personal brand.

Reach

> Reach is fairly self-explanatory, but it is the amount of people you are connected to on your social networks. How many people are you connected to on Twitter, Facebook, LinkedIn, your blog, and other blogs? It is the sum total of all your connections on every social network.
>
> —Chad Levitt

Whether you talk about friends, followers, or connections, you need to understand the difference between quality and quantity. Some argue for quality—just a few great friends—whereas others argue for quantity—the more the merrier—but you need to strike a balance between the two.

Quality Versus Quantity

You might be skeptical of the whole "quantity is extremely valuable" debate. However, it does make sense in the old marketing world. The more people you have connected to a brand, the more valuable your brand becomes. It does make complete sense to an extent—but only a small extent.

You can look at quality versus quantity in two ways according to another personal brand genius, Dan Schwabel (www.personalbrandingblog.com). "Quantity opens doors. Quality opens wallets."[1]

The quantity of your followers on your social profiles is important because you are building a network of people who can help extend the reach of your message. It's true that quantity opens doors; the more people reading your message online, the better the chances of your message being spread across the Internet. But keep in mind that quantity isn't the only metric—or even an accurate one—to measure the influence that your personal brand has on the public. (You see this idea play out again and again in this chapter.)

The quality of your network is where you can actually start figuring out if your efforts at personal branding are successful. When you measure quality, you find out if your brand moves your audience—the quantity in this discussion—to action. An *action* can be anything from retweeting your post, sharing the message on Facebook, commenting on your blog, or simply spreading your message. The quality of your network is the difference between mass communication and one-to-one conversations.

Let's say you have 120 followers on your Twitter account, and you have the opportunity to share an extremely important message through the Twittersphere. If you have a larger network (quantity), say, 20,000 followers, you have the ability to reach more people with the initial conversation. People take notice of individuals who have larger personal networks.

Visibility

> Your personal brand visibility is made up of your search engine ranking and how **many eyeballs physically see your content each day.**
>
> —Chad Levitt

What is your search engine ranking? Basically, it's your ranking on Google, Yahoo!, Bing, and any other search engine. It's where your website appears in the

---

1. www.personalbrandingblog.com/the-quantity-vs-quality-debate-revisited/.

different search engine results when a keyword is searched. It's safe to say that if you're ranked high on Google (you appear on the first page), you're doing well!

Remember, your search engine rank varies based on the different topics on your blog. Erik may rank first for "humor blog indiana" but rank thirteenth for "humor blog." Erik has to decide which keywords best promote his personal brand story. Determining which keywords are valuable involves using Google Analytics to measure how many people have clicked to your blog/website from search engines. But remember, the more you focus your blog content, the higher you are going to rank for a specific keyword.

@edeckers: Four years ago, my blog ranked #1 for "animal fart gene."

@kyleplacy: That sounds about right.

As you have probably already gathered, your visibility depends on your reach. It is safe to say that the better the quantity and quality of your network, the more visibility you'll have. Whether you share keyword-rich blog content or thoughtful tweets on Twitter, visibility depends on your content and where you share it. The more reach and visibility your brand has, the greater the chances of your followers spreading your brand message.

Influence

> Influence is a measure of how much power you have on the Internet. Influence is a byproduct of reach and visibility. It is important to take into account all systems in order to measure influence.
>
> —Chad Levitt

This idea of influence has been circulating for years and has been debated over and over again. The notion of influence is nebulous and difficult to define. Because it's more than simply the number of followers and friends you have, you need to define your influence based on your objectives.

Measuring Influence

What does it mean to be "influential" in your online community? What does it mean to push your followers and friends to action in accordance with your personal brand plan? Brian Solis, a thought leader in the world of social currency, defines influence as follows:

Influence is the ability to cause desirable and measurable actions and outcomes.[2]

Chapter 12, "How to Network: Hello, My Name Is...," talks at length about promotion, but the idea of influence needs to be defined based on your objectives. At a basic level, influence is the percentage of people who act upon a specific call to action. At an even more basic level, influence is the number of people who do what you ask of them.

A group of researchers from Northwestern University developed an algorithm that measures the influence of Twitter users.[3] By following different tweets, researchers have been able to prove that influence on social networks is no longer defined only by the overall quantity of your network but also by the quality of the information shared.

Many would say Ashton Kutcher (@aplusk) has more influence than Kyle in the world of social media based strictly on audience size. At the writing of this book, Kyle has 25,390 followers on Twitter, and Ashton has more than 11 million followers. (We rounded Ashton's number down so Kyle wouldn't feel bad about himself.) We are talking about an extreme gap. But who has more influence? It all depends on the subject matter and the goal.

It is easy to assume that if Ashton Kutcher tweets about entertainment or the next red carpet party, he is going to have more influence than Kyle. Ashton is going to get a larger number of people retweeting, sharing, and commenting on his thoughts because he's a celebrity, and that's his element. But if Kyle were to tweet something about the tech industry in Indianapolis, he would have more influence than Ashton.

This is an important distinction: Influence is not just a raw measure of fame. Your influence is based on your ability to inspire your followers to take action. Not anyone and everyone on Twitter, just your followers.

You create your personal brand story to increase your influence within your network. Whether you influence a room at a networking event or get multiple retweets from a blog post, the influence you have depends on where you focus your content and create change.

You can also measure your network's actions based on the number of visitors your blog receives: The more visitors, the more highly valued your content is. If one of the goals in your personal branding campaign is to increase traffic to your blog, you can measure progress and growth to see if you meet that goal. We discuss

---

2. www.briansolis.com/2010/09/exploring-and-defining-influence-a-new-study/.
3. www.pulseofthetweeters.com.

measuring yourself with Google Analytics later in this chapter, but it also helps to measure against your competitors. You can gauge what content is right, wrong, or indifferent to your followers and your competitor's followers.

To show you how to measure and track the change in visitors, we measured the website traffic of Jason Falls of Social Media Explorer (www.socialmediaexplorer.com), and Erik's co-author on *No Bullshit Social Media*, using Compete.com. You can use this tool to get a general idea of how your traffic compares to a competitor's traffic. Compete.com is a paid tool, but it enables you to do some basic searches like this. (It's not completely accurate in terms of actual numbers, but it's very useful for watching trends, peaks, and valleys.)

Figure 11.1 shows Jason's level of influence in terms of traffic to his website. It fluctuates in terms of the size of traffic, but you can get an idea of how well he performs. A little more research by reading his blog posts may help you figure out why it's up or down.

Figure 11.1   *Compete.com helps in measuring influence with individuals in your industry. It's not completely accurate but it's useful for measuring trends.*

 Tip

When you start reaching 60,000 to 70,000 unique visitors per month, you are doing a great job at positioning your personal brands. Congratulations, Jason!

Let's be clear. We are not saying that *only* major amounts of traffic show influence. You can spam the system to get a ton of clicks that are not worth more than the penny in your pocket. You must consider all metrics when measuring influence. After you use Compete.com to measure traffic against your competitors, try other tools (Google Analytics) to show click-through rates from social media sites and the amount of time an individual spends on your page. Remember, influence changes based on each campaign, so be sure to adjust your goals and expectations accordingly.

How Should You Measure?

From Facebook to Twitter to your own blog, each networking site and tool provides opportunities to measure your effectiveness. Armed with this information, you can then measure your effectiveness—and possibly influence—across the entire Internet.

Measuring Your Blogging Effectiveness

Remember, the blog is the central point of all content on the Internet. It is the hub of your social media branding strategy and the place where stories are told and your personal brand is built from the ground up. You need to know how to measure your effectiveness as a writer and content distributor. You must understand what posts are the most effective and what content your followers and network like and appreciate.

A blog is most effective when you monitor five extremely important metrics that help measure your personal brand influence:

- **Number of backlinks**—A backlink is basically a link that goes back to your site from an outside site. The more backlinks you have, the higher your site ranks on the search engines. That's because search engines such as Google measure a site's credibility (and therefore, rank) based on the number of backlinks. At their simplest, backlinks can come from other authors and readers via their own blog or by leaving a comment on someone else's blog and linking back to your own. Think of them as footnotes in a research paper. If Erik writes a post reacting to a post by Kyle, Erik links to Kyle's post to give him credit for the original content.

Note

Backlinks used to be a major part of search engine optimization (SEO) to help your blog rise to the top of the ranks. Because of Google's Panda update in 2011, backlinks are not as important to SEO as they were. However, we still think they're important to measuring your blog's overall effectiveness because it's a measure of how many people think your site is worth linking to.

- **Number of posts**—No one agrees on the effectiveness of posting several times during a day. The Internet gods have not laid down the law on how often you should post, but the consensus is that more often is better. Once a week is a bare minimum, but unless you're part of a media company, several times a day is going to be counterproductive because you presumably have other work you could be doing.
- **Number of comments**—Your blog's influence is directly tied to the number of comments your posts receive. When a user comments on your blog, it's like it justifies your existence and efforts. The commenter is saying that your content was worth taking the time to develop a response to and sharing with the community. (Either that or they just want to be mean and bad mouth you.) However, the reverse is not true: A lack of comments does not necessarily mean your post was bad or not worthwhile.
- **Number of feed readers**—Chapter 3, "Blogging: Telling Your Story," talked about FeedBurner as a valuable tool to let people subscribe to your blog. The number of FeedBurner readers can be a metric of your blog's success. If your blog's feed readers increase, you can say your blog has been successful.
- **Number of visitors**—This is self-explanatory: If your blog has visitors, you have some influence and are compelling people to come and read your posts. Generally, the more visitors a blog has, the more influential it is.

The best way to measure and track all this data is with analytics software. We particularly like Google Analytics, which is an application that helps you measure the effectiveness of your blog, but it's not the only system available. It's just the one we like the best. Google Analytics gives you information about the following:

- Which referring sites send you the best traffic
- Which visitors are most likely to subscribe to your email list
- Which keywords have the highest click-through rating
- Which articles have the lowest bounce rate

Using Google Analytics for Your Blog

Google Analytics can be an extremely powerful tool to increase the effectiveness of your personal brand.

- **The Google price tag**—This is the best part: It's free!

- **Usability of the application**—Google Analytics is easy to use. Unlike other analytics platforms, Google Analytics is easy to implement to your blog. There's no need for development support (who wants that anyway?), and even you, the beginner, can start to collect data that can help you. For more information, check out Michael Miller's book *Google Analytics in 10 Minutes a Day*.

- **Unbelievable amount of data**—Google Analytics organizes gobs and gobs of data at your fingertips. The system is extremely comprehensive and lets you track all forms of information from visitors or bounce rates. Although it may seem like too much data, you can pick and choose which pieces you want to look at and create a dashboard of just the pieces you want to see.

 Note

A bounce rate is the percentage of visits where the visitor enters your blog and exits on the same page without visiting or clicking any other pages on the site in between.

- **Conversion tracking**—Google Analytics generates plenty of results, but one of the more important features is conversion tracking. *Conversion tracking* helps you measure the effectiveness of your calls to action. A *call to action* is an action you want a visitor to take, like buying a product or signing up for a newsletter. You can track and cross-reference that information against other factors on your site.

  For example, a consultant can use conversion tracking to track the visitors to her blog, the campaign they follow, and how they happened upon the site. She can learn that visitors who find her through Google or Yahoo! are twice as likely to sign up for a newsletter as those who come from Twitter. This means she should focus more energy into getting additional visitors from Google and Yahoo! and cut back on the amount of time she spends bringing in people from Twitter.

- **Tweaking for success**—There's only one reason to use Google Analytics to gather all this data: to tweak your site and your content to create a better user experience. No matter what tweaks are made to your site, you can see what happened based on the changes you made. If Kyle uploads new content and switches around his ads, he can instantly see whether the new positions are more or less effective. From there, he can decide whether to move them back or leave them in their new place.

Setting Up a Google Analytics Account

Before you can use Google Analytics, you need to set up your account.

When you go to the Google Analytics website (www.google.com/analytics), you are asked to access Google Analytics with a big blue button. Click the Sign Up Now button, which is located directly beneath the blue Access button. Clicking this takes you to a page where you can sign in with your Google account. If you have not set up a Gmail or Google account, be sure to do this first. If you followed the directions for FeedBurner in Chapter 3, or if you already have a Gmail, Google Docs, or Picasa account, sign in with that account.

In the next window, provide Google with the URL of the site you want to analyze. As shown in Figure 11.2, fill out the remaining data, including country and time zone, and provide your contact information. After you provide the necessary information to Google, you are given a block of code. Copy the code, and then sign in to your blog.

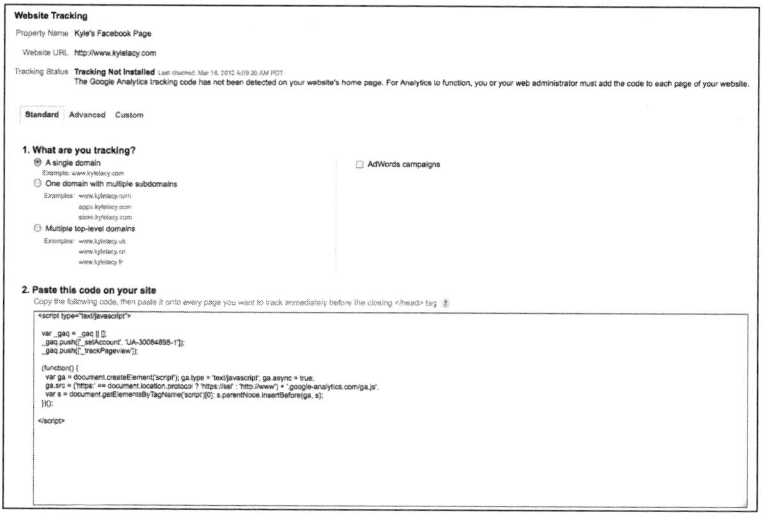

Figure 11.2   *Be sure you have the correct information on hand to fill out Google Analytics quickly and easily.*

Installing Google Analytics

Now that you have set up your account, you need to install the analytics code into your blog. By installing the necessary code, you give Google Analytics permission to pull data from your site and organize it in the analytics dashboard. Most blogs have plug-ins or easy ways to install Google Analytics. WordPress has more than 250 different easy-to-install plug-ins for Google Analytics. Kyle prefers Google Analytics for WordPress, while Erik uses Ultimate Google Analytics on his professional site. By using a plug-in on your WordPress account, you can change the setting for the Google Analytics account in your WordPress dashboard. You can also just hand-install the analytics code in your site's CSS code, but this is a little easier.

With the exception of a WordPress.com blog, most blog platforms have instructions on how to install Google Analytics code on your blog. (WordPress.com doesn't allow Google Analytics on its site, but it has its own basic analytics package.) Find those instructions on your blog platform, and follow them. We wish we could tell you more, but with more than 40 blog platforms, we can't run through every platform.

 Note

Remember the difference between WordPress.com and WordPress.org from Chapter 3? WordPress.org is where YOU host the blog on YOUR server; WordPress.com is where THEY host it on their own server. You can still put Google Analytics on a WordPress.org blog.

Getting an Overview of Your Website Performance

You are well on your way to data bliss. Your Google Analytics platform is ready to provide you with information and data discussed earlier in this section, from bounce rates to conversion tracking. However, the service may take up to 24 hours to begin pulling data from your site.

After you wait the obligatory 24 hours, you need to pull information to give you a basic overview of your site's performance. If you log in to your Google Analytics account, you are presented with a section titled Website Profiles. Find the profile you recently set up, and click the View Reports link to the right of the name. Ta-da! Your dashboard. At the top of the page is a chart (with a blue line) that gives a visual representation of site traffic over the past month. It can compare traffic over a certain period or change the data to show page views. Immediately beneath the chart is the site usage area, which gives information on everything from visits to page views. For definitions of terms in the Google Analytics dashboard, refer to Table 11.1.

Table 11.1 Google Analytics Vocabulary

Visits	How many visits there were to your page. A visit is defined as a page view when that user has viewed no other page on your site in the past 30 minutes.
Pageviews	How many times the pages on your site have been viewed.
Pages/visit	How many pages, on average, users view when they come to your site.
Bounce rate	What percentage of users left after viewing only one page on your site.
Average Time on Site	How long each user spent on your site.
New Visits	What percentage of your users have not visited your site before.

Below the Site Usage area is the Visitors Overview graph, which shows how many people have visited your site. The number is usually lower than the visits statistic because many people will be repeat visitors to your site.

You can tell from Figure 11.3—the dashboard from Erik's company page—that there is a ton of information to take in and analyze. And on the left sidebar of the dashboard window (see Figure 11.4), you can click any of the links to read a more detailed report on the information at hand. It is up to you to spend the time to fully realize the potential of Google Analytics. Google made some big improvements to Google Analytics between the first and second editions of this book, making it even more useful and powerful for both personal branding and company branding.

Google Analytics also tracks users hitting your site from referring sites, like Facebook, Twitter, and LinkedIn, that link to your blog. When you share a link on a social networking site (or someone shares it for you) and an individual clicks on the link to go to the blog post, that is an example of a *referring site*. Through the development and measurement of Twitter, Facebook, and LinkedIn, you can increase your referring sites and create a system to further your personal brand.

Measuring Your Twitter Effectiveness

Of the three social networking sites discussed in this book, Twitter is the easiest one to use to measure for your personal brand effectiveness. We are going to chalk it up to Twitter being extremely open when it comes to allowing others to build tools that help pull and organize data. Several tools have been created in the past two years to help people measure their influence. Although none of them are perfect in their measurement, they are a good gauge on how effective you are in getting your network to take certain actions.

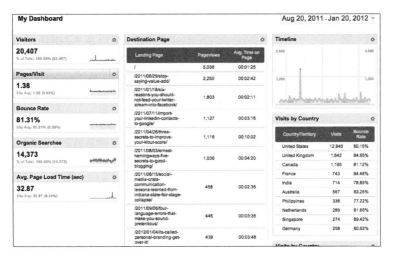

Figure 11.3   *The Google Analytics dashboard has a tantalizing amount of information for you to read and measure. This is a custom dashboard where you can choose which widgets appear on your dashboard.*

Figure 11.4   *The dashboard sidebar. This is where you can drill down to find different reports of your analytics, whether it's the country of origin, the browsers, keywords, and so on.*

Klout (www.klout.com) is a measurement system developed to help industry leaders and personal branding fanatics measure their influence online. It was the first serious measurement tool and has become the default one that most people refer to when they talk about influence measurement. One word of caution: Klout is directly tied to Twitter, as well as other social networks (LinkedIn, Google+, Facebook, Instagram, and so on). You must have a Twitter username (and other accounts) to measure your Klout. You can find plenty of things to measure by using Klout:

- **True reach**—True reach is the size of your engaged audience. This metric basically gives you an idea of how often your tweets are read, one-to-one conversations around content, and how often people add you to lists (to name a few).

- **Amplification probability**—Amplification probability is the likelihood your content will be acted upon. Klout measures your ability to be retweeted, the diversity of the people who respond to you, whether different people retweet you, and whether your tweets generate new followers.

- **Network influence**—Your network influence is the influence level of your engaged audience. This measurement is based on the influence of the people you are involved with on a daily basis.

Klout can be an extremely powerful tool in measuring your personal brand influence. Although it isn't the only way to track your reach or influence over time, it is an easy system to trend your progress. Klout can help you see if the influence of your brand increases; it is an easy-to-use scoring method to help in the progress to build your brand story.

 Note

The Twitter application HootSuite (www.hootsuite.com) pulls in Klout scores on your followers to help you determine their reach and influence in the social media world. The Gmail social media tool, Rapportive (www.rapportive.com), does too.

Other Total Influence Measurement Tools

Klout made such a splash in the last few years that other companies developed their own influence measurement tools, hoping to improve on Klout's offering and scoring system.

ProSkore (www.proskore.com) measures your reputation by looking at your Facebook, Twitter, LinkedIn, YouTube, Google+, and Klout scores, as well as your work and educational experience. You can connect with other ProSkore members and can even become a verified pro for $79 per year. The average ProSkore is approximately 20, so a score in the 40s and 50s is good. One concern is that Klout already measures the same tools that ProSkore does (Twitter, Google+, and so on), but ProSkore measures Klout and the other tools. ProSkore even lets you connect with other members and look for people who provide services you need or lets you post requests for services.

Kred (www.kred.com) is a little unusual in that it also looks at offline member-ships and activities, such as whether you're an Admirals Club Platinum member, have an advanced degree, are in Toastmasters, have a black belt in karate, or are the President of the United States. You get a score based on a possible 1,000 points. You are also given additional credit based on how someone interacts with your content, and whether someone more influential does something for you. For example, if Kyle (with 22,000+ followers) retweets one of your tweets, you get more credit than if someone with only 300 followers retweeted you.

PeerIndex (www.peerindex.com) is one of the most thorough influence measure-ment tools, looking at your authority on certain topics, your activity on Twitter, Facebook, LinkedIn, and Quora (as well as your blogs), and your audience size and their own influence. Rather than just giving you an overall, arbitrary score, it looks at the resonance rank within eight benchmark topics, including arts/media, tech-nology/Internet, sports, and politics. A PeerIndex rank of 40+ says you're in the top 10% of that community, and 90+ puts you at the top .1%.

All these tools are an acceptable way to measure your influence—PeerIndex has the advantage because it looks at a number of different factors—but none of them are perfect. We prefer Klout because it's more widely used than the others but like PeerIndex because it is a little more thorough and precise about what and how it measures.

Measuring Your LinkedIn Effectiveness

Of the three social networking sites, LinkedIn gives you the fewest tools to measure your brand's success. Unlike Twitter, LinkedIn doesn't provide code to allow pro-grammers to develop measurement applications. As you can see in Figure 11.5, you can measure your personal brand effectiveness on LinkedIn in a couple ways.

- **LinkedIn profile views**—A small section within your LinkedIn pro-file is the Who's Viewed My Profile section. In this section, LinkedIn identifies how many visitors have viewed your profile in a certain number of days by name, title, or industry. If you are looking for a job, the number of outside profile views you receive should be extremely important to you. The more profile views, the better for your LinkedIn profile. You can see up to five people who viewed your profile before you must pay the $29.95 per month fee. Occasionally, "free month" offers let you try it out.

- **LinkedIn network growth**—Next to the profile views section of your LinkedIn profile page is a section that lists how many connections you have and how many new people have joined your network in a given number of days. We care more about how many connections you have. If the connections list expands, it is important to measure how large your network grows. Kyle has 1,730 connections, which links him to 8,402,000 people. That means he's no more than three degrees separated from 8.4 million people, which means he can reach that many people via introductions.

- **Search results**—In the same area is a line that tells you how often you have shown up in searches over the past day. When you show up in searches, it means that your area of expertise or your personal information is of some importance to someone.

Figure 11.5 *LinkedIn provides a helpful panel giving you information on traffic and searches for your name.*

You can also refer back to Google Analytics to view how many people clicked through LinkedIn to go to your site and how many converted. Keep track of your referring sites to make sure you drive a healthy amount of users to your central location or blog.

Measuring Your Facebook Effectiveness

Facebook has a long way to go toward helping users measure their marketing effectiveness. You simply can't measure effectiveness with personal pages, apart from how many new friends you have. But you can measure effectiveness with Insights on your brand's fan page. (See Chapter 6, "Facebook: Developing a Community of Friends," for more information on when you might need a brand page.)

Now you can use the in-depth data analysis of Google Analytics with the demographic and personality tracker Facebook Insights. Using a free application called Facebook Google Analytics Tracker (www.webdigi.co.uk/blog/apps/fbgat-facebook-google-analytics-tracker or just go to http://bit.ly/wYGQpK), you can get Google Analytics working on your Facebook fan page. Now you can track visitor statistics, countries, keyword searches, and traffic sources.

You already have a Google Analytics account unless you completely ignored the entire first part of this section. (But we know you'd never do that, right?) You need to create a new domain profile in your Google Analytics account. Go to Google Analytics, and in the upper-right portion of the screen is a drop-down menu that boldly states: My Analytics Accounts. Click the drop-down, and choose Create New Account from the menu. Google takes you to a page where you need to click the Sign Up button because technically you are creating a new analytics dashboard. For the website's URL, type in **facebook.com**, and the rest of the boxes fill in for you. After you entered your name and country and accept the terms of the mighty Google Analytics, you are taken to a screen that asks, What Are You Tracking? and Paste This Code on Your Site. Ignore the information and click Save. Google Analytics takes you to your overview page, where you see http://facebook.com and your Google Analytics code displayed. You need that code, which usually looks like this: UA-18786286-1.

After setting up your Google Analytics account for your Facebook fan page, you need to create *custom images*. Now, understand that we have literally no idea what that means, but we know it works. Keep following the instructions. We're right here with you.

The people who brought you the FBGAT tool also made it easy for you to create your own custom images. Go to the Webdigi free custom image tool (http://ga.webdigi.co.uk) and fill in the information. Refer to Figure 11.6 to get a better idea of what to fill in.

- Analytics Code is the code you copied from Google Analytics that looks something this: UA-18786286-1. It is extremely important that you copy this exactly as it looks for Google Analytics to sync with Facebook Insights.

- Domain on Analytics is the domain name you used to create your Google Analytics account. If you followed the previous directions, we used facebook.com.

- Page Link is a name that helps you track your page on Google Analytics. We recommend naming it after the title of the page, like **/contact_form**.

- Page Title is only for your reference. Name this whatever you like as long as you can remember the name.

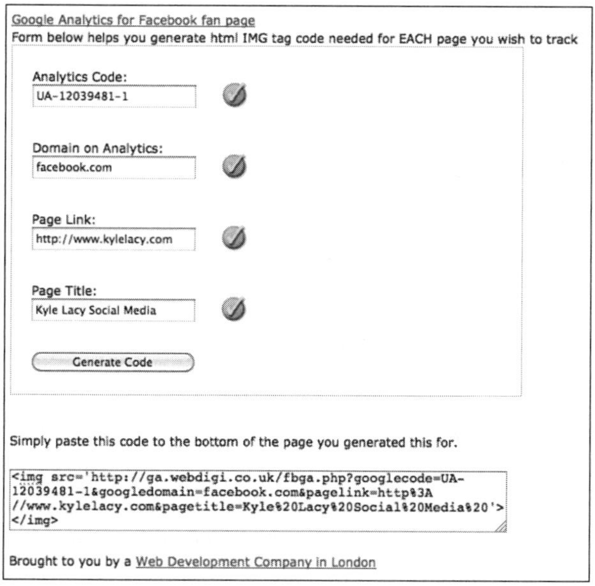

Figure 11.6   *Creating your own custom images is easy with the FBGAT tool.*

The beautiful thing about this free tool is that it helps you along the way. After you fill in the necessary custom image tags, you can click the Generate Code button. You need to copy this code to paste into your Facebook fan page.

✉ *Note*

You must generate a separate code for each fan page you want to track.

Now the only thing you need to do is add the code to your Facebook fan page. To add HTML (which is the language the code is designed in), you must use

an application such as Static FBML (www.facebook.com/apps/application.
php?id=4949752878). Paste the code into the page you want to track using Static
FMBL (either the top or bottom of the page), and that is all there is to it. After
24 hours, you should have the tracking and data you need in the world of Facebook
measurement.

 Tip

If you need additional help installing the Google Analytics system into your
Facebook fan page, try our friends at Facebook by going to this link: http://
on.fb.me/fbookhelp.

Measuring Your YouTube Effectiveness

YouTube has its own analytics tool, which lets you see not only how many views
your videos have had, but who saw them—geography, demographics, and technology used—as well as subscriber growth, likes/dislikes, and even traffic sources.

To get to your analytics, do one of the following:

- Click your name on the upper-right corner, click Video Manager in the
  drop-down menu, and then click the Analytics button on the gray bar.
  Figure 11.7 shows you which button to click.

- Go to your channel, select a video, and then click the Analytics button
  associated with that video. You can do this if you followed the previous
  step, too.

Figure 11.7   *The YouTube Video Manager bar. Click the Analytics button on the far
right. (That picture in the middle is Erik's friend and TV news reporter, Dick Wolfsie,
who has a 3-foot boa constrictor crawling inside his jacket as he interviews Jack Hanna,
circa 1984.)*

By examining a particular video's reports, you can learn a few important factors
about how people reacted to it.

- Go to the Audience Retention section (under Views) and watch your video with the audience retention graph. You can see if there are any spots where people abandon the video after a certain time. For example, if you see a spike of departures at a particular point in a video, you can either edit the video to remove the offending section, reshoot the video, or just know not to do it next time. Figure 11.8 shows the audience retention graph of a video Erik took at the 2011 Indianapolis 500 post-race press conference, after Dan Wheldon won for the second time.

Figure 11.8 *The Audience Retention screen on YouTube Analytics. You can watch your video and see when most people abandon the video.*

- Check the Traffic Sources to see where people are coming from. In Figure 11.9, you can see the traffic sources for the Dan Wheldon video. YouTube suggested videos are those videos that appear to the right of a video you're watching.

YouTube's traffic sources tells you where most people found a particular video. YouTube suggested video is always a big source, but YouTube search can tell you what people were looking for when they found your video.

YouTube search is an important piece to measure, especially considering YouTube is the second largest search engine in the world. Knowing what terms people were using when they found you can help you optimize future videos.

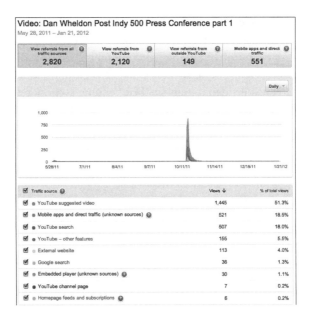

Figure 11.9 *Dan Wheldon died on October 16, 2011, in a crash at the Las Vegas Speedway. As a result, more people went to YouTube to find more information about him, and Erik's video saw more views on that day than the actual day Dan won the Indianapolis 500.*

If want to reach people with videos, especially embedding them on your blogs, you can get only so much information from Google Analytics. You need to make sure you pay attention to YouTube Analytics as well.

Nine Tools to Use for Measurement

There is so much content and data to measure and track in the world of social media that it is hard for us as individuals to keep track of it all. You can use the following tools in addition to Google Analytics, Facebook Insights, and others already covered. By using different tools and systems to track the information, it becomes easier over the long haul to become successful in this world of instant communication. Some of these are fairly accurate, others aren't as important, but they sometimes add a boost to your ego.

1. **Twitter Grader** (www.twittergrader.com) is a site that enables you to track, measure, and increase your influence in the world of Twitter. By entering your Twitter name, the system pulls data for your account. You can track the history of your follower growth or the amount of tweets that were sent. You can also track your influence among your specific location. It ranks you based on influence.

2. **Website Grader** (www.websitegrader.com) is brought to you by the same people who created Twitter Grader, HubSpot Marketing. Website Grader enables you to enter your website with a competitor and receive a report that has information such as blog analysis, blog grade, recent blog articles, Google index pages, and readability level. It also helps you optimize your content from headings to images. It is a comprehensive and worthwhile report.

3. **Twitalyzer** (www.twitalyzer.com) is an intense Twitter management, measuring, and monitoring tool that enables you to do a ton of different things in the world of Twitter. This includes automatic daily updates, full data export, email support, weekly email reports, phone support, custom URL shortener, and multiple-account tracking.

4. **Google PageRank** is an algorithm Google uses to assign numerical weighting to each element of a website with the purpose to "measure" its relative importance with other sites. Basically, it's how important your site is. To check your Google PageRank, check out the PR Checker PageRank tool at www.prchecker.info/check_page_rank.php. Just enter your URL, and the tool generates your PageRank.

5. **MyWebCareer** (www.mywebcareer.com) is a free system that works much like Klout and PeerIndex. It plugs into your Twitter, LinkedIn, Facebook, and Quora networks and then gives you a Career Score out of a possible 1,000. It also measures your reputation and search engine ranking. You can plug it into Facebook or LinkedIn for your primary data source (we recommend LinkedIn because you need to develop your professional brand) and even get a visual representation of your LinkedIn and Facebook networks.

6. **Keyword Position Monitoring Report Service** (www.kpmrs.com) is a way to check the rankings for a domain for a particular set of keywords or phrases. Thousands of tools can help you accomplish this task. Surf to Google and search for **free keyword rank checker**. After finding a suitable tool, track the progress and ranking for your particular keywords or phrases.

7. **Bitly** (www.bitly.com) offers several measuring and tracking implications. You can track single domains, multiple domains, advanced dashboard for data layout, real-time data analytics feed, and customer support. Bitly measures how many people click a specific link, and how many people you get to click that link, as shown in Figure 11.10.

8. **HootSuite** (www.hootsuite.com) is a tool that has been talked about at length throughout this book, much like Bitly. HootSuite offers an

analytics suite that helps you track links and the Klout scores of your
followers. The system is not as robust as a PostRank, but it still offers
information that is extremely valuable to the user. HootSuite has a free
version and a fee version, for the hardcore and professional users.

Figure 11.10   *Bitly shows you how many people click a link you create, and how
many people click YOUR link. For this link, 246 people clicked the link, and Erik sent
91 of them from his own Twitter account.*

9. **Twylah** (www.twylah.com) is an extremely valuable tool to aggregate
    your tweets about a particular topic, showing you (and anyone else)
    what you're talking about. It creates a magazine-like page for you based
    on those topics. You can even add and delete certain topics, so you can
    present your best image. We both had a chance to check out this tool
    while it was still in early beta, and Erik uses it quite frequently, sending
    people to his Twylah page (www.twylah.com/edeckers) instead of his
    Twitter page.

Effectively Measuring Your Personal Brand

We want to give you the necessary tools to empower you on the road to personal
branding success. The tools may seem complicated or difficult to use, but they are
intended for use by regular people, and they can empower your personal brand
story. Our heroes Allen, Beth, Carla, and Darrin are going to use the systems provided to measure their personal brand effectiveness.

Your main goal throughout this entire process is threefold:

- **Understand Facebook Insights**—Refer to Chapter 6, "Facebook:
  Developing a Community of Friends," if you need a refresher on
  Facebook Insights. This tool is briefly mentioned in this chapter
  because of the powerful force it has when combined with Google
  Analytics.

- **Use Google Analytics**—Spend some time to understand the tool of Google Analytics. A ton of information and data are processed through this system, but you need to understand the implications that the data has on your personal brand. Spend some time perfecting your understanding. If you need more help, do not hesitate to ask.

- **Use one system for each tool**—You have an overall system of Google Analytics, but you need to use at least one system for each social network. For Twitter, you have Klout or Twitalyzer, and for Facebook you have Facebook Insights. Unfortunately, you have to make up the measurement and analytics for LinkedIn, but we believe you can do it. We like Klout for a big picture view of influence, but you should look at each tool individually.

Overall, it is about the information you glean from the site and not the tool you use. Data is the most important thing you can obtain from the Internet because the numbers and metrics will tell you how influential your personal brand is (or is becoming). Check and track the data to make the most out of the time you have spent developing your personal brand story.

How Can Our Heroes Use Analytics and Measurement?

In the other chapters, our heroes have used our tools and ideas in different ways. However, for measurement and analytics, they each need to measure the same thing: how many people visit their different profiles on Facebook, LinkedIn, and their blog, where they come from, and what they look at.

One thing each of our heroes can do is promote blog posts on their different networks using Bitly and Google campaign codes. A post can be promoted via LinkedIn, Twitter, and Facebook, but using different headlines or published at different times of day as a way to see which are the most effective. Then, depending on how well a certain type of headline performs or finding the best time of day to promote the post, our heroes can improve on that.

They can also use individual Bitly links to promote their posts to specific hiring managers or decision makers and then track whether those managers have opened those links.

Finally, they can use the map function on Google Analytics to see if people from their chosen cities—again, hiring managers and decisions makers—have visited those particular links.

Even though each of the four heroes has different career goals for their personal branding efforts, they can use measurement and analytics in the same way.

Do's and Don'ts for Analytics and Measurement

- **Do measure the metrics that give you actionable data** about your social media activity, such as the posts that get the most click-throughs.

- **Do focus on metrics that help you determine your influence in your network**, like visits to your blog or number of Twitter followers or LinkedIn connections.

- **Do focus your blog's keywords** on those that give you the best visibility on Internet search terms. That could be your name, job title, or subject of your blog.

- **Don't use every measurement tool on the Internet**. Focus on just the ones that are easy to use and give you the results you need to improve your personal brand.

- **Don't measure every metric available to you.** Figure out what it is you need to know to determine your effectiveness and ignore the rest.

- **Don't obsess about your numbers.** Check once a day or even every couple of days. You don't need to focus on your numbers hour after hour. Remember, this is about trends, not actual figures. As Erik likes to say, "You want the little line to go up, not down. If it goes down, make it go up."

Analytics Tips in 140 Characters

- Don't take it too seriously. —@slicklaroo

- True influence is measured by the conversations you're having, not the # of followers, Klout score, etc. —@paigeworthy

- Use Klout's metrics, not its number. Make sure things trend upward. Pay attention to unfollows only if you follow them, too. —@allisonlcarter

- Even if you don't analyze the data now, make sure to set up the mechanisms to compile it. —@prebynski

- Drive traffic and check measurements on specific landing pages. —@lorraineball

- If you want to see how influential you are on social media, try helping someone else raise money for their cause. —@charlesbivona

- Klout is a viable all-in-one metric. I also like followers per tweet sent ratio. And LinkedIn profile visits. —@JayBaer

- Use Netvibes for a listening station. Only a human review can show you sentiment and influence. —@MariaDuron

- Klout can provide rough figures, but I don't worry about small score changes. There may be issues if your score seriously drops long term. —@joshhumble

- Be concerned more with people and productive, targeted engagement—not purely stats from machines.

- Test various SM measuring tools. Cross check for mean averages indicating RTs, mentions, etc., and find your most effective time of day.

- Keep current on your measuring tools' latest algorithmic changes and updates, and how they can impact your reported influence.

III

Promoting Your Brand in the Real World

How to Network: Hello, My Name Is...

We've spent the previous eleven chapters talking about social media and how wonderful it is. Most social media books stop right there: It's wonderful and awesome, and everyone should use it.

We agree, except it doesn't stop there. Social media is only the tip of the networking iceberg. There are personal interactions to be made and given. It's the personal touch that truly makes networking, and thus personal branding, so valuable.

You're doing pretty well so far. You've set up a blog, started using Twitter, created a Facebook account (or at least took all the inappropriate photos off your existing one), and are on your way to becoming a LinkedIn power user. Now you're going to leave the comfort of your computer and go out into the real world.

It's one thing to create your personal brand as an online persona. But you need to take the next step and get your brand out into the real world so you can leverage the brand you've been creating online.

Meeting people in the real world is important to creating your personal brand. It's so important, in fact, that we're breaking the traditional computer book role and spending the last few chapters in real life. After all, your personal brand isn't worth anything if real people don't get to react to it.

You're also going to invent or reinvent yourself into someone who speaks in public (Chapter 13, "Public Speaking: We Promise You Won't Die"), publishes articles in print publications (Chapter 14, "Getting Published: I'm an Author!"), and finds a job (Chapter 15, "Personal Branding: Using What You've Learned to Land Your Dream Job"). But for you to do those things, you need to actually meet people face to face to deepen those relationships further.

Ultimately, the human connection is what's going to propel your personal brand to great success. Similarly, a lack of human connection is going to cause it to fail.

In our story from Chapter 1, "Welcome to the Party," Erik ultimately created and grew his personal network, not solely because of his online work. Rather, it grew because of his face-to-face networking and meeting people at networking events and conferences. Sharing stories, knowledge, and experiences. Getting to know people as people, not as avatars and handles. Erik had been networking for years before that in his different roles, but this was his first time in a new city, in a new industry, and in a situation where he didn't know anyone who could be helpful to him.

Kyle has built his network the same way: by meeting people and learning from them directly, by spending his *days building research for ExactTarget and his evenings writing. He travels to other cities to network via conferences and client work, and he always tries to find time to meet with people from his online network to include them in his real-world network.*

Networking is not easy. It's hard work and time-consuming, but it's also a lot of fun. It's a great way to see your city and meet people, and it's the best way to develop the kinds and number of relationships that will lead to great opportunities for you later.

Some of you may disagree with that last sentence, thinking it's enough to connect with people on the Big Three—LinkedIn, Facebook, and Twitter—but it truly isn't. Think about the people you know online and the people you know in real life. Which of them would you rather do business with? Which of them would you rather help when they asked? Chances are, it's your real-life connections and friends, not the people you have never met, even if you are connected in several places, who you want to help more.

To build your personal brand, you need to network in person in a variety of situations and settings beyond the social networking sites.

Why Should I Bother Networking?

In Chapter 2 ("How Do You Fit in the Mix?"), we discussed how you tell your personal story. But telling someone your story doesn't mean you're now their best buddy, and that you can just call them up and ask them to do you a big favor. Far from it. They won't remember you within a few days because you were one of eight people they were introduced to, and you haven't done anything to stand out from the crowd.

That's why you need to network with people: so you can develop the deeper relationships that lead to new business opportunities, job openings, and even collaborative partnerships like writing a book together.

A Networking Case Study: Starla West

Starla West is a corporate image coach with clients all over the United States. She has a great story about how long-term networking and relationship building have paid off for her, even after she left the industry where she built those relationships.

If we've heard it once, we've heard it a million times: Effective networking is all about farming, not hunting. The goal is to cultivate relationships and gain trust. If we network only when we have to, we are way behind the game, as the full benefits of networking are most often realized after solid relationships are developed and maintained over time. I have to admit I never fully understood this until I left the corporate world to pursue my entrepreneurial dreams. Prior to starting my own business, I was a consultant for various financial institutions throughout the United States. My job was twofold: 1) help my clients obtain more than their fair share of new customers (bank executives), and 2) help them keep these customers for as long as they possibly could.

To effectively assist my clients, it was crucial that I quickly gained (and maintained) the trust and support of my clients' executive teams. Needless to say, day in and day out I called upon my relationship building skills to "win over" these bank executives. Over time, these relationships eventually strengthened. At the end of my eight years as their consultant, these executives were more than just business acquaintances; they were now my friends.

How did I know that? Well, late on a Thursday evening, as I comfortably sat with my feet propped up on the sofa, I sent an email to my clients announcing I was leaving the company and starting my own business. After pressing Send, I closed my laptop, turned, and placed my feet on the floor. No joke, no exaggeration! Within 30 seconds, my phone rang. I thought, "Wow! I just sent that!"

I answered the call. It was the senior vice president and director of marketing for a large client of mine in Florida. I assumed he was calling to wish me good luck, but I couldn't have been more wrong. He was calling to share his marketing knowledge and advertising expertise with me. He wanted to help catapult my business into full operation as quickly as possible by helping me develop a marketing plan. I couldn't believe it!

This extremely busy man who is next to impossible to catch on the phone was graciously giving me two full hours of his time and expert advice, and I didn't even ask for it!

Over the next 24 hours, I received phone call after phone call and email after email from clients who wanted to help. This is when it really hit me: Networking is simply relationship building. If cultivated and nurtured correctly, these relationships develop into lifelong friendships that include a healthy balance of giving and receiving.

The Rules of Networking

If you understand a few basic rules and practices that guide networking, you'll always know how to act when meeting new people. We have learned these rules over the years, after being involved in various Chambers of Commerce, attending small networking groups, and being regular members of Rainmakers.[1]

It's Not About You

This may be the most important rule of networking: You are not networking to help you; you are networking to help the other person. As counterintuitive as this may seem—after all, you're trying to build your personal brand—this is the best way to succeed in networking.

You have to understand that the best way to succeed at nearly any kind of business or social venture is to have it be all about the other person—to do something nice for other people or add value to their lives.

This is what's known as Giver's Gain, or the idea that by helping other people, others will want to help you in return. The philosophy was first espoused by Ivan Misner, the founder of Business Network International, or BNI, a network that has grown to more than 5,400 chapters worldwide.

Basically, Giver's Gain means that if you add value (give) to someone else's life, you have gained goodwill. If you add enough value to others' lives, the goodwill visited back on you will be returned many times. So, you, as the giver, gain more goodwill by being helpful than you will if you are selfish and try to keep all the opportunities to yourself.

---

1. Rainmakers is a small business networking group that started with a handful of people in Indianapolis six years ago but has expanded to more than 1,800 people spread across 70 hubs in Indiana, Kentucky, and Ohio.

In business networking terms, Giver's Gain means that if you focus on other people rather than focusing on yourself, other people will want to help you in return.

(What's especially fun to watch is two Giver's Gain proponents scramble to be the first to offer to help the other person. Of course, this can lead to complications.)

```
@kyleplacy:  I think it's my turn to buy lunch.
@edeckers:   No, I think it's my turn.
@kyleplacy:  No, I insist. I want to buy lunch. I'd like to do
             something nice for you.
@edeckers:   Sounds good. I'm in the mood for a steak.
@kyleplacy:  Wait a minute...
```

Let's be clear: Other people won't, or at least shouldn't, help you in exchange for your efforts. This is not a one-for-one exchange. Good networkers don't keep score; they don't tally up the number of times they have helped other people. They don't hold favors in reserve, refusing to help anyone or to even ask for small favors because they might need to "call in a favor" later.

This may sound a little odd to some people who work in industries where secrets are held close to the vest, where favors are doled out like candy from a Pez dispenser, and where people keep score of the number of times they've helped someone else. To these people, the phrase "Thanks, I owe you one" is recorded in a mental notebook and kept track of.

We want you to stop thinking that way. Life is not a zero-sum game. You don't run out of opportunities to help or be helped. Believe it or not, there are enough opportunities and money to go around for everyone. But the people who fail to realize this fight and claw for every little advantage, every small sale, every victory they can win. They end up being lonely and the ones who fall the farthest in their failures when they could have been helped by the people they used up instead.

```
@kyleplacy:  Wow, that's depressing.
@edeckers:   Sorry, I was listening to The Cure.
```

It doesn't have to be that way. The whole point of this chapter is to tell you that your career—your whole life—can be successful without keeping score or hoarding favors. In fact, your career and your life will be more successful, enjoyable, and fulfilling if you embrace the Giver's Gain philosophy.

Giver's Gain Is Not Quid Pro Quo

But this adding of value is not going to (it's not even supposed to) result in an immediate returning of the favor. It might, but don't expect it. Instead, when you provide value to other people, their goodwill can and will be returned to you in any number of ways, many of which you may not even hear about for years to come. And if we have been successful in our networking and business efforts (and thus have more influence and contacts), the favor we return is going to be even bigger than the one we were given.

Here's a hypothetical example. Let's say Erik is looking for a new speaking opportunity. He mentions this to Kyle, who just happens to know someone organizing a conference in another state. Kyle calls his friend, the conference organizer, and recommends she hire Erik for her next conference, which she does.

To some people, Erik's response is obvious: Return the favor. Find Kyle a similar speaking gig. Or give Kyle a finder's fee out of his speaking fee. But that's not how Giver's Gain works.

According to Giver's Gain, Erik's response can be anything:

- In talking to the conference organizer, Erik learns that she is looking for a new job at a company Erik knows. He puts her in touch with the appropriate person, and now she has an insider's edge into the company.
- He "pays it forward" when he meets someone at the conference who needs advice on blog writing, so Erik spends some time with him answering questions.
- Erik can bring the goodwill back around to Kyle when he meets someone who says she needs social media training for 50 customer service representatives; Erik can introduce her to Kyle, who works in email and social marketing for ExactTarget.

In these cases, Erik is willing to provide this help to other people because he was helped. But let's take it a step further. Let's say this conference organizer gets the job, and in gratitude, she outsources a project to Erik, but it's one that he is not really equipped to handle.

So according to Giver's Gain, the organizer doesn't need to give the first project she gets back to Erik—although a thank-you card or email is more than appropriate. However, she should keep him in the back of her mind for the next time she can truly help him.

Similarly, Erik shouldn't expect an immediate favor in return. Rather, he should just go about his day and his life, knowing that someday the goodwill will be returned to him, even if it happens five years later when the conference organizer needs to hire a keynote speaker at an event with a nice fat speaking fee, and she calls Erik.

This is an ongoing circle of giving and receiving, and if you wait to be helped before you help someone, you'll never receive the benefits and goodwill. (It's like when our moms told us, "If you want to have a friend, you have to be a friend.") The best way to start practicing Giver's Gain is just to step into the circle and be the first one to give.

But, here's a twist on this: Your motivation can't even be that you're going to give so you will receive something in return. This isn't a cause-and-effect relationship. If you go to a networking event or enter into a new relationship thinking, "I'm going to *really* help this person because then I'll get all sorts of goodwill, and he'll do something valuable for me," you'll be disappointed.

Instead, you just help him because you want to add value to his life. You're a good person who understands that when others succeed with your help, you succeed as well. Here's an example.

Kyle met with Mark Wilkerson, a vice president at a large insurance company, and gave him some tips on how to use social media to raise more money for a charity run Mark was in charge of. This meeting turned into a relationship of breakfast meetings just to talk about "life, business, and the world of the Internet." Mark even attended one of Kyle's training sessions to learn more about how he could use social media for the charity run and his own career.

Then, without being asked or because of a sense of obligation, Mark introduced Kyle to a board member of the large financial services company. The board member ran a nonprofit as a sideline to his main business, and Kyle was given the opportunity to produce a social media strategy for that nonprofit, creating a long-term client in the process.

Why did this happen? It all started because Kyle was willing to meet with someone and give him some pointers and ideas about how to use social media to raise more money for a charity event. It could have ended there. Or Kyle could have refused to help. Or Mark could have paid Kyle for an hour of consulting, so he wouldn't be indebted to him.

Instead, Mark and Kyle got to know each other, talked about a lot of things that weren't related to business, and formed a relationship. In turn, Kyle became someone Mark likes and trusts, and that's the key.

People buy from people they like and trust. That's an age-old adage that many salespeople are now embracing as they delve into relationship sales. But the corollary on this is that people will do favors for people they like and trust.

Be Honest Online and Offline

On the Internet, you can be anything you want. You can say you're a 6'4" model from Sweden even if you're really a 5'2" poster child for childhood baldness from Chicago.

But when you meet others face to face, they see who you really are. They realize that you're not 6'4", and you have a decidedly non-Swedish accent. And that's when your reputation and your credibility go down the toilet. Today it's easy for people to find out your true identity. If you get caught in the lie, word will spread that you don't represent yourself truthfully.

If you want to enhance your personal brand, let your online persona be who you are in real life; if you want to kill it, either lie about who you are or act like a jerk in one place and a nice person in the other.

Honesty is the key. You need to be honest with who you are, what you do, and what you think and believe. Don't try to be someone that other people want you to be. Be who you really are. It sounds trite to say it; our parents said it all the time, and it sounded trite then.

But it's true: Let people accept and reject you for who you are. If others don't like you or want to connect with you, that's fine. (They don't know what they're missing; we think you're great.) But if people do like you and connect with the real you, you know it's because they truly like you.

@kyleplacy: Are you done, Mr. Rogers?

@edeckers: Hey, Kyle, did you know that you are special? There's no one in the world like you.

@kyleplacy: Cut it out.

@edeckers: You make each day a special day, just by being you.

@kyleplacy: Seriously, if you start singing, I'm leaving.

The best way to develop your personal brand is by meeting your connections in person. Arrange a one-on-one meeting at a coffee house or cafe and get to know each other. Remember, this is about forming relationships, and although you can form relationships online, they're rather fragile and unstable. A personal relationship can go much deeper, and that's where trust and liking really develop. And because we buy from people we like and trust, we're more likely to help and be helped by the people we have relationships with.

Tip

We're not advocating that you hang out with just anyone you meet online.
If you don't feel confident meeting someone, don't go. If you do meet
someone in person who you talked to online, meet in a busy public place,
like a restaurant for lunch or a coffee shop. Use common sense, and be
safe.

You're Just as Good as Everyone Else

You already got a dose of Mr. Rogers once, so hopefully that's still fresh in your
mind when we tell you not to be afraid to meet other people, even if you think
they're "above" you in status, popularity, or fame. You're just as good as they are.
The only difference between you and them is that more people know who they are.
And that's it.

There is nothing special about people you might hold in high esteem in your
industry. Sure, they may be "celebrities" in their field: They write a popular blog,
are quoted as an industry expert in the media, give keynote speeches at conferences, and then have dozens of people who scramble to talk with them for a few
minutes afterward, or even write books and sign them.

But that doesn't make them better than you. It just means they have been practicing these personal branding techniques for a few years more than you have. But
now you have the book. You know what they have been doing for the past few
years. And you can do it, too.

Think of it this way: Chris Brogan is considered one of the leaders of the social
media industry. He's written three books, one of them a *New York Times* bestseller.
He gives keynote speeches and makes quite a bit of money doing it. He has more
than 208,000 followers on Twitter, and everyone talks about him like he's Elvis.

But he's only Elvis in the social media industry. He's not actually a celebrity. When
Chris walks into Home Depot on a Saturday morning in his baggy gym shorts and
a T-shirt, the people working there don't drop everything they're doing and shriek,
"OMG, it's Chris Brogan!" People don't flock around him for his autograph when
he goes to his kids' school play. He doesn't have screaming groupies who follow
him around whenever his wife sends him to the grocery store for half-and-half.

The point is, the people Chris meets when he's outside the social media circle
couldn't care less who he is. To them, he's just another do-it-yourselfer, proud
parent, or grocery shopper. He's approachable, whether he's inside or outside the
social media environment. That's the way he likes it, too.

We asked Chris about this, and he said "I like to consider myself approachable and I'm happy to meet other people. It's how I get new ideas, hear about new developments, gain new partners, and grow my own brand."

Avoid People Who Are Unhelpful

So what do you do if you help some people, but they do nothing for you? There are plenty of people like that, unfortunately. As long as you can do something for them, they'll be your best buddy. But once you're done or you can't do anymore, you don't hear a word from them. They don't answer your emails or return your phone calls. But when they want something from you, suddenly you're the most important person in the world to them again. How do you deal with people like that?

The short answer: Quit helping them. You might think that maybe it will be different this time. This time, they're going to connect me with that vice president of marketing I've wanted to meet or connect me to the decision maker at company X so I can pitch my idea. But they never do. And when you ask them for the favor (and ask again and again), you don't hear a word until they need your help a third time.

Just quit helping them. These people are not going to change. They've gotten this far in the world without returning favors for people, so you probably won't be the one to change them. Just politely decline their requests. Don't even bother referring them to someone else who can help, because they'll just do the same thing.

Network with Your Competition

Some of your best referrals and connections may come from the people you consider your competition. You may work in the same general industry or even compete in the same area. But before you steer clear of that person and draw black eyes and devil horns on their photos, take a long look at what both of you do.

We learned from Tony Scelzo, the founder of Rainmakers, that two small businesses working in the same market can end up being bigger resources for each other if they focus on a specific niche, picking their niche based on the types of customers they work with. We already talked about finding a niche in Chapter 3, "Blogging: Telling Your Story," so you should already understand the concept.

Let's say two independent CPAs have chosen to work with small businesses. On the surface, they may compete with each other, but if they dig a little deeper, they may find that they each have a particular type of customer they prefer and their own niche they like to practice in.

Tom likes working with professional practices, like doctors and lawyers. Dave likes working with retail businesses, like restaurants and small stores. If they discover this truth about each other, they can actually work together without ever bumping heads.

In fact, they can start referring potential clients to each other. In other words, Tom can start referring calls he gets from restaurants and stores to Dave, and Dave can refer doctors and lawyers to Tom.

This sounds crazy to a lot of "zero sum" thinkers who believe that Dave and Tom should cling to every client who crosses their path. But if they did that, Dave and Tom would not enjoy working with all their clients, and they would spend more time and energy on those clients. That could make them lose money and even burn them out. But if Dave passes to Tom the kind of clients Tom prefers and vice versa, they each enjoy the work, and they can even make more money.

Another benefit from this matchup is that now each CPA has someone else selling for him. Not only is Dave looking for restaurants and stores for his own clients, Tom is looking for him as well. Any time he gets a call from a restaurant or small retail shop, Tom can always say, "I'm sorry, I don't handle that kind of work, but let me tell you about my good friend, Dave. He specializes in an operation like yours and does a much better job than I could."

That's not to say that Tom is out beating the bushes, trying to find clients for Dave at the expense of his own business. But Tom is prepared to sing Dave's praises to anyone who fits the description of Dave's ideal client. Although this trade-off will not work for every situation, we know plenty of people who have adopted this strategy with great success.

Our friend Doug Karr owns an Internet marketing agency and is handling large six-figure projects for large corporate clients. When he started his company, he was taking on every project he could find. Doug says he was working 16–20 hours a day trying to meet deadlines, and he was not always successful.

Doug decided he wasn't going to do certain kinds of projects anymore. He passed that work off to one of his competitors who actually liked doing those kinds of projects, and he never asked anything in return. Now Doug works fewer hours per day, meets his deadlines easily, and is actually making more money with this approach than when he tried doing everything because he can take on big projects and ignore the small, time-consuming ones.

Imagine if you had a small group of people, all in cooperative businesses—say, a wedding planner, a florist, a cake decorator, and a caterer—and all working for each other as referrals. Whenever the wedding planner gets a client, she knows exactly who to recommend as a florist, a baker, and a caterer. Similarly, whenever the caterer gets a wedding client, he can recommend the planner, florist, and baker in his little group.

Now, if you work for a large corporation or for a small business in a highly competitive industry, this approach may not be possible or even allowed. You need to make those decisions yourself and abide by your company's policies. But if you ever have the chance to share work and opportunities with your so-called "competition," try it and see what happens. At the worst, you won't get an opportunity that actually aligns with your goals and preferences. But at the best, you will get an ally in your field and an extra pair of eyes to help you find the opportunities you want.

Of course, to do anything we've talked about, you actually have to meet those people. So let's talk about how you do that.

Three Types of Networking

You should focus on three different types of networking as you grow your personal brand: 1) networking groups, 2) one-on-one networking, and 3) the follow-up. These three networking types are not separate styles or techniques. Rather, they are all stages of the same process. Most likely, you will meet people in a group setting before moving on to the second and third types of networking.

We realize we have been talking about being a resource to your online contacts and how it's possible to form some good networking relationships with your LinkedIn connections and Twitter followers. This advice is not meant to discount that. But there will be times when you need to have deeper relationships with some of the influencers in your network (or even to bring new influencers into your network).

Be sure you're still using the ideas we told you about in the other chapters. But when you identify somebody you think would be especially valuable to know, try to follow these strategies.

Networking Groups

The most common form of networking for professionals is the group networking event. This may be a group strictly dedicated to networking, like Rainmakers or a Chamber of Commerce "Business After Hours" event. Or it could be the after-hours mixer at an industry conference or just a chance meeting between two people at a trade show or expo.

Regardless of where group networking occurs, if you are at a place where a lot of people have gathered for the sole purpose of making business connections with the other people in the room, you need to be ready for it.

In many ways, this type of networking is the most stressful of all networking opportunities because you may not know many people in the group, and you're looking for a friendly face. But instead of sticking to the walls or talking with your friends, now is your chance to strike out on your own and meet someone new.

Meeting People

This is the hardest part for a lot of people because they don't like meeting new people. Many people consider themselves introverts and would rather be at home in front of the TV than out in public meeting a bunch of new people.

You may even feel that way yourself, but meeting people is important. You're growing your personal brand. So let's test something: Hold this book in your left hand, and stick out your right hand. Say, "Hello, my name is _____," and then say your name.

Did that exercise work? Were you able to do it without getting light-headed or falling over? Great. You're all set.

Group networking is stressful for many of you, especially if you're shy because you're in a big room that's packed to the gills with people you don't know. You're probably too intimidated to walk up and just blurt out your name. That's understandable. The fear about public speaking is the same fear as meeting new people in large group settings. It's fear of rejection, being laughed at, or judged, especially in a large group of people.

But you need to suck it up. Nothing bad is going to happen to you. It is perfectly acceptable to walk up to someone you've never met, introduce yourself (use that handy phrase, "Hello, my name is _____," we just practiced), and just start a conversation.

Don't be a wallflower. Talk to the people you don't know, not those you do. Maybe you can start out the meeting talking with someone you know as a warm-up, but you need to move on to new people. Join a conversation already taking place between someone you know and someone you don't know. Get introduced to the new person, and use your acquaintance as the warm-up to meeting someone new.

The Networking "Dance"

Here's typically what happens at a networking group—something Erik likes to call the networking dance. Let's say Kyle and Erik are talking to each other. A third person, Lorraine, walks up and introduces herself. She starts talking to them, and as it usually happens, she subtly, subconsciously, engages one of us—Kyle—a little more. You can actually see Kyle and Lorraine square off a little more, leaving Erik as an observer.

Next, Hazel walks up to the trio, and noticing that Erik is not actually engaged in the conversation, starts talking with him. Now we have two new conversations where we had only one, sort of like an amoeba splitting. There may even be some subtle distancing of the two pairs, as they continue to talk.

After a few minutes, Doug walks up to Lorraine and Kyle and engages them in conversation. Lorraine and Doug eventually square off to face each other in conversation, leaving Kyle as the lonely onlooker, but he is soon rescued by Bruce.

The whole process continues for as long as the event runs or until the networking portion of the meeting ends.

What Should You Say?

Figuring out what to say can be difficult for some people. The question, "So, what do you do?" is used over and over at business networking events, but it can get you only so far. You'll probably run out of things to say about your job, so here are other things you can ask:

- What do you do when you're not working?
- What made you get into this field?
- How long have you worked in your industry?
- Where did you work before this job?
- What do you want to be doing in five years?
- Where did you grow up?
- What are you reading right now?
- Who are some of your business heroes?

After that, you need to listen. Don't talk, and don't answer your own question. Let the other person do most of the talking.

If you want to make others feel appreciated and happy with the conversation, let them talk about themselves. If they feel appreciated, they're more likely to want to meet with you later.

A common problem you might have when meeting others is the feeling of needing to carry the conversation. You might tell others everything you can about yourself, unloading as much information as you can and hoping some of it will stick. If you've done all the talking, you may come away feeling like you were heard, but others won't, and you may not get another chance to connect with them later.

As you're talking with someone about what it is that you do, where you work, who you know in common, and what knowledge you want to share, you may get the idea that this is someone you want to get to know better. This is not your chance to make this person your friend or form a strategic partnership. What you really want is to connect enough so the other person is willing to meet with you later, one on one, for coffee or lunch.

Just say, "I've really enjoyed talking with you. Would you be willing to meet later so we can discuss this further?" If the other person says yes, don't even propose a time (unless you both have smartphones that sync with your calendars). Just offer to email or call later and set it up then. Make sure you get your new acquaintance's business card, and email or call within 24 hours of your meeting.

Finally, help your new contact meet other people. When that inevitable third person comes up to your little duo, introduce each other. To show that you have really been listening, explain what it is the first person does, and then ask the new arrival what it is that she does. If it turns out the two work in businesses that have an obvious fit—one person is a graphic designer, the other person works at an advertising agency, or one person is a IT repair specialist, and the other person is in charge of a school's computer lab—make sure they make the connection.

Continue talking to your two new friends for as long as the three of you can manage the conversation, but be prepared for the inevitable fourth person to complete the split. If the other two are making a great connection, "take one for the team" and connect with the new person yourself, leaving the other two to continue for as long as they can.

Networking Faux Pas

If you're introducing yourself, listening to others, and being pleasant, it's hard to make too many mistakes at a networking event. However, there are two things you should never do, even though people do them over and over and they're always ineffective.

Don't Deal Your Cards

Some people think networking means passing out as many cards as they can. They whip the cards out like they're a Vegas blackjack dealer, equating the number of cards received with the number of contacts they have made. Some "card dealers" even count the number of cards they have given out, as if this is some score that will predict their success.

"I gave out 20 cards today," they boast. "And I got 18 in return." They repeat the process over and over, thinking they're making progress in their networking, before finally giving up on networking altogether, declaring it stupid and ineffective.

We have seen these people operate, and we can honestly say that we have never connected with any of them after a single event. We might find their cards a few weeks later and try to remember who they are or where we met them, but try as we might, their identity is a complete mystery.

The problem for the card dealers is that if we can't remember who they are, we're never going to know if we need their services. If we ever need a computer repaired, we're not going to call the guy who talked to us for 60 seconds, shot us his card, and then darted off in search of another hapless victim.

Now, if we ever go to networking events, we carry only a few cards with us and hand them out only to people we connected with and would like to talk to further. The card dealers always get the "sorry, I just ran out" excuse, and we never have to worry about hearing from them again.

Don't Use Clever Elevator Pitches

It's a real pet peeve of ours to hear generic elevator pitches given by people who were trained by sales coaches who don't seem to understand personal branding and marketing.

"Your elevator pitch should get people to ask questions about what you do," they're coached.

This flies in the face of everything we've talked about in this book and everything we ever tell people about personal branding. Your brand, wherever people find it, should tell people immediately what you do, not make them guess or ask questions.

We once heard a friend's elevator pitch during coffee after a sales coach gave her advice.

"We help make your company more memorable," she said.

"So does everyone else. That could be anyone from the person who puts vinyl signs on cars to marketing agencies to corporate photographers to the guy who wears a sandwich board on the sidewalk."

"But it makes people ask questions," said our friend.

"Maybe," we said, "but what if you only have 30 seconds to talk to that person? Do you really want it to be taken up by "What the heck does that mean?" Wouldn't you rather talk about how you can actually help that person?"

Elevator pitches that are designed to be clever only serve to waste time and lump you in with everyone else who "makes your company more memorable," including the guy wearing the sandwich board.

We're not actually telling you to drop your elevator pitch; just don't try to be clever. State up front what it is that you do. That way, any questions you're asked are follow-up questions, not clarification statements.

"We provide accounting services to doctors and lawyers" tells people a lot more than "We keep your company from seeing red." (However, our favorite elevator pitch was "We take the 'SH' out of IT." Anyone who has ever dealt with computer problems understood immediately what that person did.)

Figure out what it is that you do, what niche you serve, and how to explain it in less than 10 seconds. That way, when you're talking with people, your time is spent talking about how you can help the other person, not deciphering the super-secret cleverness of your elevator pitch.

The Follow-Up

After you leave the networking meeting, follow up with the people you've met within 24 hours. An email usually suffices, but give it a personal touch instead of sending a generic one to everyone you met (and even those you didn't). Mention something you talked about, send them any information you might have promised, and ask about meeting at a future date. We can't count the number of emails we've received from people we aren't even sure we met, asking us to get in touch with them if we ever need whatever it is they pitched us. Just like your networking goal is not to meet as many people as you can, your follow-up goal is not to email as many people as you can. Just email the people you have actually conversed and connected with, not the people who handed you their card and wandered off.

Follow-up is especially important if you agreed to get together during the group event. Don't wait for others to follow up; take the first step. Propose a time and day that is convenient for you, and see if it is convenient for them as well. After you settle on that time, you're ready for a one-on-one networking meeting.

One-on-One Networking

One-on-one, face-to-face, IRL (in real life), whatever you call them, these real-world meetings are where the real networking and relationship building happen. You're not going to build that relationship at a networking event; you're going to do it sitting across from each other, over coffee or food. That's one of the great things about the increased popularity of coffee shops: They're nearly everywhere, and they give you a place to sit for a while, get to know each other, and then go on your way, all for the price of a latte.

How to Set Up the One-On-One Networking Meeting

Setting up one-on-one networking with someone you met at a prior networking event is pretty easy. Just send a basic email or call the person and ask about getting together. Your note should include reminders of how you met, what you talked about, why you want to meet, like this:

> Erik,
>
> I enjoyed meeting you at the Chamber of Commerce Business After Hours event on Tuesday and talking about blogging. I was wondering if you would be free for coffee next week because I wanted to talk about blogging as a marketing tool. I have been blogging for my own personal enjoyment, but I wanted to meet with you to discuss some ideas I had for a possible blog dedicated to reviews of hamburgers at independent restaurants. How does your schedule look over the next two weeks? Mornings before 10 are usually good for me.
>
> Dick

The message can even work as a script for a phone call. Although you wouldn't read it word for word over the phone, you could use the same ideas and main points when calling the person you want to meet with.

You can take a similar approach when you're trying to set up a meeting with someone you have never met but were referred to by someone else.

> Kyle,
>
> I was referred to you by Erik Deckers, who said you would be interested in learning about a bottled water service at your office. Erik mentioned that you moved to a new location a couple of months ago.
>
> I am free to meet Monday, Wednesday, or Friday next week, any time between 1:00 and 4:30. I can meet at your office, or we can get coffee at the coffee house nearby. I'll call you in a couple days to follow up.
>
> Larry Smith

Again, this email has everything Kyle needs to know about whether to meet with Larry: how Larry knows about Kyle, what he wants to talk about, and when and where they could meet.

```
@kyleplacy:  Yeah, I haven't forgotten about that guy either. I
             ended up with an 18-month plan before he left, and I
             don't even like bottled water.
```

```
@edeckers:   Me?! You're the one who gave that vacuum salesman my
             name last fall. I had to buy one just to get him to
             leave.
```

What to Talk About During Your One-On-One

This is the part of face-to-face networking that social media can help. Think about what it's like when you meet people for the first time. You usually talk about where they live, what they do for a living, what their family is like, where they went to school, and so on.

What's great about social media is that you can find out this sort of thing without wasting valuable one-on-one time. Maybe you discover you went to the same university but never met on campus. Maybe you find out they grew up in a place where your dad worked when he was younger.

Social media lets you make these kinds of discoveries without spending time talking about them. That way when you get together, you can dig deeper into those topics rather than finding them out for the first time during your one-on-one, or worse yet, never finding them out at all. There have been several times that, for each of us, we have found out interesting connections about someone else through things like Facebook, Twitter, or a blog. Don't be afraid to talk about your personal life with others. We're blurring the lines between personal and professional lives all the time in our society. It's fairly safe to assume that the people you meet with in a business setting have a personal life as well. No one gets put back into a locker at 5 p.m. and pulled back out at 8 a.m. the next day.

Remember, your goal in networking is to find connections you can trust and respect. How can you trust and respect others when you don't know anything about them?

We're not saying you have to be involved in every intimate part of their lives, but we think it's okay to ask about their family, what they like to do for fun, and what their hobbies are. Get to know them on a personal level, and you can be a trusted resource to them—and they can be one to you in return.

When you and your acquaintances are talking, listen carefully to what they're saying. Ask them questions about how they're trying to achieve their goals you're discussing, who they want to meet to make those happen, and if there is anything you can do to help them.

This last question is an important one; not only does it let others know you want to help them succeed, it allows you to add value to their lives. Remember, adding value to others' lives will earn you goodwill—goodwill that will eventually return to you in terms of new opportunities and new connections.

Finally, depending on how well you connected and the feeling you get from the meeting, you should try to get a commitment to do it again. All you really need at this point is a "Would it be all right if we met again?" kind of commitment, although if you can get more, go ahead. When you get the okay, follow up in a month or so and set up your next one-on-one. Use that time to build on what you've already learned from this one, and help your relationship go forward from there.

No One Wants a Sales Pitch

We talked earlier about not turning an entire conversation at a networking meeting into a sales pitch. The same goes here for the one-on-one meeting. In fact, it's even more important. Both of us have sat through our share of one-on-one meetings that turned into sales pitches for whatever product or service others were selling.

What is especially frustrating about these meetings is that not only do you not get to know the other person, you missed out on a chance to talk about yourself and your goals. And wasted an hour of your time to boot.

Although we have said that it's more important to let others do most of the talking, you do need to have some time where you get to share a little about yourself. After all, we all like to feel heard and appreciated. And listening to a 60-minute pitch about small business insurance or a multilevel marketing plan is not the place where you're likely to get that chance.

So, be respectful of others' needs and goals for one-on-one meetings, and respect their time. Go beyond what's "fair," and let them do most of the talking. Ask them questions and listen to the answers.

The "Pick-Your-Brain" Meeting

Oftentimes, as you network and learn more about your industry, you should ask others if you can pick their brain about their knowledge of a certain topic. As you grow in your expertise, you will find more people are asking if they can pick your brain.

We advise that you ask as often as you can, for a few reasons. When you're the "picker":

- You can get a lot of valuable information from the experts. They have learned their lessons, learned about the pitfalls, and found the best and worst ways to do things, usually the hard way. This lets you avoid the pitfalls and allows you to grow faster because you are learning which obstacles to avoid.

- Others will feel listened to, valued, and appreciated. This is a good way to form relationships and bonds.

- Others may have recommendations for people you should meet. They may have access to people you would never meet otherwise because they don't go to networking events or move in the same circles you do.

- You may find a mentor to guide you, give you advice, and help you move up your career ladder.

- You should buy lunch or coffee because these people are giving you a lot of valuable information. The least you can do is show your appreciation by paying.

As you progress in your career, newbies and neophytes will ask if they can pick your brain. When that happens, say yes for the following reasons:

- Remember how we talked about Giver's Gain? This is your chance to continue the cycle of adding value to people's lives, as homage to the people who added value to yours. You can especially be helpful if you can connect someone you're helping to someone who helped you, maybe as a client or connection.

- It will help grow your personal brand. The more people you can demonstrate your expertise to, the more people you'll have telling their friends and colleagues about what you know. Both of us have gotten clients and speaking opportunities from doing this.

- You never know where others you help are going to end up. They may be unfamiliar with your area of expertise, but that doesn't mean they are complete neophytes at everything. They may actually be VPs of companies you would like to work for or could become VPs shortly. They may be presidents of trade associations in a field you want to work in or whose conferences you want to speak at.

Remember Mark, Kyle's VP of a large insurance firm? He only wanted some social media pointers for a charity race he organized. Now, what if he had approached Kyle in that role—"I organize a charity race each year, and I wanted to pick your brain on how we can use social media to promote it."—and Kyle had turned him down, not knowing what the man's day job was or who else he knew? Kyle would have lost out on the opportunity to get to know someone who could be a mentor or valuable resource.

The one problem with being asked over and over if someone else can pick your brain is that you could spend day after day sharing information with people, drinking latte after latte, and never get any work done.

And as much as we don't like to admit it, plenty of people don't believe in Giver's Gain. After they've gotten your information and paid for your coffee, you don't hear from them again. You may also become so wildly successful that you just don't have time to meet with people who are just starting out and run through basic how-to's and lessons learned for them.

First, try to avoid getting such a big head that you refuse to ever meet with people. We've encountered people like this, and frankly, they come off as arrogant and cocky. They've forgotten what (and who) made them successful, and think they're too important to help others.

However, we also understand that it's not always possible to meet with someone when you're pursuing your own goals and needs. But that doesn't mean you're too important to meet with others. There are a few things you can do when you reach this stage in your career:

- Limit the number of people you can meet with to once or twice a week, early in the morning. A 6:30 a.m. meeting is not out of the question, at least if you can get yourself out of bed early enough. If you schedule meetings this early, it will weed out the people who aren't as serious about learning what it is you have to offer.

- Figure out what your time is worth per hour, and charge that as a consulting fee. Keep in mind that this is not appropriate in all cases, like if you work for a corporation or government agency. Also, keep in mind that people who are approaching you may be asking for personal development and improvement, and there's something unseemly about charging a consulting fee for that. But sometimes it is entirely appropriate to charge a consulting fee, like if a corporation or business wants advice. This is something we have both struggled with for some time, and there is no easy answer. Ultimately it comes down to whatever you're comfortable with.

- Tell others you don't have time to meet with them for a few months but you would be happy to refer them to someone else who can help them. Then refer them to someone who isn't as far along in his career growth or personal branding efforts as you are. This referral will end up adding value to two people: the person who originally wanted to meet with you, and the person you refer him to.

Under no circumstances should you ask what value others would add to you as a way to determine whether they should meet with you. Erik once asked a former professional football player if he would be willing to meet for coffee.

The player emailed back saying he wasn't sure he would be able to meet unless Erik could tell him what sort of value he thought he could bring to the player. Erik had already helped arrange for the player to be paid to speak at a networking group, and he knew several conference organizers who would have been interested in hiring the player to speak at their event. Erik was put off by the question and never responded to the player, who, as a result, missed out on several possible paid speaking opportunities.

The Follow-Up

The follow-up is where you can make or break your networking efforts. You should come away from every meeting with some sort of action you need to take, even if it's a simple thank-you email or note to send to the person you just met with.

Follow-up is necessary whether it's someone you met with for a one-on-one or even someone you met at a networking event if you talked to that person for any length of time. (Unless you still have the nasty habit of being a "card dealer" and whipping out as many cards as possible. Then, don't bother.)

Forwarding Articles and Links

Forwarding articles and links is one of the easiest, yet least used, ways of building a relationship with another after your one-on-one is over. If you're doing any kind of reading and professional growth, hopefully you're reading blogs and online magazines related to your industry and the industries of the people you're meeting.

Try to find areas of overlap where you may have something in common with the other person. (This is hopefully why you're trying to get together in the first place.) If you find something new or interesting, forward your new acquaintance the link to the website or blog post, or send the entire article. Most online articles now have a Share with a Friend link of some sort that you can use. Click the link, type in a personal message—"This sounds a lot like what we were talking about a couple weeks ago over coffee."—and send it.

If you're really on the ball, you can even keep track of the discussions and articles you send in your meeting notes or calendar and use it as part of your discussion the next time you meet.

If you run across a print article, take the time to clip it and mail it with a handwritten note. As uncommon as personal letters are these days, your efforts will stand out as memorable and thoughtful. It will also show the other person that you're truly interested in getting to know him better.

Sharing Opportunities

One of the things we both like to do for friends who are looking for jobs, grants, or RFPs (request for proposals) is forward the opportunities we find as we go about our day. Whether it's a job listing in a newsletter we receive or a note from another friend who is looking to hire someone for his company, we keep our eyes and ears open for any opportunities that we can pass on to people in our network.

We're even proactive about recommending people to the hiring companies before the candidates even apply. An unsolicited letter of recommendation puts a potential candidate at the top of a pile of résumés, especially when the person we're writing to already knows and trusts us. We've both helped people find jobs this way, which also adds to our personal brand of being influencers and networkers, thus creating new opportunities for us.

Making Connections and Introductions for Others

One of the best ways to help your friends is by introducing them to someone else. If you're in any kind of sales position, you know the pain and heartache of cold-calling potential customers. That's why salespeople always appreciate an introduction (also called a referral) to other people.

A referral is one of two things. Let's say Kyle wants to meet Tom, and Tom is Erik's friend. In a proper referral, Erik can do any of these things:

- Call Tom, tell him about Kyle, and ask him to expect Kyle's call.

- Arrange a meeting for the three of them so Kyle and Tom can get to know each other.

- Make sure Kyle and Tom are at the same event, introduce the two of them, and explain why Tom should be interested in talking to Kyle.

Here is what a referral is not:

- "I know Tom. You might be able to do something for him. You ought to give him a call. I'll email you his number."

A referral lends credibility to the person who needs it (Kyle) because it's coming from someone the other person trusts (Erik). In essence, Erik is counting on Tom's trust of him to carry some weight when he suggests that Tom should meet with Kyle.

You can email this introduction to both parties (include both names in the To: field), or you can call the other person. Either way, here is essentially how an introduction message should go:

"Tom, meet Kyle. He works for a company that provides email, social, and mobile marketing software. Kyle, meet Tom Jensen. He owns a marketing agency that specializes in providing marketing services for art museums.

"Tom, you told me last week that you were thinking about adding some social media and email marketing capabilities to the services you offer to your clients. I thought you should talk to Kyle and see if he can help you develop a system to deliver his product to your agency clients."

In that email, Erik has reminded Tom about his particular need—finding email marketing software to deliver to clients—and told him why he should talk to Kyle—Kyle can do the thing it is that Tom is looking for.

But it would be a bad referral if Erik just gave Tom's number to Kyle and said, "You ought to call him." That's still a cold call, and it doesn't do either of them any good. It doesn't help Kyle to say, "Erik said I ought to call you." Dropping Erik's name during a cold call might give him a better advantage than if he didn't mention Erik's name at all, but not by much.

So if you have a chance to give this kind of referral, do it. If someone offers you a referral to a contact, ask for an email introduction, or at least call the other person first and then him let you know when it's done.

But I Just Don't Want to Meet the Other Person

Sometimes you just don't have anything in common with the other person who wants to connect with you. Or you know he just wants to sell you something and isn't actually interested in connecting with you. There's nothing wrong with someone like this, but at times someone in this category just won't fit into your plans or goals, and you aren't interested in making contact.

Be Honest

So how do you say no to someone like this without hurting feelings? Honesty is usually the best approach.

"I'm sorry, I'm not really interested in that at the moment," is the best thing to say to someone asking about getting together about his latest product. If he persists, be firm.

The prevailing sales training always tells people to be persistent, so don't be surprised if they call you back again and again. If they do, you have a few options for making them stop:

- Avoid their calls, never return their calls, and hope they go away. (We don't actually recommend this one. But it seems to be a common practice for some people.)
- Tell them you will never be interested and they can save their time and energy by not calling. (Try to be gentle if you use this tactic.)
- Go ahead and meet with them (make them buy the coffee), listen to their pitch, and then tell them no again.
- Ask them for a return favor. Tell them you'd like a separate hour to tell them about your product or service.
- Ask them for a bigger favor. Can they introduce you to the decision maker in their organization that you can talk to about your product or service?

Some of these suggestions may seem a little silly or flippant, but sometimes these are the only options that seem to work.

But What if the Other Person Isn't Honest?

What if the other person lied about wanting to meet you? Erik was once asked by a sales associate for a well-known insurance company if he would like to meet so they could "get to know each other better." Erik had met with different associates on several other occasions and usually spent more than three-quarters of the time listening to a sales pitch.

"All right, I'll meet with you," said Erik, "but I've been pitched at least four other times by people from your company, and I'm not interested. But if you would like to meet just to get to know each other, that's fine."

The other person agreed, and the two met for coffee. That's when the other person pulled out a questionnaire and began to ask Erik the questions on it, so he could "put together a quote on a life insurance plan for you."

Erik was rather annoyed by the presumption of it. If he had been a more direct person, he would have reminded the other guy he had specifically said he wasn't interested in the company's program and left the appointment. But Erik also didn't want to make the other person feel bad—the guy was still new in his job and in networking and may not have been aware of the protocol—so Erik did the only thing he felt justified in doing: He lied about his answers.

```
@kyleplacy:   Are you serious? That's pretty passive-aggressive of
              you.
@edeckers:    You really think so? I could give the guy your number
              and you could meet to discuss it with him.
@kyleplacy:   No, that's okay.
```

This won't happen that often, and we can't tell you how to respond to something like this. Should you storm out in a fit of righteous indignation because the guy lied about his intentions? Should you sit quietly and pretend to be interested while you secretly fantasize about the other's demise? Should you just change the subject of the conversation, saying you were under the impression that you weren't going to talk about the business product?

Although we lean more toward this last option, your reaction is up to you. Just remember: Even reactions in situations like this can have an effect on your personal brand. If you're rude to someone, word can get around that you're the kind of person who yells at people you meet with. Justified or not, this would become part of your reputation, and something that people may have in the backs of their minds when they agree to meet with you.

Do's and Don'ts of Networking

Here are some do's and don'ts that were shared with us on our Twitter networks. What's cool about this list is that with a couple of exceptions, we have met with all of these people face to face, especially in one-on-one situations (although some of them just at several networking events). The fact that the list turned out this way makes us think that our extra contacts with them helped them want to answer the questions.

Do

- Listen and ask questions. And say the person's name three times in your head so you remember them next time. —@courtenayrogers
- If you forget someone's name, admit it. —@jaybaer
- Design biz cards to include on back: It was a pleasure meeting you! Event___ Date___ It helps people to remember who they met, and it helps me to keep track, too! —@CourtneySampson
- Put your face on your blog/biz card so people remember who you were later. Had someone in Paris say they knew me from my pic online. —@DouglasKarr
- Do give a firm, assertive handshake when meeting people. And yes, this goes for females, too. Pet peeve: Weak handshakes. —@BeckyAPR
- Put down the gadget. —@JasonFalls
- Always phrase your work in terms of a solution for your client. Find their pain points and brand yourself as a problem solver. —@y0mbo
- When you're planning a face2face meet, find a nonthreatening locale (coffee shop, bookstore, etc.) that facilitates open conversation. —@joeystrawn

- Ask more than you answer. —@JasonFalls
- Breakfast networking beats cocktails networking—you'll remember more. —@jaybaer
- Follow up if you say you will. —@NickiLaycoax
- Tactical tip. If meeting goes well, schedule your next meeting before leaving. Always write a personal thank-you note. —@TrustHomeSense
- Always buy the drinks. —@jaybaer
- Maintain eye contact. Nothing conveys confidence and sincerity like eye contact. —@TeeMonster
- Small groups are always better than big groups. —@jaybaer

Don't

- Don't be a name dropper or look around like the person you are talking to isn't important. —@courtenayrogers
- Don't offer your card before asked or before getting theirs. —@LotusDev
- You don't have to give a card to everyone you meet. —@NickiLaycoax
- Don't assume. A person you network with may not be the connection you need, but they may know the person you want to talk to. —@ChrisAyar

How Would Our Heroes Network?

- **Allen (influencer)** was an account manager for a marketing and advertising agency for 14 years but is looking for a new job after his agency lost its biggest client and laid him off. Allen's best bet is to start attending meetings of his local American Marketing Association as well as the Public Relations Society of America chapter. As he meets other account managers and higher-level managers at agencies, he should try to connect with them one on one as frequently and as often as possible. When Allen strikes up a friendly relationship with these people, he should nurture it as much as he can. Not only will they tell him about openings at theirs or other agencies, they may influence the hiring process when it happens. Allen should also use his downtime to take a leadership role for one of these associations to make himself more visible to people and to make himself the person others want to meet with to pick his brain.

- **Beth (climber)** is a marketing manager for a large insurance company. She has been with the company for 10 years, but this is her second insurance company. Assuming there are no policies, either written or unwritten, Beth should try meeting with other marketing managers and chief marketing officers in other insurance companies. Although they may not mentor her directly, if she can provide value to them—notifying them about job openings, forwarding them notices about conferences (nothing that might give a "competitive" benefit, which Beth's supervisors may frown on)—they will remember her later, if she ever looks for a new job at another company. Beth should also consider getting involved with the Chamber of Commerce at a higher level. Many chambers have programs aimed at executives of corporations, and Beth should try to involve herself in those. This will make her supervisors notice her as being involved in the local business community, which is what every corporation wants to do but sometimes lacks the time or resources for.

- **Carla (neophyte)** is a former pharmaceutical sales rep who was laid off after eight years with her company. She is interested in working for a nonprofit, either as a program director or a fund-raising specialist. Carla would be best served trying to have informational meetings with executive directors and boards of director members of the kinds of nonprofits she wants to work for. She should ask questions like, "What kinds of qualities does a successful program director or fund-raiser have?" and "Do you know anyone else I should talk to so I can learn more?" And of course, she should always ask, "Do you have any openings coming up in your organization, or do you know of any in other nonprofits?" Carla should also add value to the people she meets by forwarding articles, arranging introductions with influential people, and volunteering for an organization or two while she is job hunting.

- **Darrin (free agent)** is an IT professional who leaves his job every two or three years in pursuit of more money. Because of the nature of Darrin's job, he is unlikely to need to attend the same kinds of networking meetings we have been discussing—Chamber of Commerce and business networking groups. However, larger cities often have IT-related professional groups and even social groups that meet after work hours. Darrin should try to attend as many of these as he can and then meet his contacts for lunch or breakfast. Just like our other three heroes, Darrin can hear about any kinds of opportunities, as well as pass them along to the people he meets with.

13

Public Speaking: We Promise You Won't Die

Maybe it's because we both have an obsessive need to be the center of attention, but we live for speaking in public.

Understandably, this gets a lot of weird looks and comments from our friends because most people hate public speaking. Hate, hate, hate it with a fiery hot passion reserved only for snakes, tobacco executives, and commies. (Our apologies to any snakes who may be reading this book.)

We speak in public for three reasons. First, public speaking is essential to building our brand and establishing our credibility. If we want companies and colleagues to realize we're experts in our field, we need to find ways to share that expertise with others. When we are seen as experts in our field, bigger clients are more willing to hire us for larger fees.

Second, we enjoy sharing knowledge with large groups of people. A big focus for Kyle's company is providing email marketing training and support; Erik taught public speaking for three years at the college level, and he nearly went into education. So, we both share a teacher's heart. (Kyle keeps it in a jar under his bed.)

Third, we like public speaking because people pay speakers to share their wisdom and knowledge. We were staggered to learn that organizations pay someone anywhere from a few hundred to several thousand dollars to come in and tell their people about stuff they do for a living. It could be a keynote at a conference, a motivational speaker at a national sales meeting, or leading a day-long seminar, but professional public speakers are well-paid to talk about what they do for a living, and to teach those skills to other people.

Think about what you do right now. Whether you're a purchasing agent, a marketing coordinator, a chef, or a license branch manager, you've probably found several shortcuts that help you do your job better, or you have some thoughts on the direction of your particular industry. Now imagine if someone handed you a check for, say, $2,000 to talk for an hour to a group of your colleagues about these shortcuts or thoughts.

Staggering.

You've probably thought about a number of ways you can do your job better. You likely think that if you had a chance to share this knowledge, your job, your company, or your industry would be a good and happy place. The fact that you bought this book is proof of that: You want to learn how to share knowledge and thus create or grow your personal brand.

But, although it seems like getting $2,000—or whatever you charge—for an hour's worth of work is the ideal job, *you're not really getting $2,000 for a single hour. You're getting $2,000 for the hour you speak, the hours you prepare, the weeks and months you've spent writing about your topic, and the years you spent learning your craft. It only works out to a few pennies an hour, but it's $2,000 more than your nonspeaking colleagues are going to get for the same amount of work.*

Case Study: Hazel Walker, The Queen of Networking

Hazel is a good friend of ours, and she's the Queen of Networking. She is a world-renowned traveler and writer, not to mention a highly sought after speaker. We won't say how much she earns speaking each year, but she has a winter Lexus and a summer Lexus. We both look up to her for inspiration on how to grow our own speaking careers, so we're glad to give her a little space here to tell us how she got started.

> *I was forced to learn to be a public speaker. I believe that you must learn more to earn more, and speaking was one of those things I had to learn.*
>
> *It became clear to me after I bought my BNI franchise that I was going to do more and more speaking. Even if it was only in front of my BNI chapters, it was important that I present my very best self. So the first thing I did was join a local Toastmasters group. Toastmasters is all about learning how to speak well—the technical aspects of speaking, and helping you overcome bad habits—which is what I needed. Toastmasters is where I honed my skills.*
>
> *To learn and practice, I began taking free speaking engagements around town; then I started landing small paid speaking engagements. Once that started happening, I decided it was time to join the National Speakers Association since I knew that I wanted to be in the business of professional speaking.*
>
> *ALL of my business comes to me by referral. I turn to my international network and ask for referrals, I go to my local network and ask for referrals, and I ask my clients for referrals. I have also landed several clients from my LinkedIn account and one or two from my Twitter account.*
>
> *Today I do not speak for free. I ask everyone I speak for to at least make a donation to my favorite charity. This allows me to help my charity of*

choice, allows me to help those who want me to speak, and shows respect for my profession.

The most important thing about being a good speaker is being GOOD at it. Learn what you need to learn to be speak effectively.

Connect with your audience. I rarely ever use presentation software since it does not really connect to the people there to hear you. Get connected to the people who organize and attend; ask for referrals.

If you speak for free, ask the organizers to write you a testimonial and put it on your LinkedIn account.

Should I Speak in Public?

Depends. Do you like money and being a minor celebrity in your field? Next question.

No, Seriously.

Yes. Because if you're looking to move to the next level in your career, gain a national reputation in your industry, share knowledge and information, and even earn more money—in general, growing your brand—becoming a public speaker is one of the most effective ways to do this.

But I Hate Speaking in Public

That's fine. Public speaking is not for everybody. We don't expect everyone to become a public speaker. Not everyone can be an expert; not everyone wants to speak to large crowds. You can still have an outstanding career and can create a great personal brand without doing it. But most leaders and rock stars in their industry are asked to speak in public.

If you don't want to speak in public because you're afraid, don't worry about it. We promise you won't die. (Hey, that's the name of this chapter!)

A lot of people are afraid of public speaking. They're afraid of being judged. They're afraid people won't like them or will find out they're frauds. They're afraid of making mistakes and looking foolish.

One year Erik was a volunteer speechwriter for a woman running for the U.S. Congress. She had been scheduled to do a recorded debate at a local TV station against the incumbent. She was so nervous that before she could even give her opening statement, she tore off her headphones and walked off.

Someone from the station calmed her down and encouraged her to try it one more time. She put her headphones on, got through her opening statement, and then lost it. "I can't do this, I just can't do this." she cried. She then ran out the door, got into her car, and drove away. That was the news clip that made national news, which Erik was able to watch while he was at a conference eight hours away.

The candidate's explanation later was that she got stage fright and let it get the best of her. She had been giving speeches around the district for a few months but came unglued when there were TV cameras involved.

There are two important points you need to remember, which Erik's candidate forgot, when you give a speech, make a presentation, or even just toast the bride and groom at a wedding:

1. Everyone wants you to do a good job. Nobody is hoping you screw up so they can leap to their feet, point their finger, and shout "See? See, I told you she was a phony!"

2. Everyone in the room is just as nervous as you are when giving a talk, so no one's going to be unsympathetic or judgmental about your efforts. When Erik's candidate left her debate, even her opponent told the papers he understood that she was nervous.

Overcoming Your Fear of Public Speaking

If you're afraid to speak in public, or you want to but just don't have the experience, you're not alone. There are organizations and opportunities for you to overcome your fear or gain valuable experience.

Toastmasters

The most popular, most useful organization for public speakers is Toastmasters. It's a great place to learn how to speak in front of groups, organize your speeches, give impromptu speeches, and even learn how to recognize what makes a good speech.

Depending on where you live, there may be one, two, or even dozens of Toastmasters clubs that meet weekly, every other week, or even once a month for 60 minutes per meeting. Each meeting has a set, regular agenda they follow. Members give speeches to earn credit toward certifications like the Certified Toastmaster and Advanced Toastmaster; they give speeches, learn to give feedback on others' speeches, which they present like a regular speech; and, even have the opportunity to compete in local and regional contests.

You can find out more information by visiting the Toastmasters website at www. toastmasters.org. Click the red Find a Location Near You link to find a club in your area. Keep in mind that some clubs have membership requirements, like working for the company where the meeting is held. The downside to Toastmasters is that it can be a big time commitment. The upside is that the clubs are filled with some awesome people who want to learn how to speak in public. You'll be surrounded by friendly people who want to see you succeed. The other upside is that dues are less than $60 per year, payable every six months. It's the least expensive of the other options, but it provides the greatest value.

Toastmasters

www.toastmasters.org

Mailing Address
Toastmasters International
P.O. Box 9052
Mission Viejo, CA 92690-9052
USA

Phone: 949-858-8255
Automated system: 949-835-1300
Fax: 949-858-1207

Classes at Your Local College or University

Taking college classes is another option for improving speaking ability. Although Toastmasters is an ongoing effort, you can give yourself a deadline by taking a course. You can take basic public speaking and even move into advanced public speaking, if you want. The downside is that a college class can be pricey compared to Toastmasters. The upside is that you can cram everything you want to learn into a single class that meets once a week, or even a few times a week, for four months, and then you're done.

Seminars and Courses

Several organizations help people learn more effective communication. Whether it's leadership training, team management, or even public speaking, you can take one-, two-, or even three-day courses on these techniques. The upside is that you get everything you need in less than three days. The downside is that they're often more expensive than a college course, and you don't get the same amount of time for practice and feedback that you do in either Toastmasters or college classes. These seminars are great for refreshers or crash courses, but they're not enough to build an entire speaking career. There are thousands of courses and seminars available from national groups, whether they're from organizations like National Seminars or Dale Carnegie or local ones organized by local groups and instructors. A quick Google search will turn up any courses and seminars in your area.

Speakers Associations

There are several organizations for professional speakers, like the National Speakers Association, the American Professional Speakers Association, the World Speakers Association, and the Advanced Writers and Speakers Association. These are geared more toward the advanced or professional speaker, and some may have an income-from-speaking requirement for applicants. Many of these organizations have meetings in larger cities, where members meet and learn how to become better speakers, how to get more speaking engagements, and how to promote their speaking events.

Private or Executive Coaches

We even know a few people who provide executive coaching for public speaking. These coaches not only teach you how to speak in public, they'll help you reshape your image, dress for success, learn how to deal with new situations, and give you individually tailored, no-punches-pulled feedback on where you need to improve. The downside is that these coaches can cost a few thousand dollars. The upside is that you get specific feedback, and you learn how to fix your issues from a professional.

We don't recommend this option until you're ready to take your speaking career to that professional level. Make sure you try the easy, least expensive option first, and get some speeches under your belt before you look at a private coach.

To find a private coach, do a quick Google search to find speaking coaches in your area. Ask notable speakers in your area who they use. Ask the potential coach if you can speak to any of their past or present clients to get testimonials.

Finding or Creating Your Own Speaking Niche

You need to discover your speaking niche. What are you good at? What is your industry or field of interest? If you've been following along in this book, you've already figured this out. If you turned straight to this chapter, just be aware that this is something you need to do. We'll show you how.

First, this needs to be something you're not only good at, but have some expertise at. If you just started your first job as a copywriter at a marketing agency two months ago, chances are you don't have the expertise to speak to a room full of other copywriters about "The Top 10 Copywriting Secrets."

So if you want to become a speaker, you need to identify that area you're not only passionate about, but you have done for a few years. When you figure that out, you need to find your niche.

Finding your speaking niche is critical to establish your speaking career. You can't just select "everything" as your subject matter, any more than you can select "everyone" as your potential audience.

Even business motivational speakers know that they only want to reach a certain group or type of people—businesspeople, salespeople, people who want to make more money, and so on. Their audience is not the general population, or nonsales-people. They only want people who work in sales and marketing.

Start with the general picture, and then drill down further. Even a specialized field may have areas of specialty.

Let's say you're a cost reduction consultant. You help companies improve their bottom line by reducing their costs. That's even your elevator speech when you explain what it is you do: "I help companies improve their bottom line by reducing their costs." (We'll ignore that this is a boring introduction to what you do.) Believe it or not, that's not your potential audience when you're trying to find speaking gigs. Dig deeper.

"I help small businesses—businesses with fewer than 100 employees—reduce their costs."

Better, but that's still a lot of businesses. According to the U.S. Census Bureau, in 2009, there were 5.1 million businesses in the United States with fewer than 20 employees. Get more specific.

"I help small manufacturing companies reduce their costs."

That's pretty good. We can live with that. We can actually go deeper into our spe-cialty (small tool-and-die manufacturers, small tool-and-die manufacturers who work in the automotive industry), but that might be a niche to pursue for a busi-ness route, not your speaking field.

Keep in mind that you don't have to live exclusively in your niche. You just have to focus on that one particular field, finding different conferences, trade shows, and expos to speak at. Then, when you're comfortable there, you can branch out to a second niche. By focusing on one niche, like reducing costs for small manufactur-ing companies, you can choose a second one—one- and two-partner law firms—without ever causing any problems for yourself because those two areas rarely overlap.

You can also have a small niche that fits within a large field. For example, we're both social media consultants/users with deeper specialties. Kyle focuses on enterprise-level email, mobile, and social media marketing with ExactTarget, and Erik focuses on content marketing. These can cross into other industries with ease. Whether its social media training or online marketing, companies from every industry can use these services.

You can create your own specific niche that crosses borders, too. Whether it's transportation safety, identity theft protection insurance, Generation Y image consulting, or executive travel coordination, you can choose such a narrow niche that you can then focus on a wide market of ideal companies, like companies that are a specific size or are based in a certain region.

Again, drill down to that same focus as in the previous section. For example, don't just pick "small business consulting" as your niche. Even "marketing for small businesses" is too big. "International sales and marketing for small businesses" is a decent speaker's niche. A good number of businesses do business overseas, and you can tap into all kinds of government programs, sales organizations, and even specific industries to find speaking opportunities.

After you identify your niche, you're ready to launch your speaking career.

How to Start Your Speaking Career

Do this: Go to your bathroom mirror, look confidently at yourself, raise your arms over your head and shout, "I am a public speaker!"

And now you are one.

```
@kyleplacy:  Is that seriously how you got started?
@edeckers:   Well, I didn't have a big mirror, but I...no, not
             really.
@kyleplacy:  We need to write more than that. We have a page count
             we have to meet.
```

If you want to get started as a speaker, first identify your goal as a speaker. Is it to make $5,000 in your first year as a speaker? To be a keynote speaker at your industry association's national conference? To speak to more than 500 people at once? Some goals can be met right away; others may take a few years, with these goals serving as milestones along the way.

For the purposes of this chapter, we assume you want to get paid as a speaker, whether you're giving talks as part of your regular job and you receive an honorarium, or you want to become a professional speaker whose full-time job is to travel around and give talks. These other steps we just mentioned will be milestones along the way.

Here's the problem: Most of your speaking gigs are going to be for free, especially in the first year. That's because you don't have credibility as a speaker, even if you just finished your third year in Toastmasters. You're still an untried, unknown quantity, and you're not going to get the same respect as the industry experts who have been doing it for several years. (And if you've spent three years in Toastmasters without speaking outside, you need to move off center just a little bit.)

Don't get hung up that you're speaking for free; learn to appreciate the opportunities. Think about all the stage time you're getting. You're honing your skills, developing your stage presence, and learning what works for you and what doesn't. This will help you achieve the speaking goals you have set for yourself.

Plus, speaking for free can sometimes produce the same results as speaking for money—getting more business, getting other speaking gigs, generating traffic for your blog, and finding a new job.

Stand-up comics work like this when they start out, building stage time, trying to get as much as they can, as often as they can. They work up 5 minutes of material and perform it over and over—for free—at open mic nights. Then they move up to showcases, expanding their set into 7 minutes, and then 10 minutes. They hone that 10 minutes until it's perfect, and they keep performing it as many times as they can, usually for free.

A lot of these new comics drive for 2 hours just for the chance to do 7 minutes onstage. Any successful comic you talk to or hear in an interview talks about how they just did the same short set over and over, for free or little pay, until they started making it to bigger and bigger venues.

That's because one club owner will see that perfect 7 minutes and offer the comic a chance to do an industry showcase for $50. Then all the other club owners assume that if the comic did an industry showcase, he's good enough to do their industry showcase for $50. Then the comic is good enough to do another showcase, after which another owner asks the comic to open for a headliner in her club, and *bada-bing, bada-boom!* One day, the comic is a headliner. And it's all because he was willing to drive 2 hours to do a free 7-minute set a few years earlier.

But the comics who do only two sets and then give up because they don't get a paying gig will be unknown, out-of-work comics who slowly grind their way to anonymous retirement at their data analyst's job in their tiny cubicle that's slowly killing them. (Oh, but we're sure it's different for *you*. Seriously, that won't happen to you.)

The lesson is the same for speaking. You need to speak for free for a while. That's the way these things work. But you won't always do that. Because in the meantime, you're still blogging about your industry, you're still growing your network, and you're blogging to your network about all the talks you're giving, which is helping grow your personal brand.

As you give more talks, more people will see you. Specifically, more people who make decisions about getting speakers will see you. There are almost always decision makers or influencers at conferences. And they'll assume that if you are good enough to speak at this conference, you're good enough to speak at their conference. (Remember how club owners hire comics for their showcases?)

We can't count the number of speaking opportunities we've had because someone saw one or both of us speak at an event, only to be invited to their event a few months later. So while we're both out of the "speaking for free" part of our careers, we recognize that it was an important part of how we got this far.

Identify Speaking Opportunities

You'll start your speaking career by giving basic talks about your niche. They'll be to small audiences, they'll be local, and they'll most likely be free. That's because you're going to talk to local business groups, local fraternal organizations, and even small seminars for your local chamber of commerce and give them a basic overview of what you know.

You need to be greedy about these small, free opportunities. Get as many as you can. Get your name and your face in front of as many people as you can by calling business groups, attending their meetings, and asking for speaking opportunities.

As you become involved with the business groups and chambers of commerce, you're bound to catch someone's attention in an area, someone who may serve on the board of a trade group or industry association, nonprofit, or they could be a conference organizer.

When you meet this person, pursue your own opportunities; don't wait for them to come to you. Ask the organizers and board members if they have speaking opportunities you could do. You can find a lot of speaking gigs this way.

That's because many of these people have a need, or will have, to find a speaker for their upcoming events. They may need to find someone to talk about your particular topic, or they may just need a speaker to fill a slot in three months. But they know that they are going to need to fill that spot, and that means asking their friends and colleagues for recommendations, putting the word out to group members, and working the phones and their contact list until they find someone.

And here you come, charging in on your white horse, shouting, "I'll save the day! I'll be your speaker for your next event."

`@kyleplacy:`   What is it with you and shouting today?
`@edeckers:`   WHY, DOES IT BOTHER YOU?!

By offering to fill the speaking slot, you're helping the organizer with a big problem. Not only will you get the speaking slot, the organizer will remember you. And when the organizer is asked by her contacts if she knows any good speakers, she'll recommend the one who bailed her out of a jam several months ago by approaching her first.

Industry Groups

Industry group events are great places to speak because you can focus your niche to such laser-like specificity, you would be surprised. We have been to conferences in which the presentations and sessions have been so esoteric, so far out, we were surprised people even came up with the ideas, let alone found a roomful of people interested enough to sit through it for an hour. But, that's the great thing about social media and the Internet: You can find a niche that interests you and then find other people who share your interests.

While some industry groups are national, many others are local. Figure out your chosen specialty area, and then see if there is a group in your area that focuses on it. It could be technical writing, visual artists, corporate travel planners, heating and cooling contractors, or left-handed actuarial scientists.

Your goal for speaking to these local groups is twofold: 1) to find new clients. Remember, if you show people how smart you are, they'll hire you to do a project for them or come work for them; and 2) to find new, bigger speaking engagements. Small speaking gigs lead to larger ones, so speak to industry groups on a local level because they can lead to national speaking opportunities down the road.

After you make your name on the local scene in your specialty, take the leap into the national scene, and try to get a speaking slot at the national conference. Check out the conference's website, find the Call For Speakers section, and submit a proposal.

You don't have to limit yourself to just speaking to industry groups you're involved in. If your topic fits outside a single industry, go for it. Just make sure your chosen subject will somehow fit within what that group is already doing, even if it's a cross-over topic. Actually, a cross-over topic can sometimes be a bigger draw than the traditional topics you usually find at an industry conference. For example, HR professionals are probably sick to death of hearing about the latest EEO hiring requirements but would love to hear a seminar on how to use Facebook for recruiting and hiring.

Table 13.1 has a list of a few cross-over suggestions.

Table 13.1   Possible Cross-Over Groups and Topics

Your Specialty	Cross-Over Industry Group	Cross-Over Topic
Tax law	Chamber of Commerce	Taxes for small businesses
Trade show displays	American Marketing Association	Pre-trade show promotion
Technical writing	Startup companies	Proper software documentation
Web designer	High school teachers	Creating a class website
Marketer	Visual artists	How to market art
Direct mail	Nonprofits	Save money on fundraising
Financial planning	High school business teachers	Financial planning for teens
Cost reduction analyst	Office managers	Cutting office expenditures
Health insurance	Human resources pros	Saving employee benefit costs

Rather than focusing your specialty on your own industry group, find other "allied" groups that might benefit from your talk.

If there's not a particular industry group in your area, or you live in a smaller area, find one that's within driving distance and make the trip.

Remember, stand-up comics are willing to drive 2 hours just for a 5-minute set, so you should be willing to drive at least 3 hours to deliver a 1-hour talk. And although it's good to get paid, don't expect to make big money when you're starting out. (But it doesn't hurt to ask for travel expenses for those multihour trips.)

Civic Groups

If you think of industry groups as a B2B (business-to-business) audience, think of civic groups as a B2C (business-to-consumer) audience. You're not going to get as in depth with a topic with civic groups as you would with industry groups. For example, instead of talking about tax law for small businesses, you may end up talking to a group of Shriners about the personal tax implications of using those little cars and scooters for parades. Or instead of talking about financial planning for young professionals, you may end up talking to a fraternity's national conference about how to pay off college debt in five years.

The two best places to find civic groups are the Yellow Pages and the Internet. Unless you're attached to your Yellow Pages, you can head straight for the Internet. Do a Google search for the civic groups you're interested in talking to, or just do a generic search for "civic groups" in your area, and then check their website to see if they have any lunches or special events where you can address the members. Send them an introductory email and see what happens.

Conferences, Trade Shows, and Expos

This is something both of us have spent the past several months doing. We're scouring conference websites in the industries we want to be known in and checking to see if they are looking for speakers. We've also been subscribing to newsletters that have different speaking opportunity lists.

You can find different trade shows and conferences with a little detective work and your favorite search engine. First, check to see if there are any trade associations or groups for your chosen industry or profession. Many trade associations have a national conference, and you can usually find that information on their website. Some will even have regional conferences or local chapters, and you might find some opportunities there, too. Submit speaking proposals when they're being accepted. Next, look for any allied, related, or even competing trade associations, and look for their conferences. Finally, be sure to blog about the hot-button issues the association members are dealing with. Then make sure the conference organizers are in your social networks—Twitter and LinkedIn, especially—and that they receive notifications about your blog posts.

When you find a trade show or conference that looks interesting, go to the speaker submission page to see what kinds of speakers they're looking for. There are four main types of presentations you could make:

- **Poster session**—You usually find these at educational conferences. A *poster session* is basically a series of 6-foot folding tables with pop-up displays and pages of your latest research taped to them. You stand around and hope that people ask you questions, but they don't. They're there for the free hors d'oeuvres being offered to bring attendees into the poster session. (Not that we're bitter or anything.) Maybe we're biased, but we don't consider these real speaking sessions. Don't waste your time with them. In many cases, poster presenters won't even get a discounted admission to the conference, which tells you how highly they're regarded. (Hint: They're not.)

- **Round table**—Imagine putting 75 people in one room with seven different tables, and presenters at each talking about seven different topics. The attendees split up and sit at different tables. Talks may take

15 minutes or an hour. Although you don't get the same benefit as speaking to your own room, at least it's not a poster session. Sometimes this may be your foot in the door for a future speaking slot at the next year's conference. When you've been a speaker for a while, avoid doing round tables unless you also get to do a breakout session. You don't get enough time to get into the meat of your topic, and the room is often too loud to be heard properly.

- **Breakout speaking session**—These are the standard speaking sessions that most speakers get. Most breakout sessions are scheduled as one of several going on during an hour, and the attendees have to choose which one they want to attend. You speak at your session for an hour, and don't need to worry about competing tables, posters, or people showing up for free hors d'oeuvres. Sometimes you may be asked to give your session more than once because there aren't enough speakers. Other times, there are so many speaker submissions that the conference can only accept a fraction of them. There is a varying degree of skill and energy in these sessions, so this is a great way to stand out from other speakers. If you can do a great job compared to other speakers the attendees have seen, you look like a brilliant orator to their 60 minutes of sucking out loud. Sometimes these are paid slots, but most often they are not. Speakers often get free admission to the conference.

- **Keynote address**—This is the granddaddy of all speaking sessions. (Actually, organizing your own seminar is, but we didn't want to discuss it here.) Although a breakout session only lets a speaker reach a fraction of the conference attendees, the keynote speaker not only gets to address all the attendees at once, he or she often kicks off the entire conference. Some conferences will even have one keynote speaker per day, which means there's more than one opportunity for you. Plus, this is a paid speaking opportunity. At no time should you agree to do a keynote session for free.

Introducing Yourself

After you identify the groups you want to speak to, write a cover letter or email that explains what you want to do, what your area of expertise is, how long you've been doing it, and where you've done it in the past. Make sure that your grammar, spelling, and punctuation are perfect, and be sure to write each letter as an individual pitch to that group. Explain why you and your session would be a good fit for them, rather than relying on a form letter. Direct the groups to your blog. (You do have a blog, right? Check out Chapter 3, "Blogging: Telling Your Story," if you don't.)

Dear Ms. Havisham:

I am interested in speaking to your Wedding Planning Professionals of Orlando organization at an upcoming luncheon. I am a direct mail planner and would like to speak to your members about how using direct mail postcards can help brides and their families save money on invitation costs.

I have been in direct mail sales for 10 years and have been speaking to wedding planning professionals and other party planners for 3 years. I recently gave a talk at the National Wedding Planning Professionals Association conference about this same topic, and it was well received, ranking as one of the top five sessions of the entire conference.

You can read more about me at my blog, http://BobScrumrunner. blogspot.com, *as well as see some videos of my past talks. My usual speaking fee is $500, plus travel expenses. I will follow up with you via phone in five days. Thank you.*

Sincerely,

Philip Pirrip

Follow this up with a phone call a few days later as you promised, to see if the groups received your letter and if they have any opportunities for you to speak.

(And give yourself 10 bonus points if you said, "Hey, that's *Great Expectations!*" when you read the letter.)

Promoting Your Talk

You've got your first speaking session arranged. Now you need to make sure people actually show up. You can always hope the organizer is going to do a lot of the promotion, but you need to do it, too. You have access to other people that your organizers may not: your blog readers and your Twitter and LinkedIn networks. Not only will you bring people from your network to your own talk, but you may end up introducing those people to the entire event, which is an added bonus for the organizer, and makes you look like a star.

What are the best ways to invite people to your talk? In this section, we're going to help you...

...Learn five ways to attract an audience to your presentation.

...Discover three secrets every professional speaker uses to increase audience participation.

Do you see what we did there? Your brain probably fired a few neurons, and your metaphorical ears perked up a little bit. We attracted your attention by promising a finite number of ways to attract attention, and three secrets that the real pros use.

This is a common technique used by professional copywriters to get people to not only read their sales material, but to get them to buy their products. If it works in a sales letter, then you should use the techniques in your promotional efforts as well.

We've discussed this elsewhere in the book, but it's worth mentioning again: There is something about a numbered list in a headline or copy that makes people take notice. It's like brain candy for humans because our minds see that information and say, "Hey, that's something I can easily understand. I want to read that!" Umberto Eco even told *Der Spiegel* (a German news magazine) in 1999 that we like lists because they establish order out of chaos.[1]

So take advantage of that little quirk in all humans and use it when you promote your talks. You can use these techniques whether you're writing a blog post, an article, or even an email.

First, write captivating copy. (Don't write the headline first. The headline is going to come from the copy.) Use the numbered list ideas, and generate Three Big Things the audience is going to learn. But then give each of those items its' own list. For example:

1. Learn five ways to attract an audience to your presentation.

2. Discover three secrets every professional speaker uses to boost attendance.

3. Learn the five free social media tools you can use to promote your next talk.

Once you have written all the text, the headline will follow. Use the same techniques we just discussed, and create a headline that covers one of the hot-button issues your audience wants to hear about. You can find this out by asking the event organizer what the hot-button issues are for their members. Then, design your presentation and write the headline based on that.

For example, if Facebook is a big issue in the human resources field, create a headline like "Five Ways to Use Facebook to Streamline Your Hiring Process."

With this headline, we have hit three hotspots for HR professionals:

- We have a finite numbered list. It's more than just how they can use Facebook but an actual number of items they can use.

---

1. www.spiegel.de/international/zeitgeist/0,1518,659577,00.html.

- Facebook is a big deal right now to a lot of HR professionals and hiring managers. In a recent survey, 75 percent of hiring managers used the Internet to get a better idea of the job candidates they're screening.[2,3] So by tailoring a title to a current issue, we are more likely to catch their attention.

- We're trying to make their job easier. Everyone has things they don't like about their jobs or things they wish were easier. The hiring process is one of those things for HR professionals, so by "streamlining their hiring process," we're telling them they can learn how to make their job easier.

Email the description of your talk to the show organizer, who will put it in the conference directory. Then post an article on your blog, and start promoting that blog post via Twitter, Facebook, LinkedIn, and any other social networks you belong to.

Promote your talk frequently, about 2–4 times per week. Don't just send a notice out once and hope people show. It's going to take a number of different messages on your different networks and your blog to people to get them to start noticing that you're going to speak somewhere, and then a few more to get them interested in coming.

When you're at a conference, don't be afraid to invite people to your session. We know, we know; you don't want to feel like you're being needy, but you're speaking in public because you crave the attention, so that ship has already sailed. Swallow the last of your pride, and start inviting people.

Remember, the fuller your rooms are, the more you can spread your personal brand and earn new opportunities or gain new clients. Visit other sessions during the day, and invite people to your session afterward, especially if your two topics are related. You can also invite the other speakers, and as a form of professional courtesy, give them some love during your talk. (That's hipster talk for "mention them.")

Your goal is to get as many people in your session as you can, which unfortunately means other speakers may have fewer attendees at their session. Don't feel bad; it just means they should have promoted their talk better. Buy them a copy of this book.

---

2. http://articles.cnn.com/2010-03-29/tech/facebook.job-seekers_1_facebook-hiring-online-reputation?_s=PM:TECH.

3. http://www.atelier-us.com/e-business-and-it/article/one-in-five-hiring-managers-screen-applicants-myspace-and-facebook.

How Does This Apply to Our Four Heroes?

Although people generally speak for the same reasons—they're often desperately craving attention and want to make some money on the side—the path they take to get there may be a little different. So how will our four heroes from Chapter 1, "Welcome to the Party," use public speaking to advance in their career path or find a new job?

- **Allen (influencer)** spent 14 years as an account manager and has a lot of expertise in account management, marketing campaigns, ad creation, and the like. He would be a valuable resource to new marketing managers and coordinators, so speaking about a niche within marketing management would be a good one to pursue. Topics like "Marketing Analytics" and "ROI Measurement" would be good subjects to present to his local chapter of the American Marketing Association. Not only can he share his knowledge, he might make good connections with potential employers there.

- **Beth's (climber)** goal is to move up the career ladder to a chief marketing officer position in the insurance industry, so she should pursue a speaking plan in one of two directions: She can either speak to the marketing industry, or she can speak to the insurance industry. And she can even do it with the same topic: "Marketing Tactics in a Heavily Regulated Industry." The talk can be geared toward any regulated industry, like finance, health care, or pharmacy. Or she can gear it back toward her regular industry and retitle it "Marketing Tactics in the Insurance Industry."

- **Carla (neophyte)** wants to change careers from pharmaceutical sales to nonprofits, so she is better off focusing on nonprofit issues rather than pharmaceutical ones. Although it would be easy to focus on a pharmaceutical audience, those aren't the people she wants to work for. Because a lot of nonprofit professionals don't think of themselves as businesspeople, business topics geared toward nonprofits tend to gather big audiences. Carla should focus on speaking to nonprofit professional organizations (that is, the Kentucky Fundraising Professionals Organization, Planned Giving Professionals of New Hampshire) and teaching people how to take a sales approach to fundraising. This will not only show her business development expertise, it will put her in contact with people who are either hiring fundraisers or know about fund-raising positions.

- **Darrin (free agent)** is a commodity as an IT professional because he "fixes computers." (Sorry, IT folks, that's the way we non-IT folks see it.) Darrin wants to start public speaking to enhance his career and job growth possibilities, so he has two choices. He can try to impress the IT hiring managers by speaking about a particular growing field, like "Walking the Fine Line Between Network Security and Social Media." Or he can do basic presentations to reach C-level hiring managers, like "Basic Computer Security for Office Staff." Either way, Darrin's talks should be geared specifically toward the right audience. And because Darrin usually only transfers laterally based on more money, giving the right kind of talk to the right kind of audience might also get him a bump up the career ladder.

Giving Your Talk

When it comes to giving speeches, there are a lot of books, newsletters, and blogs to read, besides classes to take. In fact, we already mentioned a few of the beginners' opportunities at the start of the chapter, so we're not going to go deeply into how to prepare for your talk. We're going to assume you know how to do these steps, like outlining your presentation beforehand, rehearsing your presentation, dressing appropriately, and using language effectively.

But we offer these seven ideas for organizing your talk:

- **Avoid putting a lot of text on your slides**—Our preference is you don't put more than 5 words on a single slide, in 144-point size or bigger. Use photos and graphics instead. This way, you can speed up or slow down your talk as needed. You can skip slides, spend only a few seconds on them, or even tell a 5-minute story about that particular slide. And people in the back of the room won't burst a blood vessel trying to read the tiny print on the screen.

- **Show up early**—Scope out the room. If you can go a few days early to check it out, do it. You want to get a feel for the room, see where the projector is, how the room is laid out, how much room you have to walk around, and in general to get more comfortable. But if you're speaking at a conference, you may not have that chance. Then you have to assume the conference organizers know what they're doing and be fairly flexible on your requirements and adaptability. Still, it doesn't hurt to plan for the worst, in case the organizers aren't too adept at managing technology. (See the section titled "Important Technology Tips for Presenters.")

- **Make sure the lighting is appropriate**—Under no circumstances should you allow the lights to be turned down low so people can see the screen. They are there to see you, not your images. You can give your presentation without PowerPoint/Keynote; your slide deck can't do squat without you. Lights need to stay up at a normal level. Let the people see your smiling face.

- **Treat talks like theater**—You're not relaying information; you're acting! You should consider yourself a performer, and it's okay to act like one. Actors often use the phrase, "playing to the back row." This means their projection and gestures are meant to be bigger so they're heard and seen by the back row. Although you don't have to bellow and make large sweeping gestures, don't have conversations with the front row. Make sure you make eye contact with the people in the back of the room, so they feel included in your talk. Also, new speakers often have a tendency to speak faster than they think they do. Make sure you speak at a normal rate of speed.

- **Mention other people, especially other speakers, during your talks**—This gives you more credibility, plus you come off as gracious, sharing, and noncompetitive. Speakers who do this tend to be recognized and appreciated for those qualities when it comes to future, more lucrative opportunities. (At which point, you can totally crush those other speakers and grind their souls into the dirt.)

- **It helps to have a soundtrack you sing to yourself as you're being introduced and walk on stage**—If you have time beforehand, listen to music that puts you in a good mood and leaves you feeling confident. One public speaking trainer once suggested humming the opening bars of *Rocky* to ourselves as we walked across the stage to begin our talks.

- **Record your talks, and study them afterward**—You will be your own harshest critic, so watch and listen to tapes of yourself speaking. Take notes on what you need to fix, and then fix them. Stand-up comics record themselves and then listen to the tape to see what parts of their set need to be fixed.

Important Technology Tips for Presenters

We both love using our computers for our talks, and we're both particular about what we use. We're both rabid Apple fans and use our MacBooks for everything. Despite what our friend Hazel said about presentation software, we both love Keynote because it's stable and not prone to crashing. However, we recognize that PowerPoint is widely used and is easier to transfer a slide deck to someone else's computer. (Keynote can also export slide decks to the PowerPoint format.)

Both systems have their pros and cons, but regardless of who is right, there are several technology tips every presenter needs to know before giving talks in front of people.

- **Make sure your computer is ready**—Shut down every program, hide all files on your desktop in another folder, and clear out your browser history and disk cache. While you don't surf Internet porn on your work computer, your friend probably does, and this is something your friend should know. So loan him this book (better yet, buy him his own copy), and make sure he reads this section.

  We've all heard stories about presenters who clicked the wrong button on their computer and had some rather embarrassing photos pop up on the screen for everyone to see. While the safest bet is to never look at those kinds of things to begin with, at least make sure they're not easily accessible or accidentally switched on. So clear your history and cache, hide any personal photos and documents in a safe place, and make sure all programs except your presentation software are off. You should even turn off your Wi-Fi unless you need it for your presentation.

- **Use big photos and (almost) no text**—PowerPoint and Keynote can be used effectively *if they're used correctly*. When we do slide decks, we get Creative Commons photos for slide images and put 2–4 words on a slide. Remember, as the speaker, that you are the focus of the room, not the slides. The slides are there for visual support, and perhaps a little comedy. They should not contain the important information; you should.

 Tip

Creative Commons licenses are copyright licenses from the creator of a work (photo, graphic, or text) that allows others the right to reuse the copyrighted work—without changes, and at no charge—in things like presentations or in blog posts. If you use photos from a photo-sharing site, such as Flickr or Picasa, you need to make sure they are Creative Commons photos and not "All Rights Reserved" photos (which is legalese for "Do not reuse!"). There are different kinds of Creative Commons licenses, so make sure you research before you start publishing someone else's content.

If you do use text, make the point size at least 144 (2 inches) so people in the back of the room can see it. If they're straining to see from the back, your projector isn't big enough. Hopefully you scoped out the room ahead of time, saw how huge it is, and noticed that the projector was about as effective as holding up slides and a flashlight.

But if you don't get that chance, always assume the worst when it comes to available technology. If you stick with photos and huge text, you'll be fine. If you only use photos to support your points, not make them, you're not lost if the projector fails or is too small, or your presentation software crashes. You can still speak without these props.

- **Use your computer for presentations**—A lot of well-meaning people will offer you the chance to use their computers for your presentations, but that is sometimes more trouble than it's worth. They may have an older version of PowerPoint, Keynote won't run on a PC, or they may not have a remote or the right monitor cable for their laptop. You will have tweaked your computer to perform the way you want it to, and it's hard to try to learn someone else's setup or operating system, especially if you're setting up your presentation 5 minutes after the last speaker finished and 5 minutes before you start.

  If you use someone else's system, you're at their mercy. It's also more than a little maddening to know more than the technical support guy who's supposed to "help" you but doesn't quite know how everything works. Rather than putting yourself in a situation in which your entire presentation hinges on the quality of someone else's system, insist that you use your own computer. If you can't, be gracious about it, find a way to make it work, and hope it goes well. (If it doesn't, don't apologize to your audience for not having a slide deck. There's no point in embarrassing the organizers; that will get you blackballed from speaking at future events. Instead, use your computer as cue cards, and speak without a deck. That's why the point about using big photos and almost no text is so important.)

- **Get a separate presentation computer, preferably a MacBook**—If you want to make a living giving presentations, you need a computer that's not prone to virus attacks, crashes, and glitches that can pop up in the middle of a presentation. For stability, ease of use, and graphics capability, you can't go wrong with a MacBook. And yes, there's Windows 7, which is much easier to use and more stable than all the other versions that came before it, and yes, Macs aren't immune to viruses. But a Mac is less likely to suffer these things and is less likely to crash in the middle of a presentation. And if you follow the first point's steps as well, you'll have smooth sailing with a Mac.

  And if you have the budget, get a decent LCD projector. Don't cheap out and get the smallest, least expensive one you can find. Get a good one that can *brightly* fill up a screen from 25 feet away.

- **Upload your slide deck to SlideShare.net before you give your presentation**—We've been in rooms before where everything was hardwired and bolted in place, including the computer, and we were forced to use their system instead of our own. (See the bullet "Use your computer for presentations.") Although it's possible to export a Keynote deck to a PowerPoint version, this really screws up the formatting and fonts, and it looks bad. There's nothing worse than seeing weird fonts and screwed-up slides as you're giving your talk and having no possible way to fix it. We recommend paying for the premium membership for SlideShare. It's worth it.

 Note

SlideShare.net is a presentation slide deck-sharing site. Just like YouTube lets you share movies and Flickr lets you share photos, SlideShare lets you, well, share slides.

Instead, upload your deck to SlideShare the day before your presentation (see Figure 13.1). Then, before your talk, log on to SlideShare and pull up the deck in full presentation mode. It may mean you have to stand next to the keyboard to change the slides instead of using a remote (which is wicked cool and makes you feel like a big shot). However, at least you don't have to mess around with putting your presentation on a thumb drive and hoping your presentation software isn't newer than theirs, or exporting your deck to their software and hoping the formatting isn't messed up.

Figure 13.1   *One of Erik's presentations available on SlideShare.net. Note the clever use of a numbered list in the presentation title. And you can get a Simpsons version of yourself at SimpsonsMovie.com.*

Finally, by having the SlideShare uniform resource locator (URL), you can give people the URL to your deck rather than wasting paper on printing 50 copies of handouts and giving them out to the 20 people who showed up. It wastes paper to have to bring home 30 copies of handouts that can't be used again because you created a custom deck and handouts for that particular presentation.

You can also shorten the URL at a shortening service like bit.ly (www. bit.ly). A bit.ly shortened URL is 20 characters, so it's easier for audience members to write it down. You can also ask people to email you so you can send them the URL. This helps you add to your list of contacts as well, so you can communicate with them in the future (like when you're speaking again or have a book for sale).

- **Always carry a monitor cord and extension cord with you**—Most places already have a projector available, but they don't always have a monitor cord. Carry a monitor cord (and a Mac-to-RGB adapter if you took our earlier advice and got a Macbook) to be safe. Also, get a 12-foot 3-to-1 extension cord. Then you can plug in a laptop and the projector and reach the plug across the room. Be sure to tape down the cord so attendees don't trip on it as they're filling the room. So you'll want to bring duct tape as well.

  You may even find it helpful to carry a presenter's bag. Keep the cords, colored markers, notepads, index cards, duct tape, and any props you may use in your talks. Leave it in the trunk of your car when you're not using it, so you don't forget it if you drive to your presentations.

- **Create screen shots of websites you want to use**—It's nice to pull up a live website and show it off to a room full of people. But too often, you don't have access to the conference's Wi-Fi, or it's the public Wi-Fi and everyone is on it, so it's slower than a turtle with a limp. Don't depend on having Wi-Fi access. Create screen shots of every website you need, and keep them handy. Better yet, incorporate the screen shots into your slide deck, so you don't have to jump around between applications.

  If you do have Wi-Fi access, open all the websites you're going to need ahead of time. Consider using a browser like Firefox or Google Chrome for additional stability and speed. And again, don't forget to clear your disk cache and history before you start. (See the first bullet, "Make sure your computer is ready," if you need a reminder.)

Miscellaneous Tips, 140 Characters or Less

- You're on the minute you walk into the building. The person you're gruff or abrupt with could be the person who gives your introduction.
- "Winging it" disrespects the audience. If you couldn't bother to take the time to prepare, why should they bother to pay attention? —@LisaBraithwaite
- At a conference, be friendly and helpful to everyone before/after your session. They'll remember that as much as they remember your talk.
- Ask people to email you for a copy of the slide deck. It's a great way to track the number of people interested in your topic.
- Asking people for their email is also a great way to gather names for your enewsletter. Just be sure you ask if you can send it first.
- Practice vocal variety by reading aloud. Children's books, newspapers, poetry, and comedy dialogue help you work on pitch, pace, tone, and volume. —@LisaBraithwaite
- Have a central idea to come back to if you get on a tangent. It should be something to make it seamless while you find your thoughts. —@that_girl_lola
- Start fast, especially online (e.g., webinar). Attention spans are shorter than ever. —@1080group
- Don't give a speech. Talk to your audience and add at least some element of discussion to it. —@GloriaBell
- We all have butterflies before we speak. Train yours to fly in formation, so the energy expends with purpose. —@IkePigott
- Before you start, drink something that gives you something in your stomach. —@CoxyMoney
- Use Tweetwall for Twitter comments and Q&A. —@CoxyMoney
- Make a friend (or four) in the audience by using them as repeated points of eye contact. Smile within the first 30 seconds. —@GrindTheMusical
- Keep your visual aids as free of words as possible. Use blank slides between photo slides often, so they're looking at you, not the screen. —@GrindTheMusical
- All the books, blogs, and trainings in the world don't mean a thing if you don't apply your learning. Make opportunities—get out and speak! —@LisaBraithwaite

- Q&A your ass off. —@CoxyMoney
- Put your closing AFTER the Q&A. The last thing the audience will hear is your final message, not a random or irrelevant question from the crowd. —@LisaBraithwaite

14

Getting Published: I'm an Author!

There's nothing like getting published with real ink and paper: seeing a physical manifestation of something you created with your name on it and knowing that you put something out into the world, for other people to read, experience, and react to. The minute the ink hits the paper and your work is distributed to dozens, hundreds, or even thousands of people, you're a published author. And to a writer, there's no feeling like it in all the world. It's a historical record, an artifact, and a validation of your thoughts and ideas.

@kyleplacy: What about digital publishing and online publishing? Aren't you going to talk about that?

@edeckers: Seriously? You're going to interrupt my flow
right now? I was just getting warmed up.

@kyleplacy: I just think you need to mention digital
publishing.

```
@edeckers:   Yes, it's important! Ebook sales were up 261%
             in Jan. 2010.¹ The New York Times just said
             they may stop printing in the near future.²
             So?
@kyleplacy:  You don't need to get cranky.
@edeckers:   This is the introduction. This is where we
             create imagery and set the mood, not discuss
             technicalities and details. That's for later.
```

It's the same feeling we had when we published our first-ever articles, but it's continued for the subsequent ones and even this book. In fact, by the time you read this, we will have eagerly grabbed the first copies of this book out of their boxes, gripped them tightly, giggled a little—a little more than normal for two grown men—and positively beamed at our names on the cover.

Nothing can beat that sense of accomplishment, the feeling that you've somehow made history. All writers who have ever published a book, magazine article, newspaper column, or letter to the editor know that joy; they're on top of the world for days and weeks at a time.

This feeling is nothing like that experienced from blogging. Don't get us wrong; blogging is great. It's how we make our living, and it's going to be the future of publishing. But there is permanence to printed words. Books are sacred, magazines are interesting, and newspapers carry a sense of tradition and gravitas (even as the print newspaper slowly dies). Blogs are just, well, blogs. You'll forget all about your blog the first time you see your words and byline in a print publication.

As much as we both love blogs, we realize that anyone can write them. But being published in a newspaper,

---

1. http://idpf.org/doc_library/industrystats.htm (**@edeckers**: See, and now you made me footnote in the intro!).

2. http://www.businessinsider.com/sulzberger-we-will-stop-printing-the-new-york-times-2010-9.

magazine, or book requires established knowledge and expertise. That's why there's a certain respectability that comes from being published. Someone thought highly enough of your work that he wanted to take the effort to spend money to put ink on paper, and he trusted you enough to share your ideas with his readers.

It's an awesome feeling.

Kyle was once asked to write an article called "Developing a Policy for Your Company and Social Media" for the Hamilton County Business Magazine, which he geared toward the nonsocial media community. For him, it was exciting not only to be asked—to be recognized as an authority in his chosen field—but to see his work published in a high-gloss magazine. And although that publication didn't garner him immediate recognition, we think future articles on the subject will.

We're not disparaging bloggers. In fact, we think blogging is vital to today's business world. Erik even does it for a living, and Kyle has built a business in teaching people how to do it, so we understand the importance of blogging. But right now, we want to look at writing beyond your blog and getting your work published in other venues.

Being published will boost your personal brand immensely. It shows that not only do you have a command of the language and the ability to form cohesive ideas, you have mastery of your topic (or at least the ability to completely BS an editor into thinking you know what you're talking about).

In this chapter, we're going to discuss print writing. Whether you're talking about newspapers, magazines, trade journals, or even newsletters, writing for print is a lot different than writing for a blog. With a blog, you are your own editor, and you can pick any topic you want. In a print publication, you have to write to others' standards and follow their editorial calendar. In a blog, you can make your own errors and correct them, form your own ideas, and change your mind. In a print publication, everything has to be perfect, and your thoughts need to align with the overall mission and philosophies of the publication. Conversely, in a blog, you won't get paid for writing your own articles. In print publishing, you can get paid for what you do. (It may not be much, but there are some publications that pay their writers.)

But print writing is worth doing because it will add so much more credibility to your personal brand if you're published in someone else's print publication.

Why Should I Become a Writer?

There are very few reasons you should *not* try to get published. Actually, we can't think of any. So, you know, just...do it. Just because.

@kyleplacy: I think they want a better explanation than that.

@edeckers: Fine, whatever.

There are two main reasons to start thinking of yourself as a writer, or at least not think *I hate writing, I hate writing, I hate writing* every time you have to write anything longer than a five-word email.

First, look at any job description. One of the things these descriptions always ask for is people to have "effective oral and written communication skills." Despite the fact that companies never say what "effective oral and written communication skills" actually are, it's safe to assume that you're going to be seen as "an effective written communicator" if you actually have some publishing credits to your name and maybe even a few ink stains on your fingers.

```
@edeckers:   I meant metaphorical ink stains, not actual ink
             stains.
@kyleplacy:  I wish you had said that earlier. This stuff is hard
             to wash off.
```

Second, you're always going to need to be an effective communicator, whether you want to build your résumé or expand your personal brand. Whether you're writing a blog post or communicating an idea to your co-workers and boss, you need to get your ideas across quickly, easily, effectively, and persuasively. The people who succeed in the workplace are often the people who can convey their ideas better than anyone else. (They're also good networkers, which we discussed in Chapter 12, "How to Network: Hello, My Name Is...," but we don't want to get into that right now.)

There are a few reasons you should consider becoming a published writer:

- **It builds your personal brand**—Not only will more people learn who you are, but you will be seen as an expert on your published topic.

- **You can share your knowledge, which helps you be seen as an expert in your field**—Your articles will be read by people in your industry or in a market you want to be known in.

- **You can find new sales or job opportunities**—Just as we said blogging will help you with this (Chapter 5, "Twitter: Sharing in the Conversation"), writing for print can get your ideas and personal brand in front of someone who needs your expertise. That can leverage into a sale of your product, a speaking engagement, or even a job opportunity.

- **You can make some extra money**—Most print publications pay for articles, whereas blogs and online publications typically don't.

- **There are still plenty of people who read print publications, whether they're newspapers, magazines, or books**—Although it may seem like the whole world is going digital, print still has a large audience.

Publication Opportunities

While this book is primarily about social media and blogging, a writer can be (*should* be) more widely published than just his or her own blog. There are a lot of opportunities for people to be published. You could try to appear in thousands upon thousands of print publications. You can get your foot in the publishing door in several ways, a few of which we discuss here. Later, we discuss how to write a query letter, what rights you can and should offer, and how to get paid.

Believe it or not, there is an *either/or* thing going on with print writing. It's much harder to be a print writer because you're trying to meet others' standards, trying to follow others' editorial calendar, and trying to meet their readers' wants and needs.

Before we start, we want to make sure you understand that getting published is competitive and difficult. A magazine typically publishes 12 times a year and accepts only a set number of articles from freelancers. A newspaper can publish anywhere from once a week to every day, and again, it has limited space. So although our advice may sound like "Write a story; submit it; collect $200," it's really not that easy. You're competing with other writers who also want to see their name in print.

Our goal with this chapter is to show you the basics of where to publish, how to submit for publication, and what you can expect, and tie it all back to your personal brand. There are all kinds of websites, books, and magazines about the writing life that discuss these topics in further detail. A quick check of the writing section of your favorite bookstore, or even a quick Google search, will turn up any number of writing resources.

 Tip

Get the book *Writer's Market*, published by *Writer's Digest* magazine. This is the writer's bible for learning about things like publication rights, how to write a cover/pitch letter, what rates to charge, and best of all, contact and submission information for nearly every publishing house and periodical in the United States and Canada. If you're looking for the best place to pitch your article, you need the latest copy of this book.

Local Newspapers

There are any number of pieces you can write in your local newspaper, whether it's a guest editorial, an op-ed piece, a weekly column, or even a freelance news article. If you live in a big city or your paper is owned by a media conglomerate, you may have a tougher time getting a piece in there. But smaller towns and weekly newspapers are always looking for well-written content. If you have a business-to-consumer (B2C) business, publish how-to and advice columns in your local newspaper.

Let's say you run a personal finance business in a city of 30,000 people. You could spend a lot of money on Yellow Pages ads, newspaper ads, and the like and spend a lot of time going to networking events. (You should read Chapter 12.) But you can also write a personal finance column in the paper, giving general (not specific) advice on saving money, investing in stocks and bonds, paying taxes, and so on. The upside is that the newspaper will get some well-written, informed content, and you'll be seen as more of an expert by your potential clients (people in your market) because you're "in the paper."

Send a query letter to the editor of your local paper (we'll discuss a basic query letter later in this chapter), or if your city has a larger newspaper, submit the letter to the editor who manages your chosen section. Pitch the idea of the column to the editor, and include a couple of sample columns you have written "on spec." Make sure you read the paper for several days or weeks so that you get to know their style and tone first.

If you are writing a single story, you may want to pitch your story idea to the editor in question, especially if you're not an established freelancer. Then you'll know whether you need to devote the time and energy to writing the article, rather than hoping your hard work gets accepted. (This is why a lot of writers get into blogging.)

If you aren't having much luck with one newspaper, there are likely others in your area, both smaller and larger. What about the next city or town over? How about weekly newspapers? Or smaller dailies? After you start building a reputation as a decent newspaper writer in other cities, your local newspaper is more likely to consider working with you.

Business Newspapers

Some cities and regions have dedicated business newspapers, which is great for people in business-to-business...uh, businesses (B2B). These newspapers are filled with news for the different businesspeople and industries in the city they serve. Articles analyze the economic progress of the city, real estate, business growth, and development. They discuss who's joining what company, which companies are merging or expanding, and the political issues that affect local businesses.

If you work in a B2B business, you want to get your information in front of the executives who read the paper, so getting published here is a great step toward becoming an established writer.

Our friend, Bruce Hetrick, owns Powerful Appeals Inc. and is a professor of Public Relations at the Indiana University School of Journalism. In a rare bridging of the PR/journalism chasm, Bruce also doubles as a columnist for the *Indianapolis Business Journal*, the local business newspaper. But rather than talk only about PR/marketing or even client-category subject matter, Bruce writes about bigger issues, whether it's the environmental benefits of living downtown instead of the suburbs, how BP handled (read: mishandled) its crisis communication, the importance of nonsmoking initiatives in the state, and even lessons he learned driving his sons to college one fall.

Bruce has earned a citywide reputation for being a business thought leader just by publishing his column twice a month. He is often asked to serve on nonprofit boards, to pilot nonsmoking initiatives, and to participate in citywide corporate events.

The biggest benefit? Some of Bruce's past and current clients are the biggest in the community, all of whom trust him because he writes thoughtful commentary in the city's most respected business news publication.

(Let's circle back to our opening section for a second to make its point: Did Bruce do anything special to earn these business leaders' trust? Did he change his ideas or behave differently to earn it? No, he kept doing what he was doing, but he had a *printed platform* in which to share his ideas.)

Finding a column or article writing opportunity here works just like it does in newspapers. Read the publication to get a sense of the tone and style, send a query letter to the editor pitching your idea, and include some spec column samples if necessary.

Scientific Journals

It doesn't matter what industry you're in, most established industries—scientific, manufacturing, and professional (doctors, lawyers)—have a journal. There are journals in the engineering and agricultural fields and most academic studies. Generally, if you work in the research side of any of these industries, you probably get your industry's journal. This is also the place for you to become known.

Most college departments require their professors to publish at least once a year in a peer-reviewed scientific journal to get tenure. It is rare for a nonacademician or nonindustry person to be published in these journals. That's because these publications have rigorous, demanding standards that you must meet just to be considered for publication. They're certainly no place for people who want to sell a product or provide professional advice. However, if you can be published in your industry's trade journal, you're at the top of your industry mountain and are a recognized authority.

Being published in a journal is different from being published in a newspaper. Rather than pitching a query to an editor, you write the article and submit it to the journal. There will occasionally be a call for papers, although some journals do accept submissions. Be sure to check your journal's submission guidelines. Also, read several past issues to get an idea of the tone and writing style of the journal. Past articles are good indicators of the kinds of articles the publisher will accept.

Specialty Magazines and Newspapers

A step down from the journals in terms of rigor and stuffiness, a lot of industries have their own trade newspapers and magazines rather than the more scientific journals.

When Erik worked in the poultry industry, he used to receive stacks of magazines and specialty newspapers each month about production, processing, equipment, overseas issues, and regional issues in that industry. There were magazines from Illinois and Arkansas, England and Holland. Several of these trade magazines used content from people in the field, including companies that sold poultry production products because they were the ones most knowledgeable about the industry. The only caveat was that the articles couldn't be commercial—that is, nothing about their own products or services. Sure, the articles could answer questions about problems that only their products could solve, but they had to be advisory or educational in nature, not commercial. So Erik wrote a couple of articles about problems that his product just happened to solve. From that, he generated some sales and tradeshow recognition from them. ("Hey, weren't you in that poultry magazine?")

Do a Google search for the name of your industry and "trade journal" to see if there are any magazines or journals for your field. Subscribe to them, and figure out if you can contribute articles. Some of these journals or magazines only hire writers, and some of them take "contributor" articles (that is, other readers).

If you work in an industry closely allied with other industries, see if your content would fit in their publications. Table 14.1 has some allied industry suggestions to get your mind thinking in that direction.

Table 14.1   Article Ideas for Crossing into Allied Industries

Your Industry	Allied Industries	Article Ideas
Direct mail	Nonprofits, magazines, banking, restaurants	Save money on direct mail costs; increase profits; increase customer base or donations through direct mail
Business banking	Small businesses	How to apply for credit lines; using business lines of credit to expand your business; tax implications of business credit
Recycling	Construction, city governments	City recycling programs; construction recycling programs

Your Industry	Allied Industries	Article Ideas
Personal insurance	Small business owners, entrepreneurs, and farmers	The importance of insurance for entrepreneurs; how farmers can save on insurance

By crossing over into these allied industries, you accomplish two things:

- **You find a new niche audience who may need your product or service**—By establishing yourself as the expert in your field as it relates to their field (as opposed to trying to be an expert in their field), you become much more useful and trusted.

- **You stop preaching to the choir**—It's a common desire to want to be seen as the expert among experts in your own field. We do it, too. Some of the content we create is designed to outdo other social media experts...

@edeckers: But I am better than you.

@kyleplacy: Older doesn't always mean better.

...or to see if we can write about a topic first and get everyone else to jump on the bandwagon. However, we're not going to be hired by other social media consultants. And you're never going to get work from other direct mail firms, business bankers, recycling plants, or insurance agents. (Well, almost never. See Chapter 12 on networking.) So, don't worry so much about trying to impress them, except at the national convention.

Hobby Publications

These are a good place to pursue writing about your personal passion or hobby. They let you practice your writing (in addition to your personal blog, if you're already doing that), you can learn more about your particular topic, and if nothing else, they give you another notch on your writing belt.

Some hobby publications are less stringent than other types of publications we've mentioned earlier. That's not to say they're lax and willing to accept any schlock you throw at them, but they're a little more willing to accept your contributions, especially if you're still new at the writing game. They're a great way to build up your writing portfolio as you go for bigger and better-paying writing gigs. Some of the premier hobby magazines publish articles from the leading practitioners of the hobby, so you're going to have a tougher time breaking into those.

Submitting to hobby publications is just like submitting to other publications we've discussed: Submit a query letter, and pitch an idea to the editor. If you're blogging already, be sure to tell the editor about your blog. Although this is a good strategy for any writing you're doing (except maybe for the scientific journals), it may be more helpful for hobby publications because you can demonstrate your expertise and authority in that field.

Major Mainstream Magazines

This is the pinnacle of magazine publishing. If you can make it in the general interest magazines—*Time, Newsweek, Better Home & Gardens, Sports Illustrated, Entrepreneur, BusinessWeek*—that's really saying something. The articles in these magazines are the highest caliber, the writers are the best in their field, and the pay is some of the highest in the industry.

But the competition is intense, and some of these publications don't even accept freelance submissions. So, be sure to check out the writers' guidelines before you submit a query or pitch an idea. You also want to make sure you have publishing credits in other publications before you submit to the major magazines.

Go Horizontal Instead of Vertical

There are publications geared toward people who work in a particular segment that can be covered horizontally, rather than vertically, like we've just discussed. For example, there are trade magazines for people in the retail industry, such as lumber yards, grocery stores, electronics stores, and liquor stores. There are trade magazines for people in all levels of IT, people in different facets of marketing, and people in different positions in the restaurant industry. An article such as "How to Save Money on Credit Card Processing" would work for any magazine in the retail industry. "Direct Mail Still Improves ROI" could fit in any marketing trade magazine.

 Note

A "vertical" refers to a particular industry or market, like a "publishing vertical" or "automotive vertical." If you sold software used only by book publishers, you would sell to the "publishing vertical." Going "horizontally" means you have a product or expertise that spans all verticals, like marketing or accounting.

The nice thing about these types of magazines is that you can easily tailor one article to each niche and have it run several times without being read by the same people. Your article about lowering credit card fees for restaurants can be recycled as an article about lowering credit card fees for lumber yards, grocery stores, and liquor stores.

This is also a favorite trick of freelance writers: Build one story from scratch, retool it for a different publication and market, and generate some additional revenue out of it. We discuss ownership rights later, so be sure you haven't signed over all rights to an article. Be sure to read the magazine's contract for mention of intellectual property rights and republication rights.

 Tip

> Most magazines hate simultaneous submissions. They don't want you to publish identical articles in different magazines. They don't even want you to submit the same article to different magazines. Also keep in mind that some magazines don't like reprints, although most will accept them. Check out the "Publication Rights" section later in this chapter to see what kinds of conditions you can and should sell your articles under.

Build Your Personal Brand with Your Writing

The one problem associated with writing B2B articles is if you're a completely generous team player. Your company would get all the credit for your work, your expertise, and your knowledge while you get the byline. Getting the byline is important, but sometimes you may end up giving away the credit that should build your brand. We've talked to people who have written extensively for trade publications, but they later realized they have not reaped any of the benefit. Sure, they get an item to put on their résumé, an article to include in their personnel file, or something to get more writing opportunities. But when it came to building their personal brand, they missed out on a significant opportunity.

Doug Karr said that when he worked for a newspaper publisher as a database marketer, he wrote extensively for trade publications about database marketing in the newspaper industry. The problem was, said Doug, he always wrote about the great things his employer was doing, even though *he* was the one doing it all. He wrote the articles about the company's efforts, without alluding to any of the work he had done.

Doug said that when the time came for a job search and he wanted to tell people about all the great stuff he had been doing, all of his articles—his "proof"—showed that it was a company effort. He found that although other people in his industry knew about the database marketing his old employer had been doing, no one realized that he had been the one to do it all. As such, he didn't get the benefit to his personal brand by taking more ownership of what he had written, and he may have missed out on several job opportunities because no one in the industry knew his accomplishments and reputation like he had hoped.

"I think people need to be a little more selfish when it comes to this," Doug said. "I think if I had to do it over, I would talk about my efforts more, so people knew it was me who did the work. That would have helped me in the job market more."

Although this may be a tough line to walk—how do you talk about "my" efforts versus "my team's" efforts without sounding like a glory hound?—you need to take some ownership of your knowledge and experience in your articles, whether you're writing the article in first person, using personal anecdotes, or even mentioning your efforts in the byline. Remember, this isn't just about adding a single line to your résumé; it's about building your personal brand and authority within your field.

If the magazine publishes a bio section, you will also get a chance to talk about your accomplishments. You can at least take credit there by saying you led the efforts, worked on the project, or managed the team that did everything you described in the article.

So, continue to promote accomplishments like this to your network. Twitter messages and Facebook status updates like "So excited to see my latest article in *Marble Collectors Digest* yesterday" with a link to the online version are more than acceptable. Then, assuming your network includes a bunch of marble collectors, others will see the article and associate you with it.

Promoting your published articles this way, especially if you have online versions to link to, is no different from promoting your blog posts and other accomplishments (see Chapter 3, "Blogging: Telling Your Story"). Treat them the same way, but point out that they're also available in print. As long as the people in your network see them, you can get more benefit out of them than if you limit your publication accomplishments to just your résumé.

Finally, don't forget to publish your Twitter handle or your main website in your byline so people can find you online. Make sure you write a tight bio on your website, in your Twitter profile, and in your article.

Publication Rights

We need to touch on publication rights briefly here, although you'll want to do more reading on this via other resources, like *Writer's Digest* or any of the thousands of online writing resources. You can offer several basic types of rights:

- **First North American Serial Rights (FNASR)**—These are rights you offer to a publication in North America that lets it publish your piece for the first time. These rights tell the publisher that you've never published this piece anywhere else. The work cannot be reprinted in another format or outside of North America. Often (but not always), FNASR excludes electronic rights.

- **First rights**—These specify that a publication has "first use" of the piece, but it isn't limited to print publications. Electronic markets, like websites, use first rights.

- **Second rights or reprint rights**—Second rights are the publication rights you can give to any other publisher after you have sold FNASRs, but you can publish the piece simultaneously.

- **One-time rights**—These let a publication use your work once, but not first, and sometimes simultaneously. These are similar to second rights.

- **Electronic rights**—Most writers try to avoid electronic rights because it means there is no difference in the format where your work is published (database, website, blog, and article site). Sometimes the article becomes exclusive to the publisher, which means you can never republish it anywhere else.

- **All rights**—This means a publisher buys every instance where your piece could be published—electronic, print, you name it. Writers should avoid these rights whenever possible, but if you can't escape it, figure out how much you realistically could get paid for the piece over several years, and charge that much.

Many publishers have their own contracts they require writers to sign before they accept your material. Some magazines do not negotiate on the publication rights they give the writers. So when a publisher accepts a piece for publication, you need to consider whether you're willing to live with their terms, especially when being asked for electronic rights or all rights. (*Source: Writing-World.com*[3])

Create Your Own Articles' Niche

In Chapter 3, we talked about how to find your own writing niche. We also talked about the importance of creating a rather narrow niche so you could be known for something.

---

3. http://www.writing-world.com/rights/copyright.shtml.

Note

Remember, a general topic might be cooking, a narrow topic might be
Italian cooking, but a niche is something like "Gluten-Free Italian Cooking"
or "Finance —> Personal Finance —> Personal Finance for Generation Y."

When you blog, you can just write whatever you want, and your readers will follow you and love you. But the readers of a print publication want all kinds of things and might abandon a publication if they're not getting what they want. Also, bloggers have a personality and tone that readers respond to. Most print publications have their own personality, rather than the writers', so that's a big difference when considering your readers and writing outlets.

The point we're trying to make is that it's not always necessary, or even a good idea, to focus on a single niche all the time. If you're that gluten-free Italian cooking writer, you're going to find few opportunities to write about gluten-free Italian cooking for different publications.

There will be industry health magazines, local parenting newspapers, and even national cooking magazines. But you can't publish the same article over and over. (Editors hate that and will blackball you for it.) However, you can recycle articles and reprint them in different publications; keep in mind, though, that there are only so many publications that are looking for your particular niche.

In this case, it may be more important to widen your niche a little bit. Don't focus so narrowly on a single type or country of origin of food. Rather, stick with gluten-free cooking, and you can talk about a variety of topics. For example, you could publish these articles in different newspapers or general interest magazines to fit the editorial calendar, or even the same publication:

- Gluten-free cooking for new Celiac sufferers (general)
- Gluten-free cookies for the holidays (holiday season)
- Gluten-free tailgating ideas (football season)
- Gluten-free romantic dinner ideas (Valentine's Day)
- Gluten-free cookout ideas (summer)

See, we haven't even talked about Italian food, but there are five ideas for different publications without once burying our head into our niche.

And the added benefit of doing this is that you're establishing a more impressive reputation as a gluten-free writer, and not just a gluten-free Italian cooking writer. And if you ever pursue those speaking opportunities, book opportunities, or the chance to appear on the various news and cooking shows, you're going to land that as the "gluten-free writer who *likes* Italian cooking."

Getting Started

Being published is just like getting a job. (Skip ahead to Chapter 15, "Personal Branding: Using What You've Learned to Land Your Dream Job," if you don't believe us.) You have to find a possible opening, send in your résumé (your query letter), have an interview (your completion of the writing project), and be paid. (And in some cases, you may actually be asked to send in a real résumé and do a real interview.) Here are the basic steps to follow when you have the confidence to take that first writing step:

- **Do research first**—After you figure out which kinds of publications to write for, don't just submit an article to the editor. Maybe they don't publish the kind of article you wrote, or they just published a similar one last month. Get back issues of the publication to see what kinds of stories they write and whether anyone has written about your niche before.

- **Get the writers' guidelines**—Each magazine has writers' guidelines. The ones that have joined the 21st century have them online. But the older ones may make you send a self-addressed stamped envelope (SASE) to get them. When you get the guidelines, follow them exactly! If they say to submit a query letter but no article, then submit a query letter without an article. Deviating from the guidelines will mean a certain literary death.

  Editors can be cranky and finicky...

  > **@edeckers:** Not ours, of course.
  >
  > **@kyleplacy:** Absolutely, not ours.

  ...and if editors see you deviating from their guidelines, they'll toss your submission into the trash can without the slightest twinge of remorse. Editors are often asked what their biggest pet peeve is. Almost all of them say getting queries and articles that don't follow the writers' guidelines.

  > **@edeckers:** It's death, I tell you! Death!
  >
  > **@kyleplacy:** Settle down.

- **Write a solid query letter**—This is the "résumé" we referred to earlier. There are certain pieces of information you need to include in a cover letter or query letter.

Note

A cover letter is included with an article submission. A query letter asks if you can write or submit an article.

Include a paragraph about the article you want to write and what you want it to be about. Next, cite your experience as an expert on that topic. Third, cite your experience as a writer on this topic. (This is where personal branding comes in handy.)

Several websites, magazine articles, and books discuss the best way to write a query letter. Refer to them for the particulars of the language and information to include or exclude. We especially like *Writer's Digest*, which we mentioned earlier in the chapter. You can pick up a copy of it at your local library or bookstore.

- **Do the work you're supposed to**—This is your "interview." Not only does the editor want to see if you can write, she wants to see if you can follow instructions. If you write a good article, you'll get the byline and the paycheck. If you don't follow instructions, your story may not even get published, and you won't get paid. Which brings us to our next point....

- **Invoice immediately**—You're a professional now, so act like one. Don't wait for a publisher to pay you; send an invoice. Send it with the work if you can. Although some magazines already have a well-established system in place, don't wait for them to show you whether they do or don't. Send the invoice and make sure you are paid on time. If you are not paid right away, send another invoice. If the magazine fails to pay, don't accept any more work from that magazine until you see your money. Treasure the relationships you have with the ones that pay immediately, and drop the ones that don't.

- **Once you establish your reliability, you may be able to pitch other ideas to the editor**—It's important to feel the editor out first, though. Make a couple of basic suggestions for other article ideas via a query letter or email. See if the editor is receptive to the idea. If she is, and you can continue to provide solid ideas that are up to date and follow the editor's editorial calendar, you become a valuable resource. (Remember how we talked about being a valuable resource in other chapters?) The more valuable you are, the more the editor will rely on you.

- **Continue to network with the editor and staff**—Don't be a pest, but don't be a stranger either. Keep in touch with these people via LinkedIn and Twitter, if they use them. And when they leave for another publication, keep in touch. If they loved you for their old publication, they'll love you for this one, too. At the same time, you'll need to start over with the new editor at square one. Keep in mind that although your old editor thought you were a valuable addition to the magazine, the new editor has his or her own vision, and you may not fit it. Don't take it personally if you don't.

Getting Paid

Writers are paid. They write for money, not for exposure, for contributor copies, or for the promise of more money at a later date. And despite what sites like ClientsFromHell.net (see Figure 14.1) may make you think, most editors are a good and fair bunch of people who want to see their writers fairly compensated.

@kyleplacy:	Absolutely. So good they're fattening! And very fair!
@edeckers:	And good looking, too. In fact, the best looking of any editor there ever was.
@YourDamnEditor:	Guys, forget it. You already signed the contract.

Figure 14.1 *People who offer you a chance to write for "exposure" sometimes have more grandiose expectations of what you're going to get.*

Note

Contributor copies are free copies of the magazine your article is published in, presumably so you can give them to all your friends and family.

However, there are two things you need to know about writing professionally. First, writing for magazines and newspapers is a tough way to make a living. The pay is not lucrative, and you're going to work harder doing this than you would with a regular 8–5 day job. However, from a personal branding standpoint, writing professionally is worth the time and effort.

Second, you're not going to make much money in the beginning. You're going to have to establish yourself and prove that you're a great writer and that you can turn out high-quality material on the deadlines.

Paying Your Dues

You have to pay your dues for a while. That's a given. It may suck, and you may think you're beneath it, but you're going to have to put up with it. However, depending on how good you are—don't make this assessment yourself; ask one of your brutally honest friends—your dues-paying period can be shorter or longer.

There are a few reasons why all new writers have to pay dues:

- **Every writer and editor before you did it**—They didn't get to exact revenge on those older writers and editors, so they have to take it out on the newbies. That's you.

- **No one knows you**—They don't know if you suck or if you're awesome. You need to prove your worth by being easy to work with, turning your work in on time, giving editors exactly what they want, and being a good writer.

- **You'll be paid what you're worth**—As you prove that you're better than the others, you'll get more money. As you prove that you're more reliable than the others, you'll get even more money. And as you prove that you're better at this and know more about the subject matter than anyone else, you'll get even more money than that.

This is personal branding in a nutshell. You need to prove that you're as awesome as you—and we—think you are. The only way to do that is by doing what it takes to succeed in this or any other business. Do that, and you'll start reaping your rewards.

The Myth of "Exposure"

Having said all that, you will reach the point where you should not only *ask* for money, but *expect* it. You will reach the point where you should be writing only for money. You've proven yourself and made a name for yourself, so money should be the only form of payment you receive.

This means you should turn down those who say they'll give you "exposure" instead of money.[4]

"We can't pay you, but you'll get great exposure" or "You'll get a great article for your portfolio."

Turn these people down. If you're getting paid decent money for your articles, you are beyond the need for all the benefits that "exposure" will get you. If you are getting top dollar for your articles, you've probably stopped clipping articles for your portfolio months ago. Erik has had exchanges like this with editors of small publications before, and they all usually end the same way:

Erik: How much do you pay for publication?

Editor: Well, we give you five free copies of our magazine.

Erik: And...?

Editor: Uh, and you get some great exposure for your writing.

Erik: Sorry, my supermarket doesn't let me pay for groceries with "exposure."

Editor: But more people will hear about you, and you can secure paying gigs in the future.

Erik: Or I could secure paying gigs right now.

We don't advocate writing for exposure after you have several published articles under your belt. Exposure is fine and all, but it doesn't pay the rent, and you can't eat it. We've been offered "exposure" by magazines with print runs that are measured in the hundreds. We have to wonder just how good that exposure could actually be. (Most of them fold a few months later.)

Do's and Don'ts of Writing for Publication

There are a few do's and don'ts to writing for publication, just like for anything you want to pursue. These are rules handed down from writer to writer, article to article, book to book, website to website.

---

4. Okay, there may be a few times you don't want to turn them down. They're your friends, or it's a startup publication that you want to see do well, or it's a nonprofit, or something noble and good. Or *The New York Times*. At the least you should get lunch out of it. Just remind them that you're beyond exposure, so you can feel like a big shot.

@edeckers: There, I worked in something about digital
              publishing. Happy?

@kyleplacy: Deliriously.

We have found that while most professionals are sticklers about the rules in their industry, publishers and editors are adamant about these. Ignore these rules at your peril.

- **Do read the writers' guidelines**—That's the best indication as to what the magazine or newspaper will accept from writers. These publications don't want new ideas, new topics, or new subjects.

- **Do proofread everything**—This is especially important when you're submitting your first query letter. Remember, you're submitting a story idea to a professional wordsmith. Editors take language and spelling seriously and will not look favorably upon a submission with even a single misspelling. That's not to say they'll pitch the article they agreed to purchase for a single typo, but even so, you want to avoid them.

- **Do read your submitted pieces out loud, including your initial query letter**—This will help you spot any errors or double words, like "the the."

- **Do meet all deadlines**—Nothing makes an editor go crazy like a writer who can't meet his or her deadlines. If you have a problem with time management and can't even meet the simplest deadlines at work, you may want to reconsider whether you should go into writing. At the very least, find a time management system and get better about meeting deadlines.

- **Don't get creative, wacky, or funny with your submissions, because it won't make you stand out in a positive way**—Just print your letters and your articles on plain white paper. There are websites that detail horror story after horror story of weird submissions to publishers and editors. And from what we have seen, if you just print your submissions and articles on plain white paper, you will stand out from a majority of the submissions they receive. Emailing is another acceptable option. Be sure to check the writers' guidelines to see whether your publication will accept email submissions. (Most of them do, but double-check.)

- **Don't get married to your words**—Don't think of them as your babies. Don't refuse to be edited. Even the best writers in the world are edited to a degree. If anything, an editor makes your writing better.

- **Don't plagiarize**—We shouldn't have to say this, but you would be surprised at the number of people who lift entire articles from other sources, thinking they won't get caught.

> **@kyleplacy:** It was the best of times, it was the worst of times.
>
> **@edeckers:** No! That's been done before.

Erik once caught an assistant editor of a weekly newspaper in Canada who had copied one of Erik's newspaper columns. Erik found him by doing a basic Google search on a unique phrase in that particular column, and this was before Google and search engines were so extensively used. Erik told the guy's publisher about it, and then pleaded for leniency on behalf of the offending writer. The offending editor wasn't fired, but he lost his newspaper column and was suspended without pay for two months.

While we were working on the second edition of this book, Erik learned he was plagiarized twice, once by a newspaper editor in Minnesota, and once by a publisher in Canada, both of whom had made a long-running habit of stealing from other humor writers. Both men resigned in disgrace after the stories of their serial theft made national and journalism industry news. So, in terms of stealing Erik's stuff, Canada leads the U.S., 2–1, but we're hoping the U.S. can make a comeback before the third edition.

> **@edeckers:** Actually, no we don't. That was an awful experience.
>
> **@kyleplacy:** Seriously. Haven't you people ever heard of Google?

- **Don't stray from the writers' guidelines**—We know we already said it, but we can't say it enough. Nothing will get your query letter or article thrown in the trash faster than straying from the writers' guidelines.

How Can Our Heroes Turn to Writing for Publication?

- **Allen (influencer)** spent 14 years working for a marketing agency and is considered a veteran of the industry. He has a good idea of what works and doesn't work and could write articles for the different marketing magazines. These magazines are usually read by other marketers, whether they're in agencies. Another possibility is to publish basic how-to articles for small business magazines and Chamber of Commerce publications—things that the do-it-yourself marketer would benefit from. These may also help Allen catch the eye of agency owners and business owners, which is important, because Allen is looking for a job.

- **Beth (climber)** has a plan to become the chief marketing officer of an insurance company. One way to prove that she knows her stuff is to publish marketing articles—especially case studies of her company's own marketing efforts—for trade publications. Beth will actually get two things out of this. First, she can bolster her reputation among other marketers, some of whom may want to recruit her as she climbs her way to the CMO job. Second, she can be noticed by other C-level executives who will want to hire CMOs. Her case studies will let her show off her past work in a public setting. If she uses these articles and her social networks, she can get her name in front of those C-level executives on an ongoing basis.

- **Carla (neophyte)** is a former pharmaceutical sales rep who is out of work but trying to find a fundraising or program director position at a nonprofit. Publishing in trade journals may not make as much of an impact; although it's something she should consider. Blogging may be her better and more effective outlet for showing how well she understands the nonprofit field. However, she could write career advice pieces aimed at college students who want to go into sales, especially in the pharmaceutical industry. She can also write sales advice columns for business magazines.

- **Darrin (free agent)** is an IT professional who leaves his job every two or three years in pursuit of more money. Darrin has a few industry options, like publications geared toward chief information officers (CIOs) and IT networking professionals. These tend to be more newsy than how-to focused and often rely on reviews of products. Darrin can create the "product reviewer" as part of his personal brand and review different products and services. This will do two things: 1) set him up as someone who is always forward looking and willing to try new ideas and products and 2) plug him into beta releases of software and hardware. He'll know what's coming down the pike months before the general IT community will. So when he's not writing these kinds of articles for print, he can write them for his blog and get a boost to this part of his brand. The upshot is that for less than double the amount of effort, he gets twice the benefit.

15

Personal Branding: Using What You've Learned to Land Your Dream Job

Let's just get this out of the way: If you start networking for your new job on the day you were let go from your last job, you're already behind.

If you're out of work, looking for work, and trying to create your personal brand to help you do it, you should have done this during your previous job. But it's not too late, not by a long shot. You're just going to have to develop your network much more quickly.

If you're still employed, you need to start putting the lessons in this book into practice right now, today. You need to lay the groundwork for your next job while you still have an income, not while the pressure of taking care of you and your family is looming over your head, stressing you out.

Whether you're happy in your current job or searching for your next gig, you need to start planting the seeds now for a professional network that can reach potential employers and colleagues who will give you solid job referrals. Building this type of network takes time, and you want it in place before you actually need it.

We have both received calls from people who are looking for work, wondering if we can help them, know of any openings in their field, and even introduce them to other people they should talk to. We're always willing to help as much as we can, but it can sometimes be difficult to be helpful when we're given short notice.

Erik once received a call from a friend a few days after the friend was let go from his old position.

"I'm reaching out to the people in my personal network to find a new job," said the guy.

"Who does that involve?" asked Erik.

"The people I used to work with," said the guy. The problem was he came from a fairly closed system—no outside networking, no outside meetings. In short, the only people the guy knew were just as professionally isolated as he was.

But if you don't have a job at this moment, there's still time to network. (We're just trying to scare the hell out of the people who already have a job and are wasting time watching reality TV night after night.) Building your network to find potential employers and job referral sources can take a few months, and if you're wondering about your next paycheck, this can be a scary time.

Still, you need to start building that network because 1) you might get lucky and find something right away and 2) you want to have the network in place so when you're looking for another job, you don't have this long and expensive ramp-up time.

Remember, building your personal brand is actually about building relationships. You need to build and maintain those relationships over weeks, months, and years, both online and offline. Use your social media presence to build your brand and expand your network to help with your job search when the time comes.

Our friend, Jack[1], has benefitted from having a strong social media presence and landed a couple of jobs that way.

A Fortune 100 corporation hired Jack for a social media position after reading his blog. He wrote regularly about how social media humanizes a brand and builds community with its customers. The corporation just happened to be launching a social media initiative at the same time, and they liked what Jack wrote.

In the interview, the director of global Internet marketing told Jack that he was impressed with his blog and thought Jack had the knowledge to help him launch the company's global social media initiative.

Jack's blog basically positioned him as the thought leader for leading the corporation's new initiative the company was launching. He said he got the interview because someone within the company had been reading his blog and passed the information to the global Internet marketing director.

---

1. Not his real name, but he's really our friend. No, seriously.

The only time Jack said he presented a résumé was during the interview, when he and the director discussed other points of his professional background. Jack got the job and worked for the company for several months on the new initiative.

While we were writing this chapter, Jack was contacted by a large Internet marketing solutions provider about an internal PR spot. Jack submitted a formal résumé but was told by the marketing communications director that he had already looked at Jack's social graph (the sum total of social media assets he had on the web).

It turns out the two were already connected on LinkedIn, so the marketing communications director studied Jack's profile, his blog, and other social media information. He also looked at Jack's work for a nonprofit association and the work he did for the Fortune 100 corporation. Although Jack didn't get the job, he did make it to the final round of the interview process and thinks he wouldn't have made it that far if he hadn't had the original connection with the marketing communications director.

This is what the previous 14 chapters have been leading up to. This is where your personal branding efforts are ultimately going to pay off. Using these tools, you're going to have a better opportunity to find and land the job you want in the industry you enjoy.

This is why you need to treat social media as a networking tool, not just a fun way to play Farmville or organize hookups, club hopping, and pub crawls. You need to be your own marketer and create your own buzz.

If you can create enough buzz about yourself, employers will start to imagine how much more you can do for them.

Using Your Network to Find a Job

Jack's story about being contacted by the marketing communications director is not that unusual. In Jack's case, the two were connected on a few different social networks for more than a year. They were well aware of each other, have followed each other's progress, and keep up with each other before the director took the position. Jack first connected with the marketing communications director before he took the position at the Internet marketing company.

Even though he didn't get the job, the fact that he made it that far into the company's hiring process says a lot about the online connections he made. It wasn't a position he sought; rather, he just happened to be connected to the right person at the right time.

But what's unusual about the story is that in the time since we wrote the first edition of this book, this is not so unusual anymore. We've been hearing more and more stories about how people made that first job-related connection on social media, and not on the major job boards or by mailing in a paper résumé.

We've mentioned before about social media being *faith-based networking*. The idea is that you will meet the right person with the right opportunity at the right time. Of course, this doesn't just magically happen. You must be present and participate for a long time before that right person with the right opportunity comes along. Just like the athlete who spends countless hours practicing her sport, you need to spend countless hours creating and promoting your personal brand. Those hours will eventually pay off by connecting with, not the first person, not the tenth person, not even the hundredth person, but with the person who is your thousandth connection.

And you can't rush these things. So, no cheating.

Twitter: Make Job Connections in 140 Characters

This is one of the times it's okay to talk about yourself more than a little. (See Chapter 5, "Twitter: Sharing in the Conversation.") If you're job hunting, feel free to tell your Twitter friends. Ask them to keep an eye open for any position that matches your skills and experience. Direct them to your LinkedIn profile, your blog, and your online portfolio (if appropriate and available). A lot of your industry experts will know about job openings that may not hit the job boards or may not even be widely known within the hiring company yet.

Tweet a variation of this message more than once or twice a week, and ask people to send you a direct message if they have anything. Ask them to retweet your request.

Warning

Do not tweet, post Facebook updates, make LinkedIn updates, or otherwise publicly tell your social network you are looking for a new job while you are still employed. Erik knows someone who did this. Her employer helpfully gave her an additional 40 hours a week to focus on her job search.

Use LinkedIn to Make Job Connections

While we were writing this chapter, Erik was asked by a freelance writer to introduce her through LinkedIn to a hiring manager at a publishing house. What was interesting was that Erik didn't even know the person he was supposed to introduce the writer to. But he knew someone who knew the hiring manager (HM).

The request originally came in from LinkedIn, where both Erik and the writer were connected. She saw that Erik was connected to the HM by reviewing his connections, by two degrees. In other words, there was one person between Erik and the HM.

So, she sent Erik a Get Introduced request, which not only had a message to the HM, but also another message asking Erik to make the connection. He then forwarded that on to the person *he* was connected with, who then forwarded it on to the HM. The connection was made, the writer sent her résumé, and we're waiting to see what happens next.

One of the great things about LinkedIn is that you can see who knows whom, who is connected, and what they do for their employer. You can make the decision about who to connect with.

The Art of the Connection

Making a connection on LinkedIn is an important part of the job search process. For one thing, you don't want to go peppering your entire network about whether they know of any job openings. It's okay to ask them once or twice a week, but bugging them day after day is bad form and will get you unconnected and ignored as fast as any spammer.

A LinkedIn connection is someone in your LinkedIn network. LinkedIn measures your total network by degrees of separation. Kyle and Erik are directly connected, so they are "1st degree connections." If you know Erik but not Kyle, you are a "2nd degree connection" to Kyle, through Erik. Figure 15.1 shows how you can be connected to someone in your network.

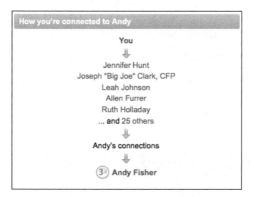

Figure 15.1   *LinkedIn will show you how you're connected to someone else in your network. This way, you can ask for an Introduction request, or in some cases, connect with someone directly, and send a message that says, "We're both connected to_____."*

Asking your networking contacts for a connection is a tricky process. For one thing, you may ask your best friend to connect you with one of his contacts (someone you don't actually know), but addressing him like you would in any other email may not be appropriate. Figure 15.2 is a good example of what *not* to say to your friend in an introduction request.

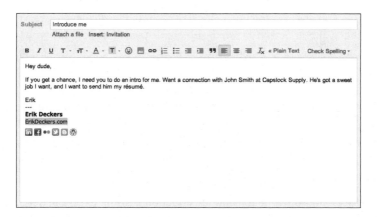

Figure 15.2   *This is an example of what not to write in an introductory email. It doesn't matter if your connection is your best friend. The person you are introducing is going to see your note to your friend.*

The person you're ultimately connecting to will see this note to your contact. So, it needs to be as professionally written as your cover note to your final connection. This means spelling, grammar, and punctuation must be perfect as well. If it helps, write your note in a word processing document, edit it a couple times, and then sit on it for 24 hours. Edit it one more time, and then send it. Do this for both notes.

Your contact may have a few errors in his note, but you can't afford that luxury.

If you need to, send a separate email to your contact telling him what you're about to do. See if he can recommend any strategies for dealing with your final connection.

Should You Connect Directly or Ask for a Connection?

Isn't it easier to contact someone directly rather than ask someone to ask someone to connect you? Sure it is. But it's not always more effective.

It's one thing to connect with someone because you're both in the same LinkedIn group, belong to the same social network, or even are part of the same trade association. You can always send a personal note that tells the other person how you're connected.

 Tip

Don't just use the default note that comes with your LinkedIn connection request. Write a note about how you know the other person or why you want to connect. Leaving the default note just shows laziness and may cause the other person to click I Don't Know This Person, which gets you in trouble with the LinkedIn administrators. If this happens, your account will be temporarily suspended until you read and sign an online form that says you promise not to try to connect with people who don't know you.

But what if that other person has no idea who you are? It's not always a great idea to try to connect with someone you have absolutely no connection with. It may be seen as annoying, as intrusive, or as some cheap way to connect because you're trying to look for a job. (Sure that's what you *are* doing, but you just don't want it to look that blatant.)

This is why asking someone for that introduction is going to be a better step to take; you're asking a trusted acquaintance to vouch for you. By forwarding a connection request, an acquaintance is, in essence, saying, "I know this person. This is someone I think you should get to know, because it will be a mutually beneficial connection."

This is why it's important to connect only with people who you have actually met or know, rather than just trying to amass as many LinkedIn connections as you can. There are some people, known as LIONs, who want to connect with as many people as they can.

```
@kyleplacy:  What does LION mean anyway?
@edeckers:   LinkedIn Obnoxious Networker.
@kyleplacy:  Really? Are you sure it doesn't mean Open Networker?
@edeckers:   To-may-to, to-mah-to.
```

Basically, a LION tries to amass tens of thousands of connections. The problem is that although they have grown this gargantuan network, they don't actually know any of the people in it. They're not good connections for you if you want to connect to a possible hiring manager. Just as you don't want to become a LION, you don't want to rely on one to make connections for you, like with a potential hiring manager. LIONs generally don't know everyone in their gargantuan network, which means the other person doesn't know them either, and that can hurt your chances. Avoid asking a LION for help.

Use LinkedIn to Get Inside Info

The best way to find out about a company is to talk to former employees. You can do a search for a company name on LinkedIn. (Select Companies in the drop-down menu next to the search box, or click the Advanced button.) Then you can look at people's profiles and pick the ones who used to work at that company. Try to pick the ones who are closest to you in terms of degrees of connectedness.

Connect directly through the usual process by asking for introductions or by joining an industry group and then connecting that way—we discuss these in Chapter 4, "LinkedIn: Networking on Steroids"—and explain that you're trying to get some insight into their former employer. After you connect, ask some basic questions about life at the company, their areas of responsibility, the sorts of issues they regularly faced at work, and a typical day at the company.

This strategy can be a bit risky if you do it the wrong way or ask the wrong questions. Make it clear that you're not looking for gossip or secrets, but you want to know some day-in-the-life type of information. Ask the former employees things like what you can expect if you work there, what the work climate is like, and what the hot button issues are that you might mention during an interview.

Don't try to find out insider information or dig up dirt on your potential boss. Your new contact may have a long-standing friendly relationship with this person, and your nosiness can get back to the HM in a few seconds.

Of course, if your contact happens to drop a little gossip about the person who might ultimately be your boss, or why they left, don't ignore it. Everyone has a bad boss now and again, and if your information gathering reveals the person you're trying to work for is a tyrannical egomaniac who could reduce Genghis Khan to tears, it's better you find out about it now than two weeks into your new job.

Creating a Résumé

Your résumé is basically a synopsis of your career, your high points, and your successes. It's evidence of your overall awesomeness, and it gives companies a reason to bring you in for an interview.

That's worth repeating: A résumé is not supposed to get you a *job*; it's supposed to get you an *interview*.

We'd love to say that you could have Jack's luck and connect with people online...

@edeckers: Actually, we are saying that. That's the point of the whole book.

@kyleplacy: I know. I just didn't want the legal department jumping all over us with their disclaimers.

@LegalBeagle: Whereas many, but not all, of your claims might possibly be taken as guarantees, we have concerns that some, but not all ###FAIL WHALE###

...but that's not a common occurrence. It happens enough times that this is a strategy worth pursuing, but it needs to be one part of a job search campaign, not the entire campaign. You need a résumé.

Should I Create a Paper Résumé?

Short answer: Yes.

Longer answer: Yes, but.

Best answer: If you have to.

Our friend, Doug Karr (www.MarketingTechBlog.com), owner of DK New Media and host of Marketing Tech Radio, says he hasn't used a paper résumé in years. He steers people toward his LinkedIn résumé, and if they don't know how to use it or still insist on a paper résumé because "that's the way we've always done it," he knows he doesn't want to work there.

Of course, Doug is in the rather enviable position of being "kind of a big deal." He co-wrote *Corporate Blogging for Dummies*, he's a highly sought-after speaker on blogging and social media, and he has his own successful social media agency. (How? By practicing everything we've been talking about here, but that's not the point right now.)

Doug's attitude may be a little unusual because much of the corporate world is still locked into using paper résumés and electronic résumés that can be easily uploaded into a company's candidate management software. But how long will it be before LinkedIn becomes the standard operating procedure for more and more companies? How long will it be before companies start allowing infographic-type websites like re.vu, visualize.me, or even the Brazen Careerist's Facebook app?

We're longing for the day this will happen—that corporate America will join the 21st century and find a new, better, more efficient way to screen candidates. Until then, right or wrong, like it or not, you should develop a regular résumé and be prepared to give it to anyone who asks. At least until you become a big shot and can afford to refuse to work for anyone who doesn't want to check your LinkedIn profile.

How Does Social Media Fit in Your Résumé?

We use social media so much these days that the question has begun to arise whether you should include it among your skills, at least for the nonsocial media positions. Another, more important question is whether you have skills, knowledge, and experience in social media that can be demonstrated?

It comes down to this: If you know enough about social media to teach an entire day-long seminar on the subject, you can list it. If you spent an entire day creating a Double Rainbow—Over the Rainbow mashup video, keep that to yourself. Table 15.1 shows some other do's and don'ts for mentioning social media on your résumé.

Table 15.1 When to Include Social Media Skills on Your Résumé

Do Include	Don't Include	Exception
You spend several hours a week creating a video reality series.	You post videos of your dog dancing to Ray Charles songs.	Your dancing dog videos have 2 million hits a month and you're in negotiations for a TV series.
You blog about Facebook marketing.	You made $1 billion in gold coins playing *Pirate Clan* on Facebook.	You made $1 billion in real coins creating *Pirate Clan* for Facebook.
You helped a restaurant create a *Foursquare* marketing campaign.	You're the mayor of your favorite coffee shop, and you get a free muffin every Monday.	Your army of *Foursquare* followers has increased revenue for your favorite restaurants by 200%.

Six Tips for Listing Social Media on Your Résumé

Social media is still new enough that there are plenty of questions about how to include it on your résumé, or whether you even should. We think social media is only going to grow in acceptance, so it's better to include it whenever necessary or possible.

- **Make sure you can demonstrate your success on past campaigns—** This is where measurement and analytics are important. You need to show the results of past social media campaigns. Mention your best ones on the résumé, but come to interviews prepared to discuss numbers. Have printouts of your results and summaries of the campaigns. Use tools like Google Analytics and a spreadsheet to show your successes.

- **Only list the social networks that you use in a professional manner—**"Started the Cougar Moms Who Love *Twilight* Facebook Page" is probably not suitable for a professional résumé. Keep things like Facebook and ChatRoulette off your résumé, unless you have a professional-looking business page for a design portfolio or similar sample page. You want to keep your Facebook profile clean and free of incriminating photos and content; a professional résumé is not the place to list your personal network. (While you shouldn't include your Facebook page on your résumé, it's still important to keep it clean because hiring managers may check out your page to learn more about you.)

 Note

There is a difference between a Facebook *profile* and a business *page*. Your *profile* is your personal Facebook page. It's where you connect with your friends and play different games. The business *page* is where you promote your business, band, or cause.

- **Make sure your personal networks are clean and devoid of any inappropriate photos or comments—**Don't worry too much about what your friends have done or said; employers shouldn't hold that against you. (You can always block them or unfriend them if they become too over the top though.) But make sure your own house is in order. You can also delete negative comments if you think it's necessary.

- **Stick with three or four social networks—**Don't list every network you belong to, but use the ones that you think an HM might be part of. Twitter and LinkedIn are the two big ones, but if you belong to an industry network, list it. Avoid the esoteric and niche networks if they're not related to the job or industry you're applying for.

- **Shorten URLs using bit.ly or another URL shortener, if you have long URLs**—Use URLs whenever appropriate to point hiring managers to important information. This can include blogs, articles, galleries and portfolios, and LinkedIn URLs.

 Tip

Bitly (www.bitly.com) can track clicks of URLs you have shortened so you can see how many people click that particular link. You can create individual URLs for different links to see if and when they get clicked, which can tell you if the HMs are actually using those links. If you want to be clever, create a separate URL each time you send a résumé. Then you can see if they ever were clicked.

- **Claim your personalized URL on Facebook and LinkedIn**—Although you won't necessarily post your Facebook URL on your résumé, you should at least try to own it. Do post your LinkedIn URL on your résumé. Following are a couple examples of what personalized URLs look like:

```
http://www.facebook.com/erikdeckers
http://www.facebook.com/kyleplacy
http://www.linkedin.com/in/kylelacy
http://www.linkedin.com/in/erikdeckers
```

Do's and Don'ts of Résumé Building

Writing a résumé is both an art and a science, and there are people who devote their professional lives to résumé writing. If you can afford to work with one of these people, it could be well worth it. But you can also read books and blogs on résumé writing. In the meantime, here are a few do's and don'ts for you to consider.

- **Don't lie**—You'd think we wouldn't have to say this, but you'd be surprised at the number of people who act like they've never heard this at least once in their lives. Do not lie on your résumé! It's as simple as that. If you lie, you will be caught. Maybe not during the job search; maybe not even during your first year. But you will be caught. And when you are, things will most certainly hit the fan.

In 2001, football coach George O'Leary left his job at Georgia Tech University to become the head football coach for the University of Notre Dame. His tenure there lasted all of 120 hours because he lied about having a Master's degree and about lettering three times in college football when he never played a single game. Five days after he was hired, O'Leary was asked to resign; he was humiliated and derided across the country.

O'Leary was lucky because he was hired by the Minnesota Vikings the next year, and he has been able to stay in football. But you won't be so lucky. Your reputation will be ruined, and you'll be forced to take a job you hate in a field you detest, all because you lied on your résumé.

- **Don't pad your résumé**—Padding is the same thing as lying. If you earned a certification, don't say you earned a degree. If you were a cashier, don't make yourself sound like an accountant. If you unloaded trucks, don't say you were in charge of shipping.

- **Don't worry about fancy paper**—Back in the early 1990s, Erik bought an entire ream (500 sheets) of fancy résumé paper, and he printed dozens of résumés and sent them out. Not only did the fancy paper not help him find a job, but he only used 100 sheets and ended up recycling the remaining paper five years later.

@kyleplacy: I was only 6 back then.

@edeckers: Shut up. Stupid punk kid.

White paper is more than adequate for your résumé. At the same time, don't use the cheapest copier paper you can find. Get something with some heft. Maybe 24-pound or 28-pound Bright White paper. Check with your local office supply store and pick up a short pack. You're not going to print out dozens of these things. You only need a few copies to take with you to your in-person interviews.

- **Don't misspell anything**—This is probably one of the most important pieces of résumé writing advice, although the fact that your résumé will be tossed because of a single typo also strikes us as one of the dumbest reasons to reject a candidate. Forget the years of hard work you've put in at other jobs, the Harvard MBA, the Medal of Honor, or the time you saved the president's dog from choking on a chicken bone. None of it matters because you accidentally missed the third s in antidisestablishmentarianism. Hard as it is to believe, some people are petty and small-minded enough to throw out the application of someone who could be the best person ever for a job, just because of a single typo. (Not that we're bitter or anything.) Don't give people that chance. Make sure your résumé is absolutely perfect and free of errors. Have a couple friends, or even a résumé writing professional, look over your résumé to ensure there's nothing that even the most officious bureaucrat could find wrong with it.

Having said all that, typos and mistakes make you look careless and not that smart. Even that one typo can make you look like you don't care enough to carefully read and proof your résumé before you send it.

- **Do keep it short**—Your résumé should be one page. Not two, not three, not five. One. Penelope Trunk, author of *Brazen Careerist*, says that HMs spend an average of 10 seconds looking at your résumé. They are most likely not going to look at a second page, and they certainly won't look at a third page. So, it doesn't do you any good to have a five-page résumé that details all your work accomplishments, including the time you were assistant substitute cashier at the Pick-N-Pay.

  Remember, your résumé is supposed to get you an interview. The interview is where you will win the job. Keep your résumé short, use bullet points to highlight accomplishments, and avoid the long narrative of what your responsibilities were. If you've been in your field for 20 years, listing your internship is not as helpful as the sentence explaining how you lead a companywide initiative that saved $5 million.

  Of course, if you're going for a position that requires an eight-page résumé, it means you're looking for the kind of position where you won't be going through HR but will deal directly with an executive head hunter or search committee. If that's the case, your résumé is going to be long because of your accomplishments over the past 15–20 years, which means you still shouldn't include your internship.

- **Do show your accomplishments**—A six-item bullet list of your job responsibilities at each position is not nearly as impressive as an explanation of how you solved a particular problem, managed a crisis, or helped your company save or make money. A bullet list of your responsibilities is not at all impressive. The goal of your résumé is to show how outstanding you are, not that you can come to work each day and perform your job description.

- **Do tailor your résumé for each position**—Remember, the résumé should be about how you can solve the company's problems, not get your own needs filled. Figure out what the company wants to accomplish by filling the position (that is, what "pain point" are you going to solve for them?), and then figure out what qualities the perfect candidate would have to solve that pain.

Tip

Most large companies now use electronic résumés and candidate software for their search processes. One of the functions of this software is to look for specific keywords in a candidate's résumé. If yours has them, you make the first electronic cut. If it doesn't, you're cast out immediately, never to be seen by human eyes. Check out the job description, figure out what keywords are going to hit the HM's hot buttons, and use them. Make each version of your résumé fit the job description.

- Do use action words and active voice—Action words are things like organized, launched, or managed. Phrases like "was responsible for" are weak and real yawners. Writing with authority and commitment shows drive and energy. Similarly, use active voice, rather than passive voice. Not only is passive voice too wordy, it's weak.

 Tip

Active voice is where the subject "does" the object: "I launched the campaign." Passive voice is where the object gets promoted to the subject position in the sentence: "The campaign was launched by me." Stick with active voice.

- **Do get creative, when appropriate**—If you're in the creative field, a creative résumé is expected. If you're in something a little more conservative, like banking or insurance, it's frowned upon. Feel free to let the creative juices flow if you think it will go over well. If you think it will cost you an interview, don't risk it.

Don't Rely on the Job Boards

If you're doing a job search, we don't want you to put all your faith, time, and energy into the job boards, like CareerBuilder.com, Monster.com, and Indeed.com. (You should spend most of your time following the steps we've discussed in the previous 14 chapters.)

Although the numbers seem to vary with who you talk to, job boards can hold anywhere from 5% to 25% of all new jobs. No one seems to have a definitive answer. The closest we found is a CareerBuilder.com press release that said 21% of laid off workers in 2009 found a new job through an online job board, whereas 22% found them through personal referrals.[2] However, according to a CareerXroads study, only 13.2% of new hires in 2009 came from job boards; 22.3% came from career sections from the companies' websites, and 26.7% came from referrals.[3] (Of that 13.2%, in the answer to the question, "How did you handle the [major] Job Boards this past year (2009)?", 35% said they reduced their contracts but made the same percentage of hires, 32.5% reduced both contracts and hires from the job boards, and 32.5% "made major efforts to switch away from major job boards to other sources, and that effort is continuing." In other words, two-thirds of an already small percentage is moving away from the major job boards.)

We're not saying you should ignore the job boards completely. Just don't spend all your time looking there. If anything, locate the individual companies' job listings instead. For one thing, posting jobs on the job boards cost money, which means some companies won't even bother putting a listing up there. Posting on their own company site is free.

Try the Company Job Boards Instead

For every job posted, an HR department can receive a couple hundred applications through the job boards. One career coach reminded us that some HR departments spend 10–20 seconds perusing each résumé, so yours isn't going to get much of a look. She said this is even more true when a résumé comes in from a job board, which can bring in 200 or 300 résumés for a single opening, and some of them aren't even remotely qualified. (This is where the need for screening software came from.)

Career sections of a website are a good idea for a company because they keep HR from being flooded with not-quite-qualified candidates. Companies are more likely to get people who are truly interested in the company through their Career sections. After all, if you take the time to check out the company's site, you have more interest than the average job seeker who clicks Apply to This Job buttons like a rat in a Skinner box.

If you want to keep track of what your target companies offer, you can try a couple of tips:

- Create RSS feeds of the different companies' job boards, and keep them in your RSS reader. Some boards have an RSS button (see Figure 15.3) on their page that lets you feed those new job listings into your RSS reader.

---

2. CareerBuilder.com press release, Feb. 3, 2010, http://bit.ly/8YCHqV.

3. http://www.slideshare.net/gerrycrispin/careerxroads-sources-of-hire-2010.

Figure 15.3   *If you see one of these on a web page, you can run the feed of that page through your RSS reader. After you set up your RSS reader, click this button, and your Internet browser will do the rest.*

 Tip

If you don't already have an RSS reader, we like Google Reader because it's easy to use. If you already have a Gmail or a Google account, you have a Reader account.

- Use Indeed.com, a Google-like job board search engine, to save searches into an RSS feed.

- Install the Morning Coffee plug-in into your Firefox web browser, and then save the jobs pages of all your target companies into Morning Coffee. Then click the Morning Coffee button at least once a day, and it will open every saved page for you to check out. You can always tell the plug-in to only open certain pages on certain days, so you can hide the pages that are updated once a week.

- Follow people in your industry who are connected and will tell everyone about the openings in their industry or community. Create a special list for them on Twitter, and keep track of them on your favorite Twitter client (that is, TweetDeck, Seesmic, or HootSuite). Some Twitterers do nothing but post jobs in their community, so it's a good idea to follow them. We discuss that in more detail in Chapter 5.

- Blogs are another great resource for job openings. Evan Finch, an advertising copywriter in Indianapolis, has a Posterous.com blog[4] that lists creative job openings (advertising and marketing) in the different agencies, firms, and large companies around town. He also features people who are looking for jobs, listing the people's skills, experiences, and a brief explanation of why they should be hired. Before he started the blog, his network was an email list that he originally ran through his company's network. He had to move to Posterous because his list

---

4. http://naptownjobswap.posterous.com/

was getting too big for his employer's email server. When he switched to Posterous, his network had grown to several hundred subscribers.

- Of course, don't forget your own industry newsletter. For example, there are several marketing newsletters and websites—Mashable.com, TalentZoo.com, and MarketingProfs.com—that aggregate marketing jobs around the country. All you have to do is search to see if you can find any you like. Again, these are jobs that don't always appear on the big job boards, so you can be sure that not everyone is going to be finding and submitting an application.

Use LinkedIn to Bypass the Job Board Process

Although we don't recommend relying on the job boards to apply for jobs, they are a useful tool for finding the jobs that are out there.

One strategy is just to do a basic job search on the boards, see which companies are hiring, and then make the connections on LinkedIn with the HMs. (We talk about using LinkedIn in Chapter 4.) Just follow the strategy of connecting with them on LinkedIn and other platforms and showing how you are a valuable resource.

Of course, this means you have to hit the ground running and start showing your value right away. The risk is that you could look like a nuisance or that you only wanted to connect with that person so you can find a job. (That is the only reason you're connecting with this person, but you don't want it to look like you're just using him or her.)

Another strategy is to find the companies you want to work for in advance and start connecting with them now, before they're hiring. Use the job boards to find out more about those companies, and then use LinkedIn's search capabilities to connect with the people who are most likely to work in the department you want to work for. Start communicating with these people like we've discussed in previous chapters, and make yourself a valuable resource to them. That way, they'll be more receptive to receiving your résumé and more interested in making sure they include you in their candidate pool.

Skip HR Altogether, and Work Your Network

Of course, you can skip HR altogether. Going through standard HR channels can be extremely frustrating. It often seems like HR's only function is to say no; to find the best people for the position and then toss their résumés out; or, to completely miss the point for what the HM is actually looking for. Okay, it's not actually *that* bad, but sometimes the best way to land a new job is by talking directly to the HM. This is where your network comes in.

One former international sales executive told us that whenever he asked the HR department for sales candidates, they made sure every candidate met the minimum HR requirements: could type 45 words per minute, and had a college degree. Of course, none of them could sell.

But the executive, because he was also the VP of the company, could insert his own candidates into the process. Although these candidates couldn't always type and may never have gone to college, they spoke two or three languages, they had sold multimillion dollar projects, and they usually already had their own extensive network in their territories.

Guess which candidates the executive hired. Every time.

You don't need to connect with an executive to get that introduction to the company. It can be anyone within the company. But the more people you know within an organization, the better your chances.

Another strategy—one that will help you avoid the masses who are still slogging it out on the job boards and in the HR department—is to follow your chosen companies in the news. Create a Google News Alert, and keep an eye out for any mentions of expansion, new programs, new funding, or rounds of venture capital. Also watch out for promotions and departures by the people in the departments you want to work in. (You know they're going because you connect with them on LinkedIn. See Chapter 4 on LinkedIn.)

As you hear about these promotions and departures, start asking your contacts at those companies if they are making plans to add new positions. Make sure you're already communicating with them like we've talked about in previous chapters, so this isn't the first they're hearing from you. Just make it part of your regular conversation.

Also, be sure to blog about the news as you hear it. Retweet the articles, and give a shout out to your contacts who work for that company so they know you're talking about them.

Using Your Network to Land a Freelance Contract

Rocky Walls and Zach Downs own 12 Stars Media, a video production company in Greenfield, Indiana, that specializes in promotional online video, specifically for use with social media. They have worked with both of us on various projects at different times. In Spring 2010, they started the "Media for Hire" reality series on YouTube as a way to show off their video capabilities, keep in touch with their network, and expand it.

Rocky's idea was to give viewers a behind-the-scenes look at the company. Rocky and Zach thought, "Why not create a whole reality series about the type of people who would make a reality series?" "Media for Hire" was born.

Through the series, they have driven on the Indy 500 track in a 2010 Chevy Camaro, interviewed James Best (Sheriff Roscoe P. Coltrane on "Dukes of Hazzard"), driven a replica of the General Lee, participated in an Air Force Reserve in-flight refueling mission aboard a KC-135 Stratotanker, and created a subplot about an errant desk leg.

The impact that "Media for Hire" and their antics have had on their business has been significant. More than 75% of the new clients they have gotten since they launched the series had heard of or seen episodes, which helped them choose 12 Stars Media. Rocky said that although it has generated new leads and helped them win new customers, its purpose has been better served by showing prospects and clients who the two really are and what they do. In short, it was their résumé and interview.

Basically, the "Media for Hire" series has been a way they can live—and show-case—their personal brand and use it to find new clients or jobs.

Freelance copywriters, graphic designers, and web designers can use these social networks in the same way. Rather than seek long-term employment, freelancers look for both short-term and long-term projects. And they have to treat client acquisition just like a job search: Get in front of the people who can hire you; show them what you can do through your blog, video, and tweets; and answer LinkedIn questions and other content-sharing networks. Create the same kinds of relationships that a full-time employee would, use them to get an interview, and get hired. If freelancers adopt the same mindset and techniques as a job seeker, they'll find the same success.

How Can Our Heroes Find a Job Through Networking?

- **Allen (influencer)** spent 14 years working for a marketing agency, amassed a large network with contacts in the agency world, and is a member of a professional marketing association. Because his aim is to stay in the industry, he needs to spend time cultivating and deepening his online relationships with people he is already connected to and making new contacts with other industry people. If he's willing to move, Allen should also expand his network to the cities he would like to move to, using Twellow.com. Allen needs to connect with these people on LinkedIn and Twitter, write blog posts about his industry, and share them with his network.

- **Beth (climber)** has a plan to become the chief marketing officer of an insurance company, but she prefers the one she is in. Still, this doesn't mean she is guaranteed to stay in the company, especially since she's willing to switch jobs to move up her career ladder. Beth should focus on connecting with people who are one and two steps above her, as well as people outside her company but in the same industry. The people a step above may eventually move up their own ranks or leave the company. If she knows early on about her colleagues leaving (they would tell her before the opening ever hits the internal job listings), she is in a good position to get her résumé into the hands of that person's manager, who is two steps above her current position. The same is true with connections in other companies. People often share with their industry friends when they're moving on; they can still get a résumé into their supervisor's hands.

- **Carla (neophyte)** is a former pharmaceutical sales rep who is out of work but is trying to find a fundraising or program director position at a nonprofit. Not only should she connect with people who work for nonprofits, she should connect with their board members. These people often know about open positions before they are made public, and Carla can ask them for a direct referral. Although Carla may be a neophyte in terms of industry connections, she has a head start because many corporate pharmaceutical executives sit on the boards of nonprofits.

- **Darrin (free agent)** is an IT professional who leaves his job every two or three years in pursuit of more money. He should communicate with IT workers in other companies via email and Twitter direct messages. These people often know about new positions opening before HR does and can alert Darrin to the fact, as well as pass his résumé to their managers. The logical thing to do is to work LinkedIn and any industry discussion boards to tell people he's interested, but this could be a problem if Darrin's current manager is connected to him as well.

A Social Media Case Study

Jeff Stanger, from the Salvation Army, Indiana Division, told us about the time the Salvation Army used social media to find a social media intern. Here's what happened, in Jeff's own words:

> We had posted to the usual intern job boards at the area colleges and universities, but I wasn't thrilled with the résumés I was receiving. Most were filled with the boring clichés that so-called job experts tell young

people to include. Knowing I couldn't stand to read another page of "goal oriented," "team focused," "results driven" drivel, I called in my intern coordinator.

"Elizabeth, I hate all these résumés. I'm going to write a new job description. I want you to post it on Craigslist, our Facebook page, and then on the intern boards."

Here is what we posted:

Do you have what it takes to be the Social Media Intern for a 140+ year old nonprofit organization? Do you have the social media savvy to help us build and lead a tribe? I don't want your résumé. I don't want a cover letter filled with clichés. I want you to find me, friend me, tweet me, and comment on my blog. I am the development director of the Salvation Army in Indiana. Go to work!

We posted the copy, and I left for the airport. Arriving in St. Louis, I checked my email and two people had already taken up the challenge. Now I was under pressure. I thought it would be a couple of days before someone responded, and that would give me time come up with a few exercises for candidates to complete. I quickly posted a note on Facebook and directed the people who found me on LinkedIn, Twitter, and even MySpace (forgot I still had a profile there!) to read it for instructions. Here is the note:

(For my regular friends, this won't make any sense!)

Okay, you've found me on Facebook. Did you find me on either of my blogs? (Disregard Smaller Indiana for now.) Did you find me anywhere else?

Well, this isn't about me. But, I did want to test your research skills. So here is your homework assignment:

1. Find me on two more places on the web.

2. Create a Squidoo lens, or Facebook Cause, or a blog about a cause. Any cause. You can make it up or it can be real. I want to see how creative you are.

3. Tell me three reasons why anyone would follow us on Twitter.

4. Go to salvationarmyindiana.org and tell me how to make it better.

I will be back in Indy on Wednesday morning and will start setting up interviews. Go to work!

I followed that up with this:

First, I want to say thanks for taking part in this unique way of recruiting our social media intern. I had sorted through a stack of boring résumés and decided there had to be a better way to find a candidate. It's working! So many of you are letting your creativity shine through in this process and that makes the process better and certainly more fun!

If you haven't done so already, see my Note with the homework assignment. You won't be called for an interview unless you complete the tasks in that note.

And now for a bonus assignment:

Tell me how to build a Tribe, create a Purple Cow, and avoid a Meatball Sundae. And tell me what they have in common.

When it was all done, Jeff said the company learned several valuable lessons:

- By advertising for a social media intern in this fashion, the company was able to prequalify all the candidates before choosing the ones it wanted to interview. The candidates had to show they knew how to do the work just by following those instructions. If they couldn't do it, they weren't considered.

- Communication skills are the most important when it comes down to the final decision. Jeff said, "I can teach a good communicator to be tech savvy much easier than teaching a techie how to communicate our case for support."

- You shouldn't have candidates friend your personal account. (Jeff said he picked up a stalker.)

- You can learn many things about a prospective candidate who friends you that you could never legally ask about in an interview. The Salvation Army realized this could create all sorts of legal and ethical issues that companies and organizations would have to deal with in the future. However, while those questions are being decided, let this be a reminder to you that you need to keep inappropriate and negative content off your social networks, especially Facebook.

- Many younger students gave up midway through the process. If you are presented with an opportunity like this, seeing this all the way through will help you rise above most of the candidates in the pool.

- The candidate who emerged was a single mom in her 40s who had returned to school. The Salvation Army was so pleased with her work that it hired her part time after her internship completed. She became a full-time member of their team in fall 2010. "It's just a reminder to always look to field the best team possible and throw out any preconceived notions about where you will find the players," said Jeff.

Another Social Media Case Study

Dan Schawbel is Mr. Personal Branding. Not only is he one of the leading voices of personal branding—he wrote *Me 2.0*—he writes the most popular personal branding blogs around (PersonalBrandingBlog.com). Kyle was a contributor to the PBB for a while; Erik is a contributor now. We'll let Dan tell you how he got started on his own personal branding mission, which led to him being recruited for a job, and ultimately for him to create his own job.

> *I worked at EMC (a Fortune 200 technology company) for a year and a half before stumbling upon Tom Peters' famous "Brand Called You" article, after leaving a training class. I realized that his words echoed what I had been preaching on my blog at the time. It was in that moment when I recognized that I was truly passionate about personal branding and I started searching online for experts in the field.*

> *I noticed that no one my age (I was 23 at the time) was writing about personal branding so naturally I felt like I could assume the role of helping young people develop their own brands. I started a new blog called "Personal Branding Blog," where I posted ten to twelve times a week outside of my full-time job. From there, I developed a video podcast series, where I interviewed business people to get their career advice, as well as the Personal Brand Awards, which gave recognition to those who were building strong brands online.*

> *At the same time, I started writing for blogs and online news sources, speaking at colleges, and commenting on every single blog post that mentioned "personal branding." This allowed me to grow a community, market my brand, and be positioned as an expert in this space. Each article and speech increased my exposure, reinforced my expertise, and opened up better opportunities. In effect, while I was teaching people how to build their brands, I was doing it myself at the same time.*

> *Eventually, Fast Company profiled me for my work. EMC wasn't aware of what I was doing because it was more of a hobby at first. The Fast Company article was picked up by EMC PR and sent to a VP who then recruited me to be the first social media specialist, which inspired my book Me 2.0 and eventually my company, Millennial Branding.*

Job Searching Tips in 140 Characters

@ChrisBrogan is fond of saying, "You live or die by your database." That means keep your DB of contacts up to date. —@edeckers

Start a Gmail account. Keep your work DB synced with your Gmail account. You know, in case you suddenly no longer have access to it. —@edeckers

Follow companies in the industry in which you would like to work. Then engage! Comment, reply, and retweet their posts. —@jlisak

Become a valuable follow, with good insight and something you can offer to the table! I did, and now I'm living my dream job! —@jlisak

Create a Twitter list of businesses and influential people. Start to make intelligent connections with this group. Be subtle. —@LeilanMcNally

For recruiters, you are what you tweet. —@MaryBiever

Audit your social media footprint before a job recruiter does. —@MaryBiever

Learn about the company's culture by following the company and the staff, if possible, on Twitter. Decide if you fit or not. —@MaryBiever

Let your mail/UPS/FedEx person know you're job hunting. They may know of unadvertised or little-known opportunities. —@PamelaReilly1

Follow hashtags on twitter to find opportunities not advertised on job boards. —@sandrulee

Get active with network groups and set up meetings w/influencers in field of your choosing. —@IndyBethG

Be professional; a feed full of racist/sexist comments isn't a good thing to show a potential employer. —@McMullen_Greg

Don't wait until you're thirsty to dig a well. —@CynthiaSchames

Your résumé is your first impression. You have 10 seconds to stand out from the crowd—Be sure the good stuff "rises to the top." —@AprilLynneScott

Index

Try Safari Books Online FREE for 15 days

Get online access to Thousands of Books and Videos

FREE 15-DAY TRIAL + 15% OFF*
informit.com/safaritrial

> ### Feed your brain
>
> Gain unlimited access to thousands of books and videos about technology, digital media and professional development from O'Reilly Media, Addison-Wesley, Microsoft Press, Cisco Press, McGraw Hill, Wiley, WROX, Prentice Hall, Que, Sams, Apress, Adobe Press and other top publishers.

> ### See it, believe it
>
> Watch hundreds of expert-led instructional videos on today's hottest topics.

WAIT, THERE'S MORE!

> ### Gain a competitive edge
>
> Be first to learn about the newest technologies and subjects with Rough Cuts pre-published manuscripts and new technology overviews in Short Cuts.

> ### Accelerate your project
>
> Copy and paste code, create smart searches that let you know when new books about your favorite topics are available, and customize your library with favorites, highlights, tags, notes, mash-ups and more.

* Available to new subscribers only. Discount applies to the Safari Library and is valid for first 12 consecutive monthly billing cycles. Safari Library is not available in all countries.

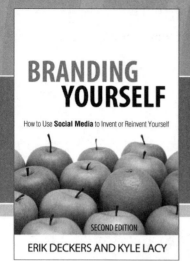

Safari
Books Online

FREE
Online Edition

Your purchase of **Branding Yourself: How to Use Social Media to Invent or Reinvent Yourself** includes access to a free online edition for 45 days through the **Safari Books Online** subscription service. Nearly every Que book is available online through **Safari Books Online**, along with thousands of books and videos from publishers such as Addison-Wesley Professional, Cisco Press, Exam Cram, IBM Press, O'Reilly Media, Prentice Hall, and Sams.

Safari Books Online is a digital library providing searchable, on-demand access to thousands of technology, digital media, and professional development books and videos from leading publishers. With one monthly or yearly subscription price, you get unlimited access to learning tools and information on topics including mobile app and software development, tips and tricks on using your favorite gadgets, networking, project management, graphic design, and much more.

Activate your FREE Online Edition at
informit.com/safarifree

STEP 1: Enter the coupon code: XMWYQZG.

STEP 2: New Safari users, complete the brief registration form.
Safari subscribers, just log in.

If you have difficulty registering on Safari or accessing the online edition,
please e-mail customer-service@safaribooksonline.com